Guide to America's Outdoors

Far West

Guide to America's Outdoors
Far West

By Geoffrey O'Gara
Photography by Phil Schermeister

NATIONAL
GEOGRAPHIC
WASHINGTON, D.C.

Contents

Cover: Channel Islands National Park *Page 1:* Desert marigold, Valley of Fire State Park
Pages 2-3: El Capitan and Merced River, Yosemite National Park
Opposite: Prairie Creek Redwoods State Park

Treading Lightly in the Wild

Camping, Sequoia National Park

NATIONAL GEOGRAPHIC GUIDE TO AMERICA'S OUTDOORS: FAR WEST takes you to some of the wildest and most beautiful natural areas in a region celebrated for its spectacular coastline, rugged mountains, ancient trees, and diverse ecological regions.

Visitors who care about this region know they must tread lightly on the land. Ecosystems can be damaged, even destroyed, by careless misuse. Many have already suffered from the impact of tourism. The marks are clear: litter-strewn acres, polluted waters, trampled vegetation, and disturbed wildlife. You can do your part to preserve these places for yourself, your children, and all other nature travelers. Before embarking on a backcountry visit or a camping adventure, learn some basic conservation dos and don'ts. Leave No Trace, a national educational program, recommends the following:

Plan ahead and prepare for your trip. If you know what to expect in terms of climate, conditions, and hazards, you can pack for general needs, extreme weather, and emergencies. Do yourself and the land a favor by visiting if possible during off-peak months and limiting your group to no more than four to six people. To keep trash or litter to a minimum, repackage food into reusable containers or bags. And rather than using cairns, flags, or paint cues that mar the environment to mark your way, bring a map and compass.

Travel and camp on solid surfaces. In popular areas, stay within established trails and campsites. Travel single-file in the middle of the trail, even when it's wet or muddy, to avoid trampling vegetation. Be particularly sensitive in boggy or coastal areas, and avoid stepping on mussels, sea stars, and the like. When exploring off the trail in pristine, lightly traveled areas, have your group spread out to lessen impact. Good campsites are found, not made. Travel and camp on sand, gravel, or rock, or on dry grasses, pine needles, or snow. Remember to stay at least 200 feet from waterways. After you've broken camp, leave the site as you found it.

Pack out what you pack in—and that means *everything* except human waste, which should be deposited in a cathole dug 200 feet away from water, camp, and trail, and then covered and concealed. When washing dishes, clothes, or yourself, use small amounts of biodegradable soap and scatter the water away from lakes and streams.

Be sure to leave all items—plants, rocks, artifacts—as you find them, especially in tide pools. Avoid potential disaster by neither introducing nor transporting non-native species. Also, don't build or carve out structures that will alter the environment. A don't-touch policy not only preserves resources for future generations; it also gives the next guy a crack at the discovery experience.

Keep fires to a minimum. It may be unthinkable to camp without a campfire, but depletion of firewood does harm the backcountry. When you can, try a gas-fueled camp stove and a candle lantern. If you choose to build a fire, first consider regulations, weather, skill, and firewood availability. At the beach, build your fire below the next high tide line, where the traces will be washed away. Where possible, employ existing fire rings; elsewhere, use fire pans or mound fires. Keep your fire small, use only sticks from the ground, burn the fire down to ash, and don't leave the site until it's cold.

Respect wildlife. Watch animals from a distance (bring binoculars or a telephoto lens for close-ups), but never approach, feed, or follow them. Feeding weakens an animal's ability to fend for itself in the wild. If you can't keep your pets under control, leave them at home. Finally, be mindful of other visitors. Yield to fellow travelers on the trail, and keep voices and noise levels low so that the sounds of nature can be heard.

With these points in mind, you have only to chart your course. Enjoy your explorations. Let natural places quiet your mind, refresh your spirit, and remain as you found them. Just remember, leave behind no trace.

MAP KEY and ABBREVIATIONS

National Park		N.P.
National Historic Site		N.H.S.
National Monument		NAT. MON.
National Natural Landmark		N.N.L.
National Preserve		
National Recreation Area		N.R.A.
National Seashore		N.S.

National Forest		N.F.
State Forest		S.F.
Forest Reserve		F.R.

National Wildlife Refuge		N.W.R.
National Conservation Area		N.C.A.
National Estuarine Research Reserve		N.E.R.R.
National Wildlife Range		
State Wildlife Area		S.W.A.

State Park		S.P.
State Beach		S.B.
State Historical Park		S.H.P.
State Recreation Area		S.R.A.
State Reserve		S.R.
Recreation Area		R.A.

Indian Reservation		I.R.

Military Reservation		
Air Force Base		A.F.B.

National Wild & Scenic River .... N.W. & S.R.

U.S. Interstate — 5

U.S. Federal or State Highway — 50 33

Other Road — J59

Trail

Fault Line

National Marine Sanctuary

BOUNDARIES

STATE or NATIONAL

FOREST   I.R.   N.P.   WILD.

POPULATION

- **LOS ANGELES**   above 500,000
- **Santa Barbara**   50,000 to 500,000
- Elko   10,000 to 50,000
- Derlo   under 10,000

ADDITIONAL ABBREVIATIONS

B.A.	Botanical Area
BLVD.	Boulevard
Cr.	Creek
Ctr.	Center
DR.	Drive
Educ.	Education
Fk.	Fork
Ft.	Fort
Hts.	Heights
HWY.	Highway
I.-s.	Islands
L.	Lake
MEM.	Memorial
Mid.	Middle
Mt-s.	Mount-ain-s
N.	North
NAT.	National
N.M.S.	National Marine Sanctuary
N.S.T.	National Scenic Trail
Pk.	Peak
Pt.	Point
R.	River
RD.	Road
Rec.	Recreation
Res.	Reservoir
WILD.	Wilderness

□ Point of Interest		✝ Falls	
⊛ State capital		⌇ Spring	
+ Elevation		⋈ Dam	
⤳ Pass		Intermittent River	
△ Campground		Intermittent Lake	
⊟ Picnic Area		Dry Lake	

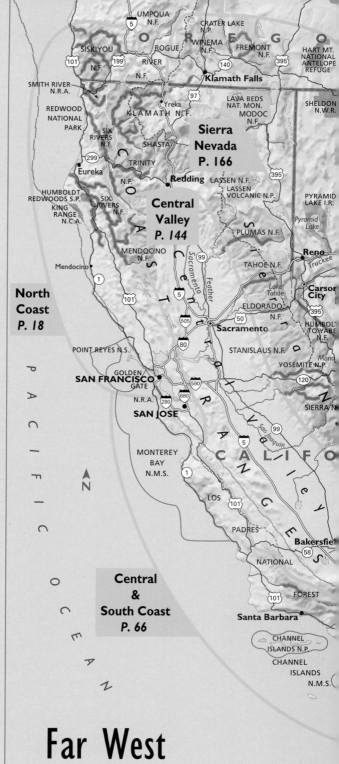

O R E G O

UMPQUA
N.F.

CRATER LAKE
N.P.

WINEMA
N.F.

FREMONT
N.F.

HART MT.
NATIONAL
ANTELOPE
REFUGE

SISKIYOU
N.F.

ROGUE

RIVER

N.F.

Klamath Falls

SMITH RIVER
N.R.A.

Yreka

SHELDON
N.W.R.

LAVA BEDS
NAT. MON.
MODOC
N.F.

REDWOOD
NATIONAL
PARK

KLAMATH N.F.

SIX
RIVERS
N.F.

SHASTA

**Sierra
Nevada
P. 166**

Eureka

TRINITY

N.F.

Redding

LASSEN N.F.
LASSEN
VOLCANIC N.P.

PYRAMID
LAKE I.R.

HUMBOLDT
REDWOODS S.P.
KING
RANGE
N.C.A.

SIX
RIVERS
N.F.

**Central
Valley
P. 144**

*Pyramid
Lake*

MENDOCINO
N.F.

PLUMAS N.F.

Mendocino

Reno

Truckee

TAHOE N.F.

**North
Coast
P. 18**

ELDORADO
N.F.

*Lake
Tahoe*

Carson
City

HUMBOLT
TOIYABE
N.F.

Sacramento

STANISLAUS N.F.

POINT REYES N.S.

GOLDEN
GATE

SAN FRANCISCO

YOSEMITE N.P.

Mono

N.R.A.

SAN JOSE

SIERRA N

MONTEREY
BAY
N.M.S.

San Joaquin

**Central
&
South Coast
P. 66**

LOS

PADRES

Bakersfie

NATIONAL

Santa Barbara

CHANNEL
ISLANDS N.P.

CHANNEL
ISLANDS
N.M.S.

P A C I F I C

O C E A N

N

C O A S T

C e n t r a l

S i e r r a

C A L I F O

R A N G E S

V a l l e y

Far West

| 0 | miles | 100 |
| 0 | kilometers | 150 |

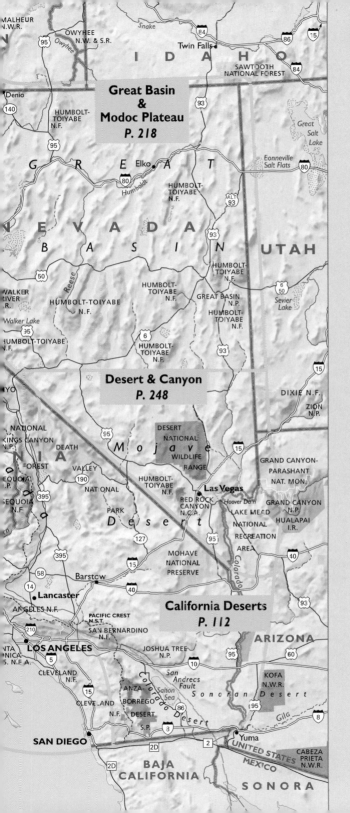

Great Basin & Modoc Plateau
P. 218

Desert & Canyon
P. 248

California Deserts
P. 112

IDAHO

Twin Falls

MALHEUR N.W.R.

OWYHEE N.W. & S.R.

Snake

Owyhee

SAWTOOTH NATIONAL FOREST

Denio

HUMBOLT-TOIYABE N.F.

Great Salt Lake

Elko

G R E A T

Humboldt

HUMBOLT-TOIYABE N.F.

Bonneville Salt Flats

N E V A D A

B A S I N

UTAH

WALKER RIVER R.

Reese

Walker Lake

HUMBOLT-TOIYABE N.F.

HUMBOLT-TOIYABE N.F.

HUMBOLT-TOIYABE N.F.

HUMBOLT-TOIYABE N.F.

GREAT BASIN N.P.

HUMBOLT-TOIYABE N.F.

Sevier Lake

HUMBOLT-TOIYABE N.F.

DIXIE N.F.

ZION N.P.

NATIONAL KINGS CANYON N.P.

DEATH VALLEY

DESERT NATIONAL WILDLIFE RANGE

M o j a v e

FOREST

NATIONAL PARK

HUMBOLT-TOIYABE N.F.

Las Vegas

RED ROCK CANYON N.C.A.

Hoover Dam

LAKE MEAD

NATIONAL RECREATION AREA

GRAND CANYON-PARASHANT NAT. MON.

GRAND CANYON N.P.

HUALAPAI I.R.

SEQUOIA N.P.

SEQUOIA N.F.

D e s e r t

MOHAVE NATIONAL PRESERVE

Colorado

Barstow

Lancaster

ANGELES N.F.

PACIFIC CREST N.S.T.

SAN BERNARDINO N.F.

ARIZONA

LOS ANGELES

NTA NICA S. N.F.A.

CLEVELAND N.F.

JOSHUA TREE N.P.

KOFA N.W.R.

San Andreas Fault

Salton Sea

S o n o r a n   D e s e r t

CLEVELAND N.F.

ANZA-BORREGO DESERT S.P.

D e s e r t

Gila

SAN DIEGO

Yuma

CABEZA PRIETA N.W.R.

UNITED STATES

BAJA CALIFORNIA

MEXICO

SONORA

Discovering the West

I GREW UP in San Francisco and Monterey, and one of the joys of researching this book was that it let me hike, paddle, and (less happily) drive around the state where I was born—trying at the same time to read a library of natural history and flora and fauna manuals. You would find me punched into a snowbank amidst the ancient bristlecone pines of the White Mountains with John Muir's memoirs in my hand; or up to my neck in Sykes Hot Springs in Big Sur wearing nothing but Phillip Fradkin's *Seven States of California*. As I write this, I sit among the redwoods by a murmuring creek in Fern Canyon on the far north coast. My office is a "nurse log"—a fallen redwood as old as ten centuries that nurtures lichen, lady ferns, trillium, and my muse.

Over a century ago, my mother's family operated a gold mine that burrowed into the Sierra Buttes near Downieville. My family's history in California thus coincides with a century of exponential population growth that has ratcheted up the pressure to use ever more natural resources, whether we're talking about timber, gold, or the trail through a pretty mountain meadow. Though I feel a twinge of nostalgia when I hike along the old wooden flume that brought water to the family mill, there's nothing sentimental about mines that still bleed minerals into the streams, or clear-cuts that have never re-seeded. Places that were wild in my childhood are less so now, not just because of the way natural resources have been extracted, but because of changes in recreational preferences as well: Many of today's Californians have little experience in, or taste for truly wild places. Many people want easier access and more amenities, and the agencies that manage public lands respond with "improvements." Personally, I can do without the creature comforts of wider roads and flush toilets in parks; I'd put my money into bringing back the discomforting creature on the state flag, the grizzly bear.

But I'll save that gripe for my curmudgeon years. For now, conservation in the Far West more often is a holding action, trying to protect what remains, whether it's a rare Torrey pine, a salmon spawning stream, or a desert mountain. Fortunately, Westerners are pretty skillful at grassroots conservation—this is, after all, the birthplace of the Sierra Club—which is why we still have ancient redwood stands and California sea otters.

A book of this length can't cover every square inch of a region that embraces 274,724 square miles. But we'll take you to famous sites such as Yosemite and Death Valley and the Channel Islands, with some insights and updated information you won't find elsewhere. And we'll visit other locales, smaller in scale and subtler in their rewards, such as the Tijuana River Estuary, where you can ride horseback along a windswept beach, or Nevada's Cathedral Gorge State Park, where you can wander through a maze-like natural sand castle of gargantuan proportions. I confess even so that there is much more that I've yet to discover. That can be your job, too.

Geoffrey O'Gara

California poppies

The West on the Edge

IN THE ROCKY MOUNTAINS, some folks refer to California and the Far West as "Beyond" West—a crowded Hollywood beach world alien to the rugged, thinly populated landscapes of the "real" West. But California is "beyond" only in the sense that much of it was once literally out to sea, and only recently, geologically speaking, joined the North American continent. Unlike the Atlantic and Gulf Coasts, where the gradual submergence of the continent's edges produced gently sloping seashores, the sheer cliffs and raised terraces of the California coastline were created by abrupt faulting and uplift. The collision and subduction of the Northern Pacific and North American tectonic plates brought islands ashore, seabed to the surface, and the Sierra up into the skies in a series of events that unfolded some 200 million years ago.

Morning sun on Mount Whitney, Sequoia National Park

The result is much more spectacular than anything Hollywood has produced. California's landscapes include vast desertlands and soaring snow-covered peaks, swampy valleys, and deep-canyoned rivers. The rugged headlands along the north and central coast attest to coastal rock that has withstood the erosive power of crashing waves, wind, and winter storms. Softer shales and sandstone, by contrast, make up the erosion-prone bluffs that characterize the coast from Mendocino County to San Diego. And just offshore, an array of rocks, pinnacles, and remote islands offer protected breeding sites for migrating seabirds and marine mammals. Few places in the world provide such varied habitat, such a range of wildlife—such a precious storehouse of nature.

Of course, California and Nevada are no different from other regions of the country where the natural environment must compete with agricultural and commercial interests. For thousands of years, for example, wetlands in California's Central Valley were stopping places for millions of birds traveling the Pacific flyway from the Arctic to the tropics and back; today most of those wetlands are farmed or subdivided. Steelhead that once migrated up the rivers by the millions to spawn now find their way blocked by concrete dams. And some species—the Roosevelt elk, the California condor, the southern coastal dune scrub, the green abalone, the island fox, the Xerces blue butterfly, the California grizzly bear—are either gone forever or clinging to existence in scattered fragments of habitat.

The draining of wetlands and diversion of rivers and a sad record of species extinction over the last two centuries hardly give rise to optimism for the natural worlds of Nevada and California. And yet, there is a positive side. A century and a half of mining, damming, logging, and subdividing has been tempered in recent years through a series of conservation programs. In January 2000, for example, President Bill Clinton proclaimed the islands, rocks, and pinnacles off the entire western coast a biological treasure to be protected as the California Coastal National Monument. The revival of the sea otter; the captive breeding and reintroduction to the wild of the California condor; and the restoration of small pockets of wetland habitat in the Central Valley are further evidence of a turning of the tide. And groups such as the Nature Conservancy, the Big Sur Land Trust, and the Paiute Indians have fought to protect vital acres and watersheds in California and Nevada.

Although presidential decrees and donations by conservation groups will expand many of the sites described in this book, the conservation battle is far from over. Huge open-pit mines have proliferated in the Great Basin in recent years, and irrigation projects continue to divert the streams that once replenished wetlands and groundwater; what water is

Snow-laden evergreens, Lake Tahoe

Sea kayaking off the coast of Redwood National Park

returned to the streams often carries farm chemicals. And as the Far West economy shifts more toward tourism, even that relatively "clean" industry will have a growing impact on the environment

What's at stake in trying to strike a balance between economic growth and environmental protection becomes clear when we attempt to divvy up California and Nevada into sensible, geographically distinct natural regions for a book like this. At the simplest level we might do it this way: the coast, the Central Valley, the mountains, the desert. But when you look closer, it gets more complicated. For instance, there are several quite different mountain ranges in California: The coastal mountains alone constitute four geological regions, including the Klamath Mountains in the north, the northwest-trending Coast Ranges, the east-west trending Transverse Ranges, and the Peninsular Ranges that head south from Los Angeles and into Baja. And distinct from all these is the huge granite wall of the Sierra Nevada, whose eroded residue filled the Central Valley and gave rise to both extensive agriculture and the 1849 gold rush.

Even the experts disagree, depending on which natural science is emphasized. The Nature Conservancy identifies 12 ecoregions in California, three of which extend into Nevada. Consult the meteorologists, however, and they describe nine climatic regions with completely different boundaries. Meanwhile, the state Department of Fish and Game recognizes 11 biogeographic regions, while geomorphologists see it differently still, puzzling over how to categorize small but distinct environments such as the Modoc Plateau in California's northeast corner or the man-made waterworld of Lake Mead in Nevada.

We note these options not to confuse, but to pique your curiosity about the many interesting ways we can define our bioregions. In this book, we've divided the Far West into seven areas, each distinct enough that a traveler could tour any one of them and find environments intertwined in ecologically interesting ways. Each also provides a modicum of intriguing biota, beautiful scenery, and recreational opportunity.

The coast is treated in two sections, separated by the natural division of San Francisco Bay: First the rugged North Coast, with its tall headlands, crashing surf, and wild rivers draining the Klamath Mountains; then the Central and South Coast, including the steeper Big Sur country, the gentler beaches below Point Conception, and the magnificent Channel Islands. Then comes the underappreciated California Deserts region, including Death Valley and such gems as Anza-Borrego Desert State Park. The fourth chapter covers the Central Valley, once a great swampy wildlife paradise and now an agricultural cornucopia. The Sierra Nevada chapter includes both the great ramparts of the Sierra Nevada and the Cascade Range in the north, while the Great Basin and Modoc Plateau chapter captures California's Modoc Plateau as well as the vast expanses of northern and central Nevada. Finally, there is the Desert and Canyon area, Nevada's little piece of the great Colorado River landscape.

In each of these sections, the editors, photographer Phil Schermeister, and I have selected places that offer experiences for readers eager to appreciate the grandeur, the infinite variety, and the infinitesimal subtlety of the Far West's natural worlds. It is such a diverse region that travelers must adjust their clothing lists and time their visits differently depending on where they're going. A beautiful time to visit the Mojave Desert country, for instance, is March through May, when the wildflowers are up—and it's worth checking to see how wet the winter was, because that affects spring blooms. But March would not be the best time to visit Big Sur, because it rains heavily there in the spring, and the roads are often in serious disrepair from winter storms. Rather, you should take to the coast in the summer, hitting the south beaches in late spring and moving north as the year progresses. If you love birds, you'll want to visit wildlife refuges in the Central Valley during the spring and fall migrations. If you like whales, you'll migrate to the coast for the gray whale sightings between November and February, or the humpback and blue whale views in the spring. In the Sierra, snowfields will block the higher elevation trails as late as June—but you may prefer to visit the high country in the winter, aboard skis or snowshoes.

Like the weather, the landscape of the Far West can surprise you. You may stumble into a spring-fed canyon near Las Vegas where the vegetation blooms lushly tropical, or find a coast redwood taller than a skyscraper less than an hour's drive from downtown San Francisco. As the California geologist Eldridge Moores told writer John McPhee: "Nature is messy. Don't expect it to be uniform or consistent." Rather, expect it to be surprising, beautiful, scary, breathtaking, and so richly varied in the Far West that your explorations will never end. ■

Ponderosa pines at sunset, Lassen Volcanic National Park

North Coast

A foggy sunset, King Range National Conservation Area

CALIFORNIA'S NORTH COAST still has the shaggy, salty, soggy, slanty character of an uncivilized frontier—the prow of the continent thrusting out into the surf of the Pacific Ocean. Dense coniferous forests gird the state's northwest mountains where they flank the sea, an undulating wall of green broken only by the mouths of big rivers—the Smith, the Klamath, the Eel—pouring down out of steep canyons. If the coast seems raw and gangly, it's because the land is, in fact, young, in geologic terms. A mere 30

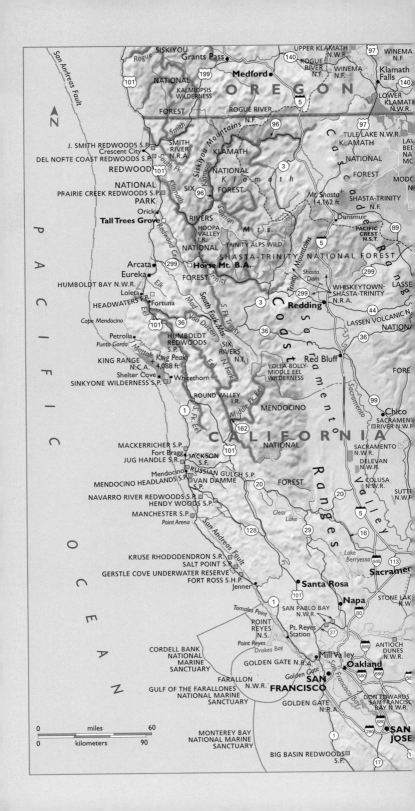

million years ago, two major plates of Earth's shifting crust—the North American plate, which holds the continent, and the Northern Pacific plate, beneath the ocean—began slipping laterally against each other along the infamous San Andreas Fault, a fracture that runs 750 miles northwest to southeast, nearly the length of the state. Along this slippage zone, folding of the seafloor against the edge of the continent produced the Coast Ranges, a series of low mountains paralleling the coastline. While the coastal lands south of San Francisco and west of the fault (see Chapter 2 map, pp. 68-69) are on a slow-moving journey northward aboard the Northern Pacific plate, you can count on the redwood forests, the beaches, and the big rivers north of San Francisco and east of the fault to remain firmly anchored to the North American plate.

In the northernmost part of the state are the older Klamath Mountains, formed some 140 million years ago as tectonic pressures forced molten rock up from the planet's interior. Powerful rivers fueled by heavy winter rains rolling in off the Pacific have divvied the Klamaths into smaller ranges: the Siskyou, the Salmon, the Trinity Alps, and the South Fork Mountains. As you travel south along the coast, no sign tells you when you have left the Klamaths and entered the much younger Coast Ranges, although Eureka is about where it happens. All along the coast are terraces where geological uplift has periodically raised the shore, creating different vegetation zones 100 feet apart in elevation. And there are sections of the coast where few roads come near the seashore, allowing the sea and land to play out their ancient battle on an elemental stage.

California's coastal mountains are the realm of the tallest tree on Earth, the coast redwood, which often towers more than 300 feet above the forest floor. Sharing the land with Sitka spruce, Douglas-fir, and hardwoods such

Sailing on San Francisco Bay

White pelicans

as alder, the redwoods are a remnant of ancient forests that covered much of North America, Europe, and Asia in the wetter world of a million years ago. The survivors—some as old as 1,500 years—are here because rain and fog keep this world damp all the time, creating a temperate rain forest that extends north into Oregon and Washington. But the giant ancient trees that made it to the modern era came under assault by the timber industry. Over the course of two centuries, logging has reduced the acreage of coast redwoods from two million to about 80,000 acres.

Also much affected are the numbers of the region's salmon and steelhead trout—both anadromous species that are born in fresh water, spend their adult life in salt water, and return to fresh water to spawn. During the rainy months, these fish swim upstream from the ocean to spawning beds in the higher reaches of freshwater mountain streams of the Northwest. There they lay and fertilize eggs and then, in the case of salmon, die. The fish keep coming, particularly up the Klamath and Trinity Rivers, but the variation in their numbers from year to year can be tremendous. Since the mid-1970s, when the California Department of Fish and Game first began recording run-size estimates, fluctuations in their populations clearly show

Rhododendron, Jedediah Smith Redwoods State Park

the impact of both favorable—and unfavorable—conditions. When the numbers are down, fingers point in all directions: logging practices, dams, overfishing, and even the weather phenomenon known as El Niño, which may disturb spawning by warming the water.

All things considered, we should be thankful for what's still here. Much of the remaining redwood forest is now protected by Redwood National and State Parks, where you can wander in a sea of ferns beneath a cool canopy hundreds of feet above. Young salmon still make their way to the ocean when the runoff rises in the spring, and find their way back years later. Near the Oregon border, the Smith River runs without inter- ference from dams. Indeed, the Klamath, Salmon, Smith, and Eel are now all federally protected as designated Wild and Scenic Rivers. Moodily wrapped in fog, the rugged headlands and sheltered beaches of the north coast are less crowded, than the state's urbanized southern beaches. Wherever you go, though, from the remote headlands of the Lost Coast to the breezy trails in Golden Gate National Recreation Area, you are never far from the powerful natural forces that formed this region. Any- one who lived in San Francisco in 1906—or 1989—can tell you that. ∎

Redwood National and State Parks

■ 105,516 acres ■ Northern California, from Crescent City to Orick on U.S. 101 ■ Year-round; most crowds in summer ■ Camping, hiking, backpacking, walking, guided walks, boating, white-water rafting and kayaking, canoeing, tide-pooling, swimming, scuba diving, tubing, fishing, biking, mountain biking, horseback riding, bird-watching, whale-watching, wildlife viewing, wildflower viewing ■ Contact the parks, 1111 Second St., Crescent City, CA 95531; phone 707-464-6101. www.nps.gov/redw

REDWOOD NATIONAL AND STATE PARKS—three state parks linked by stretches of federal parkland—protect what is left of the tallest forests in the country. What remains of the thick-barked coast redwoods today amounts to less than five percent of the two million acres that cloaked the area as recently as two centuries ago. From southern Oregon to south of California's Monterey Peninsula, these skyscraping conifers survive in a fairly narrow strip of habitat generally extending no more than ten miles inland, but sometimes a little farther along streambeds. Redwoods need to be in the range of the year-round coastal fog—which collects on the needles and branches of the trees and keeps them well watered during the

Crescent Beach, Redwood National and State Park

dry summer months. (You won't find redwoods right next to the ocean, however, because they can't tolerate too much salt.) Fallen needles and other litter from the trees are deep and wet beneath the shady canopy, providing fertile soil for ferns, mosses, and shade-loving plants such as redwood sorrel and pink-blooming huckleberry. Wildlife in the parks is both abundant and varied, including such animals as black bears, deer, coyotes, bobcats, mountain lions, skunks, foxes, beavers, squirrels, chipmunks, river otters, and Roosevelt elk. Bird-watchers have spied bald eagles and pileated woodpeckers, as well as two species dependent on old-growth forest, the spotted owl and the marbled murrelet.

To preserve and extend this habitat, federal and state park officials, along with the Forest Service managers of the adjacent Smith River National Recreation Area (see pp. 36-38), are focusing on repairing the damage done in the watersheds by clear-cuts and logging roads. And the United Nations, recognizing the value of the parks, named each of them both a Biosphere Reserve and a World Heritage site.

Redwood National and State Parks offer visitors a lively mix of beaches and hiking trails, but the trees are the main attraction. People approach them like children in the presence of dignified elders, ancient sentinels that novelist John Steinbeck called "ambassadors from another time."

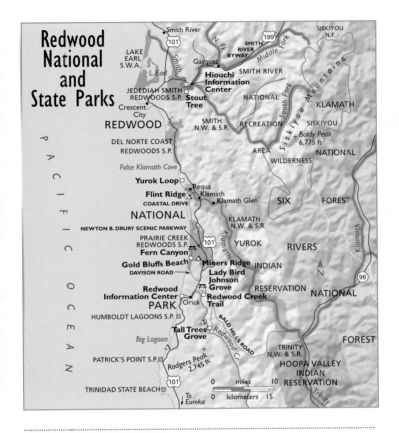

Redwood
National
and
State Parks

SISKIYOU
N.F.

Smith River

LAKE
EARL
S.W.A.

101

L. Earl

Gasquet

SMITH
RIVER
BYWAY

199

Middle Fork

N. Fk. Smith

SMITH RIVER

SISKIYOU
Mountains

Hiouchi
Information
Center

JEDEDIAH SMITH
REDWOODS S.P.

NATIONAL

Crescent
City

Stout
Tree

South Fork

KLAMATH

REDWOOD

SMITH
N.W. & S.R.

RECREATION

SISKIYOU

Baldy Peak
6,775 ft

DEL NORTE COAST
REDWOODS S.P.

AREA

NATIONAL

WILDERNESS

False Klamath Cove

Yurok Loop

Requa

Flint Ridge
COASTAL DRIVE

Klamath

Klamath Glen

SIX

FOREST

NATIONAL

KLAMATH
N.W. & S.R.

Klamath

NEWTON B. DRURY SCENIC PARKWAY

PRAIRIE CREEK
REDWOODS S.P.

101

YUROK

RIVERS

Fern Canyon

Gold Bluffs Beach
DAVISON ROAD

Miners Ridge

INDIAN

N

96

Lady Bird
Johnson
Grove

Redwood
Information Center

Orick

RESERVATION

Redwood Creek
Trail

NATIONAL

PARK

HUMBOLDT LAGOONS S.P.

Tall Trees
Grove

BALD HILLS ROAD

Redwood Cr.

FOREST

Big Lagoon

TRINITY
N.W. & S.R.

PATRICK'S POINT S.P.

Rodgers Peak
2,745 ft

HOOPA VALLEY
INDIAN
RESERVATION

101

0   miles   10

TRINIDAD STATE BEACH

0   kilometers   15

Trinity

To
Eureka

What to See and Do

This complex of parks begins at the
south end, with a stop at the national
park's Redwood Information Center *(1 mile S of Orick off US 101).*
Here you can pick up trail maps,
park information, and free permits
*(issued on first-come, first-served
basis)* to visit the Tall Trees Grove.

Redwood National Park

From the information center drive
4 miles north on 101 to Bald Hills
Road, which takes you east into
some of the most beautiful redwood groves in the park. Only 2.5
twisty miles up the steep road
you'll find a parking area for the

Lady Bird Johnson Grove, where
the former First Lady dedicated
the park in 1968. A 1-mile loop
nature trail here introduces families to redwoods as tall as football
fields are long, some of them
hollowed out by fire, others blown
down by wind. If the fog that
sometimes shrouds this area
blocks your view of the treetops,
there is much life in the understory, where rose-flowered
salmonberries, ghostly western
hemlock trees, forest ferns, and
rhododendrons grow.

   Continue east on Bald Hills
Road another 6 miles to the access

road to the **Tall Trees Grove.** From the parking area, a steep trail drops 1.6 miles down to the grove *(permit required for trail access, available from any park visitor center).* Those who would rather hike and camp can take the 17-mile round-trip **Redwood Creek Trail** *(Trailhead on Bald Hills Rd., less than 1 mile E of jct. with US 101),* which follows Redwood Creek to the Tall Trees Grove.

Less than a mile north of Bald Hills Road off US 101 is the trailhead to a 30-mile section of the ambitious **California Coastal Trail** (see sidebar p. 63), which starts on the beach at the Oregon-California border and ends on a beach at the Mexican border, hewing as much as possible to the coast in between. If you're short on time, save yourself for the shorter Flint Ridge section in the north.

Prairie Creek Redwoods State Park

Back on US 101 and continuing about 3 miles north of Bald Hills Road, you'll come to the **Newton B. Drury Scenic Parkway,** which leads you on an 8-mile journey through a lush strip of coastal redwoods. One mile after leaving US 101, you'll reach the visitor center for 14,000-acre Prairie Creek Redwoods State Park *(707-464-6101, ext. 5301),* the southernmost of the three state parks in the system. Right before the visitor center, you'll often see white-rumped, big antlered Roosevelt elk grazing in the meadow just west of the road.

From trailheads near the visitor center, you can take some of the best day and longer hikes in the park—up into the foothills, down into ferny canyons, and out onto the beach. One of the prettiest is a 4.5-mile ramble down the **James Irvine Trail** to Fern Canyon. From here an unmarked trail leads down to Gold Bluffs Beach. The jaunt becomes an 11-mile loop if you add the **Miner's Ridge Trail.**

Continuing north on the parkway, you'll pass out of Prairie Creek Redwoods State Park and back into the national park again. Here you can take the **Coastal Drive,** an 8-mile, alternately paved and unpaved road *(not for RVs or*

Lichens, Jedediah Smith Redwoods SP

Mushrooms, Prairie Creek Redwoods SP

trailers) that skirts the mouth of the Klamath River and takes you along wave-battered cliffs with great ocean views. Gray whale-watching is one of the lures that brings people to the coast in the spring and fall. To cross the Klamath River, which is bounded by Yurok reservation lands, you must turn inland to rejoin US 101. Once across the river, you can return to the north side of the Klamath estuary on Requa Road, about 3 miles north of the Klamath River Bridge. Again you'll have cliff-top views of the ocean and river mouth.

The California Coastal Trail, interrupted by the river, heads north along the shore here *(from Klamath Overlook, marked on all park maps)*, a segment of about 4 miles that takes you to **Lagoon Creek,** where you'll meet US 101 again. Around this freshwater lagoon, and climbing to high ocean views, is the 1-mile **Yurok Loop.** When you're not looking for whales, there are also brown pelicans in the summer, puffins and cormorants on the cliffs, sea lions just outside the surf, and sea stars and anemones in the tide pools.

Del Norte Coast Redwoods State Park

Back on US 101 and continuing north, you'll come to 6,400-acre Del Norte Coast Redwoods State Park *(707-464-6101 ext.5120),* with 8 miles of coastline and great ocean views. Steep cliffs make most of the rocky sea coast inaccessible except by **Damnation Creek Trail** *(Trailhead on US 101 at Milepost 16).* The trail drops you down through a redwood forest where rhododendrons bloom in the spring. Just south of here is a half-mile of sandy beach known as **False Klamath Cove.** The steep slope, rough seas, and cold water make the beach unsafe for swimming but at low tide the tide-pooling is excellent. (Remember that marine organisms are easily destroyed; if you pick something up, replace it exactly as you found it.)

Jedediah Smith Redwoods State Park

The northernmost park is 9,500-acre Jedediah Smith Redwoods State Park *(8 miles NE of Crescent City on US 199; 707-464-6101 ext. 5112 in season, ext. 5101 off season).* Through it flows the emerald green **Smith River,** the last major

---

There's a Difference

The redwoods in Sequoia and Kings Canyon National Parks (see pp. 172-177), and the redwoods along the California coast are not the same tree. The coast redwood *(Sequoia sempervirens)* grows taller (up to 367 feet), lives up to 2,000 years, has bark about a foot thick, and can reproduce from seeds or a sprout. The giant sequoia *(Sequoiadendron giganteum)* grows thicker (up to 41 feet in diameter), can live more than 3,000 years, has bark up to 31 inches thick, and can reproduce only from seeds. A third member of this family, the smaller dawn redwood *(Metasequoia glyptostroboides),* is found in central China.

Exuberant surfer, Crescent Beach, Redwood National and State Park

undammed river in California and also the cleanest. The Smith slows down after spring runoff to provide good swimming and some beachfront. The aptly named **Stout Tree**—a coast redwood with a 16-foot girth—is here at the **Stout Grove,** across the river from the park's visitor center.

Near the Jedediah Smith campground, a 0.6-mile self-guided nature trail emphasizes the park's vegetation. Besides redwoods, you'll find western hemlock, Sitka spruce, grand and Douglas-fir, and the less common Port-Orford cedar, with tanoak, madrone, red alder, bigleaf and vine maple, and California bay in the understory. A wide range of species and varieties of shrubs, flowers, ferns, mosses, and lichens make up the dense ground cover.

The park offers some horse and bicycle paths, as well as numerous hiking trails. A favorite is the 1.5-mile **Simpson Reed Trail** *(2 miles SW of Jedediah Smith campground on US 199 at Walker Rd.),* an easy, double loop that passes through a superb redwood grove. And for driving scenery, you can't beat the 33-mile **Smith River Byway** (Calif. 199), which begins at the junction of US 101 and Calif. 199 east of Crescent City and ends at the Collier Tunnel near the California-Oregon border. Deep green pools, waterfalls, and white-water rapids compete for your attention with the rhododendrons, azaleas, and ferns in the redwood forest. From November through April, you can fish for chinook salmon and steelhead (Steelhead are catch-and-release.) Kayaking and rafting enthusiasts float the rivers, too, tackling some difficult white water in the spring. ■

Six Rivers National Forest

■ 980,000 acres (Smith River NRA 300,000 acres) ■ Northern California, access 20 miles east of Crescent City on Calif. 199 ■ Year-round ■ Camping, hiking, backpacking, walking, orienteering, boating, white-water rafting and kayaking, canoeing, swimming, scuba diving, tubing, fishing, mountain biking, off-road vehicle riding, horseback riding, cross-country skiing, snowshoeing, bird-watching, wildlife viewing, wildflower viewing ■ Contact the national forest, 1330 Bayshore Way, Eureka, CA 95501; phone 707-442-1721. www.r5.fs.fed.us/sixrivers

SIX RIVERS NATIONAL FOREST LIES "behind the redwood curtain," very much in the shade of its neighbor to the west, Redwood National and State Parks (see pp. 24-29). Still, its many rivers, rich cultural heritage, and solitude offer visitors fine recreational opportunities. A narrow strip of inland forest stretching 140 miles south from the Oregon border, Six

South Fork, Smith River

Rivers extends up to the 6,500-foot elevations of the Trinity Alps Wilderness. Because of its fairly remote location in the northwestern corner of the state, it's not very heavily visited even though it contains Smith River National Recreation Area (see pp. 36–38), one of only three congressionally designated National Recreation Areas in California.

Created in 1947 from parts of three national forests to the north and east, Six Rivers National Forest encompasses a mix of topography, soils, and localized climates that produce an unusually rich and varied flora. Through it runs about 9 percent of California's total runoff, flowing in 1,500 streams, rivers, and waterways. Of its six rivers—the Smith, the Klamath, the Trinity, the Eel, the Mad, and the Van Duzen—the first four are designated Wild and Scenic Rivers. Well-known for rafting and kayaking, the Smith, Klamath, and Trinity Rivers also offer good fishing, although some restrictions on taking salmon and steelhead exist. Three nationally designated scenic byways pass through Six Rivers National Forest, which also includes four wilderness areas.

What to See and Do

At Six Rivers, you can plunk your-self down at a sandy beach on any of the rivers that cross the bound-aries of the forest. One nice spot is **Hawkins Bar** on the Trinity River *(from Willow Creek, go E 6.5 miles on Calif. 299, turn N onto Hawkins Bar river access road)*, where a trail leads to a small sandy beach for sunbathing and swimming. Rafters can put in from this day-use area, which also allows access to fishing.

Six designated botanical areas protect wildflower displays, conifer diversity, distinctive plant communities, and several species of rare plants, such as the Califor-nia lady's slipper orchid and Bolander's lily. An easy one to get to is 1,077-acre **Horse Mountain Botanical Area** *(Calif. 299 30 miles E from Arcata to Lord Ellis Summit; follow FR 1 S)*, where you'll find stunted Jeffrey pines, colorful stonecrops in summer, and golden fawn lilies in spring, as well as a view of the ocean to the west and the Trinity Alps to the east.

If you want more vigorous activity, some 200 miles of trails offer hikes on which you'll encounter few other humans. Among these are three national recreation trails, including the historic 32-mile **South Kelsey National Recreation Trail** *(From jct. of US 101 and Calif. 199 just N of Crescent City, go 7.2 miles E on Calif. 199, then left on South Fork Rd. for 13.7 miles to FR 15, 1 mile past Steven Bridge. Go S for 3.5 miles on FR 15, then left on gravel road FR 15N39 and 2 miles to trailhead)*. Originally 200 miles long, the trail was built by Chi-nese laborers in 1851 to connect Crescent City and Fort Jones. For the first 7 miles the trail follows the South Fork Smith River, then climbs through tall pine and fir forests. About 10.5 miles from the trailhead, you'll reach the former fire lookout site on **Baldy Peak,** with 360-degree views of the Pacific to the west, the rugged Siskyou Mountains to the north, the Marble Mountains to the

Drift-boat fishermen, Smith River

Steelhead caught in net, Smith River

A Primer on Salmon and Steelhead

Commercial and sport fishermen prize the Pacific salmon, which once swam up California streams as far south as the Ventura River, but now are found largely in the Northwest. The salmon and its cousin the steelhead trout are anadromous fish, which means they live in salt water most of their lives but are born in fresh water and return there to spawn. The three most significant species—the chinook or king salmon, the smaller silver or coho salmon, and the steelhead trout—have suffered declines over the last century. Among the arguable reasons: Dams that block migration routes, heavy commercial fishing at sea, silt in the rivers from logging and mining operations, water pollution, and drought. Even rivers that run clean and uninterrupted, such as the Smith, have seen lean runs.

The big king salmon born in the rivers migrate down to the ocean, where they live for five or more years before returning to spawn. Most of them make the upstream journey in the fall, but some find their way up the Sacramento River in winter, thanks to cool water released from Shasta Dam for irrigators downstream. Once they've made their run, they die. Silver salmon follow a similar pattern but use smaller streams and sometimes survive in fresh water for a year or two. Steelhead politely stay out of the salmon's way, spawning from December to April in the Smith. Unlike salmon, they survive parenthood to make several trips to the ocean and back to their spawning grounds.

The mystery of how these fish find their way "home" elicits a lot of theories. Research has shown that in their travels the fish appear to recognize marine landmarks and light patterns. Scientists believe the key to finding their spawning stream, though, is its odor. There's no smell like home.

Following pages: White-water kayaking, Middle Fork Smith River

south, and—on a clear day—Mount Shasta to the east.

For greater solitude, try **Yolla-Bolly-Middle Eel Wilderness** (707-983-6118) on the Middle Fork of the Eel. A number of trails into the wilderness start along Forest Road 27 (from Bridgeville, E on Calif. 36 past Dinsmore. Right on Cty. Rd. 501; in 20 miles it becomes Cty. Rd. 504. Follow Cty. Rd. 504 to Three Forks and follow FR 27). More heavily visited is **Trinity Alps Wilderness** (707-442-1721), but entry from the Six Rivers side is much lighter than from the Shasta-Trinity side (from Willow Creek, E on Calif. 299 to Hawkins Bar. Left on FR 2, then 1.5 miles to Cty. Rd. 402. Go 13 miles on Cty. Rd. 402, left on FR 7N15, then 5 miles to New River trailhead).

Driving

If you happen to be heading toward the Central Valley, the **Trinity Scenic Byway** (Calif. 299) is a winding and picturesque route largely along the Trinity River that takes you from the junction of Calif. 299 and US 101 in Arcata east 150 miles through Bigfoot and historic mining country to Redding. You'll traverse coastal plains, steep granite cliffs, arid manzanita, and digger pine hillsides. Look out for digger pinecones in fall; these hard, heavy cones can be as dangerous as falling rocks. In the spring the redbuds are spectacular.

Visitors with off-road vehicles might enjoy the forest's 149-mile segment of the **California Backcountry Discovery Trail** (From Mendocino Cty., go trough Covelo on Cty. Rd. 503 and follow Discovery Trail signs). This good quality dirt road is a jump-off point to many recreation opportunities in the southern part of the forest. Parts of the route are quite remote, so be sure you have adequate fuel, food, and water to carry you through to the next facilities.

Smith River National Recreation Area

Tucked into the northwest corner of the state, Smith River National Recreation Area's 300,000 acres encompass the largest undammed wild and scenic river watershed in the country. Dropping steeply from their headwaters (mostly in the Siskyou Mountains), the three forks of the Smith pass through a thick forest of pines and firs and madrones, and their waters deepen the jade color of serpentine rock that lines their beds. Year-round clear water is testimony to the health of this watershed, which supports one of the better spawning runs of steelhead and salmon in the Northwest. Your first stop should be the headquarters in Gasquet (18 miles E of Crescent City on US 199; 707-442-1721), near the confluence of the river's North and Middle Forks. Paddlers can get valuable information on river conditions, and others can get maps for hiking.

Paddling

All three forks of the Smith have navigable stretches, depending on your skill level and the time of year. Because no engineer is controlling a spigot on a dam, the Smith's steep runs can rev up to

Rushing waters, South Fork Smith River

Class V white water in early spring, then subside to a bottom-scraping trickle by midsummer. All three forks of the Smith pass through rugged country, with rough roads and unmapped trails. Paddlers and others should be sure to get maps and specific directions from NRA headquarters in Gasquet.

You'll find some challenging water on tributary creeks such as **Baldface Creek,** a tributary of the North Fork *(accessible via Wimer Rd. in Oregon);* **Hurdygurdy Creek,** within the South Fork drainage *(accessible off of Fox Ridge Rd. in California);* or **Hardscrabble Creek** in the Middle Fork drainage *(accessible via Low Divide Rd./Cty. Rd. 305 in California).* These stretches are only for well-prepared experts. For a more relaxed Class I-II paddle, put in on the main stem of the Smith where the Middle and South Forks meet *(from US 199 at Milepost 7.2 turn onto South Fork Rd. and drive 0.5 mile to the River Access sign),* or downstream a little way at Hiouchi Bridge.

Nature Walks
The North Fork Smith River is known for a designated botanical area that includes some unusual plant communities. Species that have adapted to the region's mineral-rich but nutrient-poor serpentine soils include Port-Orford cedar, brewers spruce, Alaskan yellow cedar, and the rare Bolander's lily. One place to visit—for great swimming holes as well as unusual plants—is the **North Fork River Access** *(From Calif. 197 near Hiouchi or from Rowdy Creek Rd. near town of Smith River on Calif. 101, take Low Divide Rd. to the bridge across the North Fork at Milepost 25. River Access road is on NW side of bridge).*

On the Middle Fork of the Smith, the 2-mile round-trip **Myrtle Creek Interpretive Trail** *(N side of US 199 at Milepost 7)* takes you through a conifer forest that is home to the rare insect-eating California pitcher plant. For a closer view, visit the **Darlingtonia Trail** *(N side of US 199 at Milepost 17.9).* ∎

Humboldt Bay National Wildlife Refuge

■ 3,000 acres ■ Northern California, 7 miles south of Eureka off US 101
■ Best months Nov.-Dec., March-April ■ Hiking, walking, sea kayaking, canoeing, bird-watching, wildlife viewing ■ Contact the refuge, 1020 Ranch Rd., Loleta, CA 95551; phone 707-733-5406. pacific.fws.gov/visitor/california.html

THIS IS THE LARGEST NATURAL bay north of San Francisco, once fringed by deep old-growth forests, marshes, and mudflats that provided a rest stop for thousands of birds on the Pacific flyway. The 14-mile-long bay, protected by a sandbar, formed 10,000 years ago, at the end of the last ice age. During Eureka's heyday as a busy port for the timber and logging industries, bird traffic plummeted. But since 1971 the U.S. Fish and Wildlife Service has begun acquiring lands and restoring the marshes, mudflats, willow groves, and open water sought by aquatic life and the migratory birds that are thickest from September to April.

Key to the refuge are the extensive beds of eelgrass in the mudflats. The eelgrass provides food and supports a large portion of the total world population of black brant, a small, black-headed goose, during winter and spring. Sandpipers, curlews, egrets, and herons are also among the 200 bird species seen here. There are dungeness crabs and clams in the mud, and at high tide ocean fish such as sanddabs and salmon enter the slough. Every first and third Saturday, interpreters guide visitors through the rare plant community of the **Lanphere Dunes,** where you'll see beach layia and Humboldt Bay wallflower.

Trails through the refuge include the 3-mile round-trip **Hookton Slough Trail** from the Hookton Road visitor contact point, and the 2-mile **Shorebird Loop,** scheduled by mid-2001 to become a 0.75-mile trail with a 3-mile seasonal loop. The refuge is set to expand to more than 9,000 acres, and a new visitor center is to be completed in summer 2001. ■

Headwaters Forest Reserve

■ 7,400 acres ■ Northern California, 1 mile south of Eureka off US 101
■ Best season summer ■ Hiking, walking, guided walks, bird-watching, wildlife viewing ■ Contact Arcata Field Office, Bureau of Land Management, 1695 Heindon Rd., Arcata, CA 95521; phone 707-825-2300

A 15-YEAR BATTLE OVER the fate of northern California's last large unprotected stand of old-growth redwoods was resolved in 1999 when the federal government and the state of California bought these forested lands in the Coast Ranges from the Pacific Lumber Company. Public protests over plans to log the property, and concerns over spawning streams and birdlife in the area, led to the 380-million-dollar purchase, a price that some conservation groups labeled extortion by the timber company's Texas owner, Charles Hurwitz.

More than half of the reserve's acreage is old-growth redwood, which provides shelter for the endangered marbled murrelet, a chubby black-and-white seabird that nests inland in trees. The reserve also protects sections of the **Elk River,** a spawning stream for coho salmon that drains into Arcata Bay. Management plans are still being developed, but the emphasis is on habitat protection, not recreation. Hikers can take day trips into the north end of the reserve on the 5-mile **Elk River Trail** (via Elk River Rd. exit off US 101, 1 mile S of Eureka), where they can approach but not enter old-growth areas. Hikes at the south end are guided by BLM interpreters (707-825-2300 for reservations. 20-person limit 4 days per week May-Nov.). The 4-mile round-trip (access from Newburg Rd. in Fortuna) travels the edge of an old-growth forest along **Salmon Creek.** ■

Humboldt Redwoods State Park

- 53,000 acres - Northern California, 45 miles south of Eureka off US 101
- Best season summer - Camping, hiking, backpacking, walking, guided walks, orienteering, kayaking, canoeing, swimming, fishing, biking, mountain biking, birdwatching, wildlife viewing, wildflower viewing - Contact the park, P.O. Box 100, Weott, CA 95571; phone 707-946-2409. www.humboldtredwoods.org

SINCE 1921, WHEN THE SAVE-THE-REDWOODS LEAGUE purchased the first plot of land here, Humboldt Redwoods State Park has grown grove by grove to include 17,000 acres of old-growth redwoods and nearly all of the Bull Creek watershed. At the heart of the park is Rockefeller Forest, named for John D. Rockefeller, Jr., who gave 2 million dollars to help the league purchase 10,000 acres of redwoods along Bull Creek from a logging company. Here, trees rise from green pockets of redwood sorrel and lady fern on the forest floor. The largest remaining old-growth coast redwood forest in the world, Rockefeller Forest holds trees that are thousands of years old and have never been logged—a mesmerizing world as pristine as it was 100 years ago.

What to See and Do

The main road through the park is the 32-mile **Avenue of the Giants** *(From the north, take Weott exit off US 101 and turn right; go 1.5 miles to visitor center. From the south, take Myers Flat exit and turn right; go 4.4 miles to visitor center).* Various groves with distinctively big redwoods are within easy walks of the roadway.

For example, **Founders Grove** *(4 miles N of visitor center, off Avenue of the Giants on Dyerville Loop Rd.)* is home to the ancient **Dyerville Giant,** a mammoth specimen, more than a thousand years old, that stood 362 feet tall before it toppled in 1991. At 17 feet in diameter, the tree still dwarfs mere humans, even on its side. Or take the short trail from the **Big Trees Area** parking lot on Mattole Road *(8 miles W of visitor center)* to the **Giant Tree.** At 359 feet, it is the tallest in the park since the Dyerville Giant went down.

The park is laced with trails where you can hike, ride horses (your own), or mountain bike. Most of the mountain bike routes are located in the **Bull Creek** area of the park *(8 miles NW of visitor center).* Note that mountain bikes are restricted to the park fire roads and are not allowed on the many hiking trails.

For more ambitious hikers, a strenuous trail heads out from the Big Trees Area to 3,379-foot **Grasshopper Mountain,** the highest point in the park, with panoramic views of the landscape and the redwoods. About a 7-mile trek one way, it's a good choice for an all-day or overnight hike. ■

Founders Grove, Humboldt Redwoods State Park

Roosevelt elk, Sinkyone Wilderness State Park

Lost Coast

■ 73,367 acres ■ Northern California, 50 miles of coast between Petrolia (mouth of Mattole River) and south end of Sinkyone Wilderness State Park (mouth of Usal Creek), off US 101 ■ Best season summer ■ Camping, hiking, backpacking, walking, fishing, bird-watching, whale-watching, wildlife viewing, wildflower viewing ■ Adm. fees ■ Some roads impassable in wet weather. Call Bureau of Land Management for current road conditions. Beware of black bears in King Range ■ Contact Arcata Resource Area, Bureau of Land Management, 1695 Heindon Rd., Arcata, CA 95521, phone 707-825-2300, www.mtnvisions.com/Aurora/krange.html; or Sinkyone Wilderness State Park, P.O. Box 245, Whitethorn, CA 95589, phone 707-986-7711. parks.ca.gov/north/ncrd/swsp.html

TRAVELERS USUALLY DESCRIBE the coast of northern California as rugged and wild, but they often express that opinion from behind the wheel of a car. But there is still one lengthy section of California coast where the roadbuilders shied away, a craggy-cliffed, surf-smashed, fogbound, rain-plastered, off-the-map place where stiff winds chill to the bone, trails climb abruptly to 4,000-foot ridges, and rogue waves rise from nowhere to mow down anything on the beach: the Lost Coast. Nearly 300 species of native and migratory birds have been spotted along this remote stretch, including the spotted owl and the threatened bald eagle.

Most of this remote place is encompassed by 66,000-acre King Range National Conservation Area. Here the King Range crowds the ocean along a bulge of coastline between the mouth of the Mattole River and

Shelter Cove. Severely folded and faulted by pressures of the tectonic plates grinding together just offshore, the mountains have been forced upward some 66 feet in the last 6,000 years. Young as it is, the range is already weatherworn. Wind and surf attack the shore, and streams fed by heavy rainfall of up to 200 inches annually have cut deep canyons through the cliffs. Most of the rock here is graywacke, a dark, crumbly sandstone that makes up the coast's famous Black Sands Beach. Abutting the conservation area to the south is Sinkyone Wilderness State Park. The park's 7,367 acres include grasslands, coastal bluffs, small groves of coast redwoods, and old-growth Douglas-fir forests.

What to See and Do

A network of dirt and gravel roads will allow four-wheelers into various corners of the Lost Coast, but by far the best way to explore the region is on foot. Indeed, the California Coastal Trail (see sidebar p. 63) runs the length of the Lost Coast although at times it heads inland for lack of continuous trail on the coastline.

King Range National Conservation Area

Probably the most popular trek in the King Range is the **Lost Coast Trail,** which follows the coast from the north end of the conservation area 25 miles to **Shelter Cove** in the south *(from US 101 in Humboldt Redwoods State Park, take Bull Lake Creek Rd. 23 miles W to town of Honeydew; go N on Mattole Rd. 18 miles to Lighthouse Rd., then W for 7 miles to trailhead at mouth of Mattole River).* It's best to hike north to south to keep prevailing winds at your back. The now abandoned **Punta Gorda Lighthouse** is 3.2 miles down the trail.

The Lost Coast

A favorite camping spot about halfway along is **Big Flat,** on a meadowy coastal terrace above a creek. Bears have been a problem here, so take care not to attract them. Bring dried rather than fresh, fragrant food, and leave toothpaste, shampoos, and lotions at home. Don't leave food in your tent or backpack. Suspend food, garbage, and all scented items in a tree at least 12 feet high and 10 feet from the trunk, or store in bear-proof containers. Clean up any spills, and don't leave dirty dishes around. These precautions protect both you and the bears.

If you're hiking this trail during the spring and fall, you'll have less company, but whenever you hike it, you're likely to spy harbor seals and sea lions in the offshore rocks and kelp beds. Now and then you'll have to climb over talus piles or outcrops, or avoid the surf as it covers the beach at high tide. In fact it's wise to carry a tide table, and to hike stretches such as the area near Punta Gorda from Sea Lion Gulch to Randall Creek; and from Miller Flat to Gitchell Creek during an outgoing tide to avoid being trapped. The whole hike should take three to four days.

For a much shorter trek—and sweeping views of the coastline and inland mountain ranges—try the **Chemise Mountain Trail,** 1.5 miles one way from the Nadelos and Wailaki Campgrounds to the 2,598-foot summit of **Chemise Mountain.** It's best to get maps and directions from the BLM's King Range Administrative Office in Whitethorn *(707-986-5400).*

Another good walk—one that is infamous for its steep grade—is **Buck Creek Trail** *(N on King Peak Rd., off Shelter Cove Rd.).* This 4-mile one-way trek takes in 4,088-foot **King Peak**—only 3 miles from the coast, with great views both oceanward and inland—and follows an old logging road through forests to the coast.

From the coast you can keep going 5.2 miles to the isolated community of **Shelter Cove,** completing what is perhaps the most popular of the King Crest/beach loops. Those who don't want to backpack can take Shelter Cove Road off US 101 to Shelter Cove, and visit Black Sands Beach and **Abalone Point.**

Sinkyone Wilderness State Park

This remote park , with many of the same features as the conservation area, was created in 1975 when the first 3,430 acres were acquired at Needle Rock, where the park visitor center is today *(36 miles SW of Redway and Garberville via US 101 and Briceland Rd.; last 9 miles are unpaved).* Expanded in 1986, Sinkyone now totals 7,367 acres, with nearly 40 miles of trails for hiking, bicycling, and horseback riding. Be aware that some of the interior roads are impassable in wet weather.

Roosevelt elk that once roamed in this area were hunted out about a hundred years ago, but a transplanted herd of about 85 animals is back in the park today. From the visitor center, a short walk takes you down to **Needle Rock Beach,** where you can walk either way for views of cliffs, offshore rocks, and seashore wildlife. ■

Western gulls, Mendocino Headlands State Park

Mendocino State Parks

■ 16,542 acres ■ Northern California, small coastal parks along Calif. I
between Fort Bragg and Point Arena ■ Best months April-Nov. ■ Camping,
hiking, walking, guided walks, boating, kayaking, canoeing, tide-pooling, swimming,
scuba diving, surf-fishing, biking, mountain biking, bird-watching, whale-watching,
wildlife viewing, wildflower viewing ■ Adm. fees ■ Contact Russian Gulch State
Park, P.O. Box 440, Calif. I, Mendocino, CA 95460; phone 707-937-5804.
www.mcn.org/1/mendoparks/mendo.htm

THE MENDOCINO COAST IS a gentle inward curve between Point Arena
in the south and Punta Gorda in the north, pocked by bays, creek-made
canyons, and beaches. This section of coast, with its run of small parks,
provides excellent examples of what naturalists call an "ecological
staircase," wave-cut terraces stacked atop each other on the mountainsides facing the sea where each terrace represents a different era and a
quite different set of flora and fauna. As you climb from the first terrace
near sea level to the highest, about 650 feet above, you're traveling
100,000 years back in time at each of the five levels. From the grassy
terrace just above the beach and tide-pool zone, the staircase rises
through forests of redwood and fir to pine forests, sometimes stunted by
poor soil and weather. Along with these pygmy forests, the terraces also
sometimes feature mossy, acidic bogs where insect-devouring California
pitcher plants grow.

   Most visitors are here to see the surf crashing against the headlands,
and the sea lions and seals on the rocks offshore. During spring and fall,
gray whales are also spotted spouting farther out at sea. The variety of
terrain—including sand dunes, grassy bluffs, lakes, waterfalls, and redwood groves—makes the frequent stops worth it.

What to See and Do

From north to south, the parks in this stretch of the Mendocino coast are: MacKerricher State Park, Jug Handle State Reserve, Caspar Headlands State Beach and Reserve, Russian Gulch State Park, and Mendocino Headlands, Van Damme, and Manchester State Parks. Montgomery Woods State Reserve and Navarro River Redwoods and Hendy Woods State Parks, though inland, are also part of this group. *(Contact all the parks at 707-937-5804.)* With beaches, redwood groves, creeks, camping areas, headlands, and marine sanctuaries, these Mendocino parks offer snapshots of the natural coastal environment spaced among picturesque seaside towns. Whichever ones you choose to visit, you can't go wrong.

Just 5 miles north of Fort Bragg on Calif. 1, **MacKerricher State Park** surrounds **Lake Cleone,** a tidal lagoon that is stocked with trout and is a favorite stop for migrating birds. The park's trails are open to bicyclists, horseback riders, and hikers, and a handicapped accessible path, **Laguna Point Boardwalk,** leads out to seal- and whale-watching spots on **Laguna Point.**

Jug Handle State Reserve, 8 miles south on Calif. 1, is small but interesting for the 2.5-mile **Ecological Staircase Trail** that climbs up five terraces, going back in time 100,000 years as it rises 100 feet between terraces. The third terrace features a pygmy forest, where a Mendocino cypress, which might grow 100 feet high elsewhere, will

Bull kelp washed up on the beach, Mendocino Headlands State Park

be only 2 feet tall; it may, however, have as many as 80 growth rings.

Four miles south of Jug Handle is **Russian Gulch State Park,** a 1,300-acre park featuring bicycle and equestrian trails, a beach, dramatic headlands, and the **"Punch Bowl,"** a sea cave you can look into through its collapsed roof. Inland hiking trails lead to the 36-foot-high **Russian Gulch Falls** in the pine forest along the gulch.

The next stop heading south is **Mendocino Headlands State Park.** At the **visitor center** you can view historic and naturalist exhibits and pick up maps. If you're in the mood to stretch your legs, you can hike the trails that wind around the cliffs overlooking sandy coves and offshore rocks where waves crash through arches. Below the bluff, accessible by trail or car, is **Big River Beach.**

Van Damme State Park, 3 miles south of Mendocino Headlands, offers a spacious campground, a **visitor center** with exhibits, and the half-mile **Bog Trail** from the visitor center to a fern-framed bog. The 10-mile **Fern Canyon Trail,** which also starts at the visitor center, loops by a pygmy forest. The beach, easily accessible from Calif. 1, is a haven for scuba and abalone divers.

From Calif. 1, head 23 miles inland on Calif. 128 into the Anderson Valley, where **Montgomery Woods State Reserve,** and **Navarro River Redwoods** and **Hendy Woods State Parks** protect groves of mostly second-growth big trees. Both state parks are set along the **Navarro River,** which attracts anglers for fall steelhead runs and kayakers during spring runoff.

Back out along the coast, **Manchester State Park** is 7 miles north of Point Arena, where the San Andreas Fault runs into the sea. Anglers come here to surf-fish or catch salmon and steelhead during spawning runs. Others come to walk the driftwood-strewn beach, bird-watch for tundra swans and other species, or check out the rampant wildflowers. ■

Abalone

Commercial harvesting of abalone is banned along the California coast, and you can't even collect them for sport south of San Francisco. But there's still a great hunger, particularly in Asia, for this delicacy—which is actually a large, single-footed ocean-bottom snail in a pretty shell. The black market pays poachers $75 a pound for abalone. Divers north of the Bay Area who go after red abalone for sport—and there are plenty of them in the rough waters of the Sonoma Coast near Salt Point—must "free dive" without scuba gear.

Once upon a time you could buy an abalone sandwich for $1.50, but that was before the population plummeted in the 1970s. Of the eight species of abalone along the California coast, two are on the endangered list and two are threatened. The white abalone, for instance, found around the Channel Islands, went from a population of 4 million 30 years ago to fewer than 2,000 today, making the creatures too far-flung to reproduce.

Salt Point State Park

■ 6,000 acres ■ Northern California, 90 miles north of San Francisco on Calif. I ■ Year-round ■ Camping, hiking, walking, guided walks, tide-pooling, scuba diving, fishing, horseback riding, whale-watching ■ Adm. fee ■ Contact the park, 25050 Calif. I, Jenner, CA 95450; phone 707-847-3221. parks.ca.gov/north/russian/spsp248.htm

NAMED FOR THE SEA SALT deposits that coast Indians found here, this park has a number of attractions. Among them is **Gerstle Cove Underwater Reserve** *(Calif. 1 to park entrance, then 0.5 mile W)*, tucked into a steep-walled cove where currents eddy and kelp beds sway. Many divers come to the park to harvest red abalone in the rough waters outside the cove (see sidebar

Pearly interior of abalone shell

opposite), where they take their chances with the occasional great white shark. Those who simply want to experience the rich underwater world do their diving in the reserve. Non-divers can walk the beach and explore the tide pools during low tide. (Please leave rocks unturned; fragile marine organisms can be damaged or destroyed if simply exposed to the sun.)

At the top of the coastal ridge is a large open prairie and a pygmy forest of madrone, 4-foot-tall, single-branch cypress, and even the normally gigantic redwood. Accessible on a 3-mile loop hike *(start at Woodside Campground, E of Calif. 1)*, the forest is one of only a few isolated patches in northern California, where the trees are stunted by nutrient poor, highly acidic soil with an iron hardpan only 18 inches below. Hikers or mountain bikers *(allowed on paved or fire roads)* can look for encounters with such critters as long-tailed weasels, wild pigs, black-tailed deer, raccoons, coyotes, and a variety of rodents.

On the park's north side is the **Kruse Rhododendron State Reserve** *(3 miles N of Gerstle Cove entrance on Calif. 1, turn E on Kruse Ranch Rd.)*, a 317-acre plot where rhododendrons burst into pink bloom every May. The bushes took hold after a severe fire near the turn of the 20th century burned the mixed redwood, fir, and hardwood forest, clearing the understory and allowing the rhodies to thrive. Second-growth redwoods and other trees now growing up around the rhododendrons will eventually take over again.

After the fall rains, another attraction is mushroom collecting. Because Salt Point is the only state park in the area that allows it, mushroom hunters flock here in search of edibles such as King Boletes and Chanterelles. (Be sure to correctly identify any mushroom before eating it!) There is a five-pound limit per person per day, and collecting is prohibited at Kruse Rhododendron State Reserve. ■

A barefoot walk, Limantour Beach, Point Reyes National Seashore

Point Reyes National Seashore

■ 71,000 acres ■ Northern California, 45 miles north of San Francisco off Calif. I ■ Year-round ■ Hiking, backpacking, guided walks, canoeing, tide-pooling, mountain biking, horseback riding, bird-watching, whale-watching, wild-flower viewing ■ Contact the national seashore, Point Reyes Station, CA 94956; phone 415-663-1092 or 415-633-8054 (camping reservations). www.nps.gov/pore

TOMALES POINT, THE NORTHWEST TIP OF THE triangle-shaped peninsula that is Point Reyes National Seashore, is like the bow of a schooner, pointing in the direction the ship is traveling. The schooner in this case is the Northern Pacific plate, which is inching northward each year (see sidebar opposite). Everything west of Tomales Bay, the narrow finger of water that separates the peninsula from the mainland, is also west of the San Andreas Fault and thus resides on the Pacific plate. The geologic journeying began some 100 million years ago in the vicinity of the Tehachapi Mountains in southern California, and it's been a wild ride. As the Northern Pacific plate slid laterally against the North American continent, the peninsula rose and fell beneath the ocean surface a number of times, gathering layers of ocean-floor sediments atop the granite pushing up from beneath.

These different layers of soil, combined with the area's temperate climate, support a variety of plant communities seen in few other regions of North America. Marshland, coastal strand, and marine algal areas are cheek by jowl with Douglas-fir forest, bishop pine forest, and northern scrub. Species endemic to the reserve include Point Reyes lupine, Point Reyes bent grass, San Francisco's owl clover, and Marin manzanita.

A diversity of animal life thrives here as well. Harbor seals, elephant seals, and sea lions cluster on the craggy rocks of Point Reyes itself, and gray whales surface offshore during their migrations (see p. 54). A wealth of birds—more than 470 species, including egrets, ospreys, and belted kingfishers—are drawn to **Drakes Estero,** an estuarine salt marsh opening into Drakes Bay, both named for Sir Francis Drake, who stopped here in 1579. Formed where freshwater streams meet the sea, creating brackish water, estuarine environments are essential buffers, reducing shoreline erosion and improving water quality by assimilating pollutants such as sewage outfalls and agricultural runoff. The estuary here is home to a large harbor seal breeding colony, while the warm shallow waters of neighboring Tomales Bay also are a well-known nursery—for great white sharks, which feed on sea lions.

Over the years, commercial enterprises such as ranches and logging operations have left their scars, and exotic plants such as European beachgrass have reduced the area's biological diversity. Since its establishment as a national seashore in 1962, however, Point Reyes has regained much of its earlier peacefulness. What you find there today is typical of this coastal area: headlands with crumbly cliffs above breaking surf and offshore rocks where birds and pinnipeds find safe refuge. Estuarine plants such as pickleweed and saltgrass abound in Drakes Estero in the reserve's western half, and the woods and meadows in the eastern half offer numerous campsites.

What to See and Do

When you start your visit at the **Bear Valley Visitor Center** (*Calif. 1 to Olema, go N on Bear Valley Rd.*), don't be put off by the crowds—the visitor center is the locus of educational programs throughout the year, including naturalist talks on everything from sharks to mushrooms. Also nearby is a re-created village, **Kule Loklo** (*0.5 mile from visitor center*), of the indigenous Coast Miwok, who were wiped out after Europeans arrived.

A number of trailheads begin at the visitor center as well. The **Earthquake Trail,** for example, takes you on a half-mile loop, pungent with the scent of bay laurel trees, that straddles the San Andreas Fault near the epicenter

San Andreas Fault

At Point Reyes the power of the San Andreas Fault is vividly on display. Walk the Earthquake Trail and you see the displaced earth left by the great quake of 1906. In the Five Brooks area, streams a stone's throw apart run in opposite directions, their paths jumbled by earthquake-caused shifts of grade. On the west side of the fault, Point Reyes National Seashore, riding aboard the Northern Pacific plate, is traveling north at about 2 inches annually—a rate that has moved Point Reyes 40 miles in a period of 15 million to 20 million years.

Tule Elk

Somewhat smaller than their mountain cousins, tule elk once moved in big herds through the Central Valley of California, and in coastal areas like Point Reyes—until they were hunted nearly to extinction. Then, in 1875 a small group was discovered on a private ranch near Bakersfield and protected. Gradually the herd was rebuilt, and in 1978, 10 tule elk were transplanted to Point Reyes.

The coastal scene must suit them: Reproduction in the Point Reyes herd, now about 500, is too prolific. To slow the growth rate, park officials have begun innoculating female elk with contraceptives. In addition, a group of elk have been moved from the protection of a fenced off area at Tomales Point to fend for themselves in the wilderness on the south end of the island at Limantour.

of the earthquake that leveled San Francisco in 1906. The fault looks like a deeply ploughed furrow, running right through an old farm.

Also leaving from the visitor center, the popular 4.2-mile **Bear Valley Trail** takes you into **Philip Burton Wilderness,** which protects about a third of Point Reyes from development, and all the way to the western shore at **Arch Rock,** where Coast Creek tunnels through to the sea. If you prefer a shorter hike, take offshoots from the main trail up to **Mount Wittenberg** *(4 miles round-trip from visitor center),* from whose summit you'll enjoy views of the Pacific and of the long, curving beach of peaceful **Drakes Bay.**

You can go straight to the bay via Limantour Road *(off Bear Valley Rd., 1.5 miles N of visitor center)* or stop at the Clem Miller Environmental Education Center and hike to the beach along the **Coast Trail.** From the beach, a network of trails will lead you to birderheaven lagoons and some of the forested country where only hike-

Ice plants

Marbled godwit

Point Reyes Lighthouse

in camping is allowed. Try the **Woodward Valley Trail,** or hike the beach to **Alamere Falls,** which cascades down the rocks to the ocean.

You can drive out to hammer-headed **Point Reyes** on **Sir Francis Drake Highway** (*N from visitor center; Bear Valley Rd. becomes Sir Francis Drake Hwy.*). Stop along the way at **Johnson's** (designated "oyster farm" on the park map) if you want to pick up some fresh oysters. Once you reach the point, check out the **Point Reyes Lighthouse,** a favorite whale-watching spot, and the **Sea Lion Overlook.** A short hike out to the eastern end of the point on the quarter-mile **Elephant Seal Overlook Trail** takes you past the historic Point Reyes Lifeboat Station to **Chimney Rock** where you can watch the elephant seals sunning or cavorting on the rocks below. From December to March, the seals migrate here to mate, and in summer they come to molt. Remember, even though they may look comical, the 5,000-pound males are not to be messed with, so all viewing is best done from a distance.

A real treasure of a hike is the 8-mile round-trip **Tomales Point Trail,** at the park's north end. To get there, follow Sir Francis Drake Highway to Pierce Point Road and turn right. Along the way you're likely to see cattle grazing the coastal grasslands, part of working ranches that continue to operate in the park. Park at historic Pierce Point Ranch and head north. The terrain is rolling enough to give you a good workout, and you'll probably see tule elk lounging in the coastal shrubbery en route. As the peninsula narrows, the views grow increasingly dramatic, with the Pacific Ocean on your left and tranquil Tomales Bay on your right—until the two waters meet at a craggy, windswept bluff. ■

Looking for whales, Mendocino Headlands State Park

Whales and Whale-Watching

All up and down the California coast, people climb the headlands or put out in boats in hopes of seeing whales spouting, flipping a fluke, or just showing a little barnacled skin. The whales oblige: They are surprisingly nonchalant about the boats full of humans that chase them around and sometimes the whales seem actually to show off.

Between November and February, Pacific gray whales, the most commonly seen cetacean along the California coast, head south from their summer feeding grounds in Alaska. Hunted nearly to extinction until international treaties protected them in the 1930s, Pacific grays have bounced back and now number about 23,000. Usually led by pregnant females, followed by adults and adolescents, the whales make the 6,000-mile journey to lagoons along the Baja coast, where the females give birth.

An adult gray of about 40 years is 45 feet long and weighs about 50 tons. Its mottled body has no dor-

sal fin but a series of ridges along its back near the tail. Not surprisingly, a newborn calf can be as large as 20 feet long. Born underwater, the babies are surrounded by "midwife" whales who shepherd them immediately to the surface for their first breath.

By May, the whales have begun the return migration, now led by newly pregnant females and mothers keeping a close eye on their young ones. The whales often pass within half a mile of shore, much to the delight of the humans who flock to see them.

Another whale species seen along the coast is the humpback, smaller and darker than the gray, or the even larger blue whale, with long flippers. Humpbacks also migrate to Baja, but they don't come in as close to shore as the gray; you're more apt to see them from a boat near the Channel or Farallon Islands. Have your camera ready: Acrobatic humpbacks often leap from the water, rolling and smacking their fins.

Mount Tamalpais State Park

■ 6,300 acres ■ Northern California, 13 miles north of San Francisco off Calif. 1 ■ Year-round ■ Camping, hiking, walking, guided walks, orienteering, rock climbing, fishing, biking, mountain biking, horseback riding, hang gliding, bird-watching, whale-watching, wildlife viewing, wildflower viewing ■ Adm. fee ■ Contact the park, 801 Panoramic Hwy., Mill Valley, CA 94941; phone 415-388-2070. parks.ca.gov/north/marin/mtsp239.htm

FOR MORE THAN A CENTURY, Bay Area residents have made pilgrimages to "Mount Tam" and climbed to its 2,571-foot East Peak to get the big picture. From the grassy top of the mountain on a clear day, you can see the Sierras, San Francisco Bay, the Marin Headlands, and the Farallon Islands 25 miles off to the west.

Formed by plate tectonics (not volcanic activity, as many people assume), **Mount Tamalpais** is home to more than 7,500 species of plants, including the coast redwood, Douglas-fir, California laurel, calypso orchid, and California poppy. And sharp-eyed (or lucky) visitors may glimpse such wildlife as raccoons, gray foxes, squirrels, bobcats, mountain lions, coyotes,

Joggers, Mount Tamalpais State Park

black-tailed deer, red-tailed hawks, and spotted owls.

Get oriented by making your first stop to pick up maps at the Pan Toll Ranger Station *(from US 101 take Calif. 1 to Stinson Beach turnoff, turn right on Panoramic Hwy. to park entrance)*. Although many people are more than happy simply driving to East Peak *(from the ranger station, cross Panoramic Hwy. to Pantoll Rd. and go 1.25 miles to Ridgecrest Blvd. Turn right to end of road)* and walking less than half a mile to the lookout tower on top, Mount Tam also offers the pleasures to be discovered on its more than 50 miles of hiking trails. The 4-mile round-trip **Steep Ravine Trail** *(Begins near ranger station),* for instance, follows a creek through redwood groves, taking you past several cascades on the way to the coast. (Camping at the Steep Ravine Campground is especially popular; reservations are recommended.) Off Ridgecrest Boulevard you can also hike a section of the **California Coastal Trail** (see sidebar p. 63) for about 4 miles in the park, following the contour of the land at about 1,500 feet above sea level with sensational views. ■

Big-leaf maple edged with California polypody ferns, Muir Woods NM

Muir Woods National Monument

■ 560 acres ■ Northern California, 12 miles north of Golden Gate Bridge ■ Year-round ■ Hiking, wildlife viewing ■ Adm. fee ■ Roads to park steep and winding; vehicles over 35 feet long prohibited. Limited parking; no RV parking facilities ■ Contact the monument, Mill Valley, CA 94941; phone 415-388-2596. www.nps.gov/muwo

As the San Francisco Bay Area filled up with people in the 19th century, the appetite for lumber gobbled redwood forests that had grown for centuries in the valleys along the coast. Congressman William Kent, intending to develop the area for tourism, built an inn and a gravity car railroad amidst the giant trees across San Francisco Bay along Redwood Creek. But as he saw the ancient trees toppling all around, he decided to give his land to the federal government as a preserve. In 1908 President Theodore Roosevelt declared it a national monument. Kent insisted it be named after the noted conservationist John Muir.

Today, Muir Woods, on the south side of Mount Tamalpais (see p. 55), is the only forest of old-growth redwoods close to San Francisco (*from US 101 take Calif. 1 to Stinson Beach turnoff, follow signs to Muir Woods*). The park attracts one million visitors a year, some of whom don't get much farther than the ice-cream stand by the entrance. But numerous short hikes and a few longer ones will take you on unpaved trails to adjacent natural areas such as Mount Tamalpais and the Marin Headlands. Depending on the season, you might see trilliums in bloom, vibrant red toyon berries, and spawning steelhead trout.

What to See and Do

From the visitor center, the **Main Trail** follows Redwood Creek upstream, with informative signs about the age and size of the redwoods all around you, as well as about the creek and the coho salmon and steelhead trout that come up the stream to spawn from January to March. This is an easy stroll on a wide paved path (*wheelchair accessible*) and you can change sides of the stream on any of several bridges to make longer or shorter loops. After a half mile you'll reach **Cathedral Grove,** where you'll stagger backward as you gaze up at trunks that begin wider than 10 feet and rise to tower more than 200 feet overhead.

Pause to note the abundant life on the moist forest floor, rich with ladyferns, lichen, mushrooms and other fungi, and a carpet of redwood sorrel. In addition to salmon and steelhead, you might see crawfish in the creek. Because of the forest's shaded conditions, food is scarce and so are large mammals. Look for Sonoma chipmunks, gray squirrels, black-tailed deer, and an occasional bobcat.

Other trails branch from the Main Trail. **Fern Creek Trail** begins about a quarter-mile beyond Cathedral Grove. Generally flat, the trail runs along the creek for 0.5 mile before climbing to Alice Eastwood campground. Once the terminus of a gravity railcar to Mount Tamalpais, Eastwood has drinking water, rest rooms, and a picnic area. The trail then swings around and back down to Redwood Creek, about 3 miles altogether.

For a chance to have the redwood forest to yourself while enjoying expansive vistas, take the 4-mile **Ben Johnson-Dipsea Loop.** Start at the visitor center and walk 1 mile up the Main Trail to the **Ben Johnson Trail** at Fourth Bridge. After climbing steeply up the canyon to the ridge, turn left onto the **Dipsea Trail.** You will be rewarded with spectacular views of the coast and meadows of wildflowers. The last half mile descends through ferns back to the park entrance. If you're game for a longer hike, stay on the Dipsea Trail to Stinson Beach. ■

Following pages: Coast redwoods, Muir Woods National Monument

Golden Gate National Recreation Area

■ 73,183 acres ■ Northern California, on both sides of the Golden Gate Bridge ■ Best months Sept.-Oct. ■ Camping, hiking, backpacking, walking, guided walks, kayaking, swimming, windsurfing, fishing, biking, mountain biking, horseback riding, hang gliding, bird-watching, whale-watching, wildlife viewing, wildflower viewing ■ Contact the recreation area, Fort Mason, Bldg. 201, San Francisco, CA 94123; phone 415-556-0560. www.nps.gov/goga

A LOT OF PEOPLE WHO HIKE, hang glide, and hang out at historic sites around the mouth of San Francisco Bay have no idea that they're actually visiting a national recreation area. The 73,183-acre Golden Gate National Recreation Area is a patchwork of public lands stretching from the meadows of the Olema Valley near Point Reyes to the cliffs of Fort

Golden Gate Bridge, from western shoreline of Golden Gate National Recreation Area

Funston south of the San Francisco Zoo. Within the citified Bay Area, the GGNRA preserves a linkage of green spaces, including wildlands such as Muir Woods National Monument (see pp. 56-59), along with Alcatraz Island, Marin Headlands, Fort Funston, Fort Mason, Fort Point National Historic Site, and the Presidio of San Francisco.

It doesn't really hang together in an ecological sense—interspersed as it is with fences, posh neighborhoods, and art galleries—but it offers Bay Area residents the chance to escape city life without having to go far for a walk beneath towering redwoods or a stroll along the beach. And it provides habitat for such creatures as sea lions, bobcats, and hawks. The GGNRA also counts among its sites historic fortifications, farms, and museums, as well as nude beaches and the theaters at Fort Mason. If parts of the GGNRA seem too citified for lovers of wildlands, look to the other parts, which allow you to escape for a drive through the peaceful Olema Valley, hang-glide from the cliffs at Fort Funston, or trek the windy beaches of the Marin Headlands.

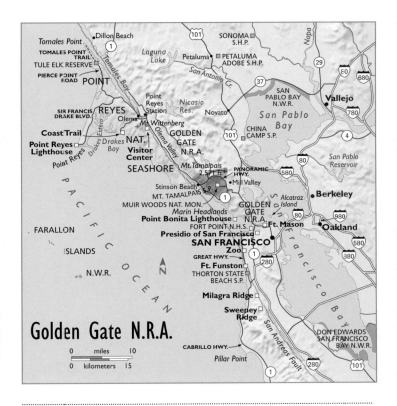

Golden Gate N.R.A.

0   miles   10

0   kilometers   15

What to See and Do

The great variety of sites grouped within the GGNRA means a visitor can choose according to personal interests: History buffs may opt for an array of coastal fortifications, windsurfers will set sail at Crissy Field, and joggers can follow the shady paths through the Presidio or join wildlife lovers heading in for the hills and beaches of the Marin Headlands.

Choose first which side of the bay you want to be on: GGNRA locations on the south side of the Golden Gate offer more history, more developed sites, and more pavement, while visitors to the north side get more open space, more wildlife, and more dirt under

their feet. If you choose the north side of the bridge, stop at the Marin Headlands Visitor Center *(from US 101, take Alexander Ave. exit to Field Rd.; visitor center 1 mile from beach)* for maps and information on the entire area. On the San Francisco side, get the same material from Fort Mason *(4.7 miles SE of Golden Gate Bridge via Lombard St., at intersection of Franklin and Bay Sts.).*

North of the Golden Gate

The **Marin Headlands** form the craggy northern face of San Francisco Bay, a rampart of steep cliffs that face south toward the city and west toward the Pacific Ocean, interspersed with beaches and fertile valleys stretching inland. Heading north from San Francisco, turn off US 101 at the Alexander Ave. exit just north of the bridge and drive along the cliffs on Conzelman Road. This spectacular, steep, one-way, 5-mile drive *(not recommended for RVs)* follows the cliff tops over **Hawk Hill**—a topnotch place for spotting raptors during the fall migration—to the southernmost tip of the headlands.

A short jog north on Field Road brings you to an old military chapel that is now the **visitor center,** with exhibits on the area's history, wildlife, and vegetation. You can then choose one of two short hikes nearby. The **Lagoon Trail** *(Trailhead at west end of visitor center parking lot)* is a 1.7-mile loop around a bird-happy lagoon that takes you to pebbly **Rodeo Beach** *(Wheelchair accessible bridge across lagoon to the beach),* where you may see brown pelicans, cormorants, and gulls.

Continue south on Field Road about a mile and you can walk the **Point Bonita Trail** half a mile through a tunnel, across a suspension footbridge, and along a ridge to the **Point Bonita Lighthouse** *(Open Sat.-Mon. p.m.),* which still warns ships away from the rocks below with its beacon and foghorn.

Back at Rodeo Beach, hikers can take off north on a 1-mile segment of the **California Coastal Trail** (see sidebar below). Parts of the trail have been moved inland from the towering oceanside cliffs because of dangerous erosion, but there are still places where, if you're careful, you can creep to the edge and look down steep walls into narrow coves and beaches.

You can also get a dramatic ocean view from the ridges farther inland: Hike a loop beginning at Rodeo Beach and climbing to the **Wolf Ridge Trail,** which runs east to connect with the **Miwok Trail** and back to the lagoon—about 4.5 miles. From the ridge you'll look north into the Tennessee Valley, and on a still day eavesdrop on the walkers on trails 500 feet below. Military history buffs will appreciate the disarmed gun implacements—so, unfortunately, do graffiti artists —

The California Coastal Trail

In the early 1970s, the audacious idea of walking the coast of California from Oregon to Mexico struck reporter Don Engdahl as a good way to call attention to its beauties and win support for its protection. His effort (and articles he wrote for the *San Francisco Examiner*) fueled the movement that led to the passage of the 1972 Coastal Initiative and to the 1976 California Coastal Act. This landmark piece of legislation, envisioning a healthy coast open to public enjoyment, included provisions for a state-long Coastal Trail. Although the trail is not yet complete, its patchwork quality—incorporating parts of federal, state, and local trails as varied as the city of Monterey to the 60-mile King Range/Sinkyone backpacking trail—is part of its appeal.

that guarded the harbor during World War II.

If you have more time, hike into the **Gerbode Valley,** the Headlands' most remote and wildlife-rich sector. You can take the **Bobcat Trail** from east of Rodeo Lagoon up the center of the valley, which is also a popular trail for mountain bikers. Or you can loop around the valley on the **Rodeo Valley Trail** and the Miwok Trail, about an 8-mile round-trip journey. In the valley's swaths of grass and chaparral you may see deer, bobcats, and birds, including soaring hawks and vultures.

Next, drive out of the park on Bunker Road back to US 101, then north to the Calif. 1 turnoff. Less than a mile from the freeway, take a left on Tennessee Valley Road, which takes you into one of the recreation area's beautiful valleys. At the end of road you can take a gentle hike 3 miles west to **Tennessee Cove,** or you can ride a horse from Miwok Stables *(415-383-8048).*

Drive back to Calif. 1 and turn left: You're on the **Shoreline Highway,** which will take you on a windy journey back to the coast and north toward popular Stinson Beach and Point Reyes National Seashore (see pp. 50-53). This drive is packed with views of California's famously rugged coast; there's an overlook above **Muir Beach** where you sometimes see whales and porpoises in the Gulf of the Farallones.

The long reach of the GGNRA takes you still farther north on Calif. 1 toward the **Olema Valley,** peaceful farm country that connects the Marin Headlands area to Tomales Bay and Point Reyes. On the way there you'll pass **Stinson Beach,** which attracts a crowd with its deep sand and good surfing waves. The beach is edged by vacation homes and patrolled, more often than you might like, by great white sharks, which are attracted to the area in late summer by congregations of seals and sea lions that come to feed on nutrients welling up in warm water.

South of the Golden Gate

The southern half of the GGNRA is more about providing space for people to recreate and less about preserving natural areas, though it's got some nice spots. There are more sunbathers than sea lions, though, and it includes tourist attractions such as **Fort Point,** the prison island of **Alcatraz,** and the **San Francisco Maritime National Historic Park.** You can stroll the 4-mile **Golden Gate Promenade** from the Aquatic Park just west of Fisherman's Wharf to Golden Gate Bridge—and then you may want to join the throngs who walk across the bridge on a sunny day.

The **California Coastal Trail** passes through here, too, continuing west from the bridge through the Presidio and past nudist Baker Beach, through the wealthy Seacliff neighborhood, and then around the bluffs near Lands End to the ruins of the Sutro Baths and the **Cliff House**—about 3.5 miles one way. A **visitor center** at the Cliff House *(415-556-8642)* has exhibits that tell about the sea lions, the shipwrecks, and the various spas that have come and gone from this

The view of San Francisco from Marin Headlands

spot. **Lands End** is the closest thing to wild that San Francisco can offer: windblown, eroded headlands, below which you can spot occasional sea lions. You can also reach Lands End via an easy, 1-mile round-trip hike from the parking lot next to the Palace of the Legion of Honor (follow Lincoln Blvd. S along coast from Golden Gate Bridge through the Presidio; Lincoln becomes El Camino Del Mar, which passes by the palace), going west on El Camino Del Mar until it becomes a dirt path.

From Cliff House, it's 4 miles south to **Fort Funston,** whether you walk it on Ocean Beach or drive the Great Highway that runs alongside the beach. Funston was another coastal battery with 16-inch guns; today, instead of launching artillery shells, it's hang gliders launching from the bluffs, climbing air currents and sometimes flying far out over the water before landing on the beach. After a windblown walk on the beach, you'll know why the gliders like it here. There is a wooden viewing deck by the parking lot, and various trails leading to the beach and along the bluffs.

Farther south are two additional GGNRA lands: **Milagra Ridge** and **Sweeney Ridge,** 5 miles south of San Francisco just east off the Cabrillo Highway. From Sweeney's 1,200-foot-high ridge you can view the bay on one side, the Pacific on the other, and landmarks such as Mount Tamalpais and the Farallon Islands. ■

Central and South Coast

Waves crashing against the rocks, Point Lobos State Reserve

IF THE WORDS "SOUTHERN CALIFORNIA" conjure visions of
soft sand, suntan lotion, and plenty of beach volleyball,
here's a thought to make you feel a little wobbly on your
beachcombing feet: The coast from just south of San
Francisco Bay all the way to San Diego is on the move.
This long chunk of rock and sand on the western side of
the San Andreas Fault system is sliding northward on the
Northern Pacific plate. Not to worry, though: The journey
is happening in geologic "slo-mo," with the plate shifting

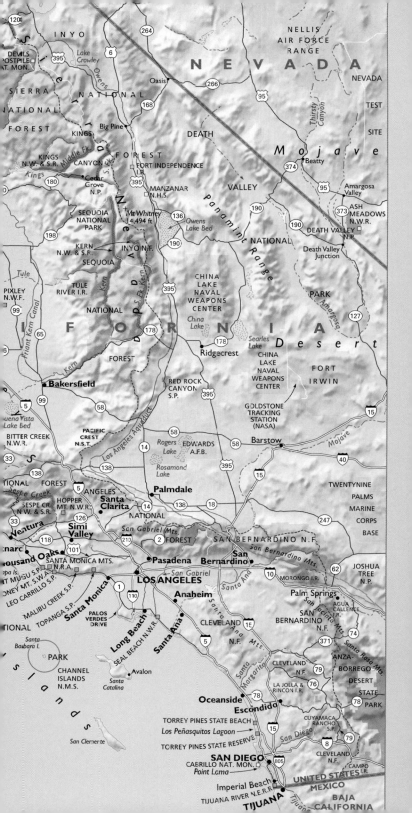

Santa Cruz Island, Channel Islands National Park

only an inch or so on average each year. You still have plenty of time to enjoy the many beauties of one of the world's most exhilarating coastlines.

Like the north coast, the central and south California coast is a product of the vast tectonic forces that have been at play for millennia, folding, twisting, and uplifting the land to create knife-edged ridges, sheer cliffs, chains of offshore islands, rocks, and pinnacles, and the undersea equivalent of the Grand Canyon. Interacting with this dramatic landscape to produce the region's climatic diversity is the other major player on the California stage: the Pacific Ocean. The cooling of moist air over the cold ocean lapping at the edge of the continent acts as a veritable fog machine, not only keeping the slopes of the coastal ranges green but also moderating the heat of summer at lower elevations and in inland valleys.

Fog aside, the climate in much of the central and south coast may be described as Mediterranean—dry in the summer and wet in the winter, with moderate temperatures year-round. This balmy clime is especially typical south of Point Conception, 40 miles north of Santa Barbara. Here the coastline makes a sharp turn eastward, leaving colder waters to circulate north of the point, while warmer waters in the relatively shallower basin curving south to Los Angeles help produce warmer temperatures onshore.

This interplay of sea and land creates a region of sudden contrasts. Whether you're taking in the cool forests of Big Basin Redwoods State Park near Santa Cruz, or winding along the breathtaking cliffs of Big Sur, where crucial habitat is home to the protected California condor, or investigating the salt marshes of Tijuana River National Estuarine Research Reserve south of San Diego, you'll find that climate, vegetation, and wildlife can change drastically within just a few miles of the coast. In the eastern portion of Ventana Wilderness in the Santa Lucia Range, for example, you can hike through stands of mixed conifers and dry chaparral, while the western edge of this same reserve puts you within a quarter-

Nipomo Dunes

mile of the foggy coast, where sea otters float in the kelp beds. State parks and national forests protect the Santa Lucia mountains and most of the beautiful steep-sided coves, preserving a rich intertidal world of sea-weeds, crustaceans, and birds. From Monterey all the way south to San Diego, these narrow bands of coastal habitat also support unique trees such as the Monterey and Torrey pines.

Like Point Conception, another natural barrier between the central and south coast is the series of east-west trending mountains called the Transverse Ranges. More products of the region's tectonic upheaval, they include the Santa Monica and San Gabriel Mountains, which run east from Santa Barbara to end in the San Bernardino Mountains, whose highest peaks rise 10,000 feet and whose bases flank the Mojave Desert.

While the San Bernardinos bracket Los Angeles on the east, the Santa Monica and San Gabriel Mountains hug the sprawling city on the north. If you could dry up the ocean off Santa Barbara, you'd see that the northern Channel Islands of Santa Cruz, Santa Rosa, and San Miguel are actually the westernmost peaks of the Santa Monicas. Likewise, if you followed the southern islands of Santa Barbara, San Nicolas, and San Clemente east-ward, you'd find them linked to the Santa Ana and San Jacinto Mountains, part of the northwest-trending Peninsular Ranges and the third mountain-ous side to the Los Angeles Basin. Cut off from the mainland millions of years ago by rising seas, the plants and animals of the Channel Islands evolved into nearly 150 species found nowhere else in the world.

Both the Transverse and Peninsular Ranges are semi-arid, with abun-dant chaparral and isolated stands of mixed conifers. In fact, the dry slopes of the Peninsular Ranges might remind the well-traveled visitor of Mexico's backcountry. This would not be surprising: As recently as 5 million years ago, these ranges were 200 miles south—a reminder that their presence in southern California is, geologically speaking, only temporary. ■

Forest along Redwood Creek, Big Basin Redwoods SP

Big Basin Redwoods State Park

■ 18,000 acres ■ Central California, 20 miles west of San Jose in the Santa Cruz Mountains on US 9 ■ Best months March-Nov. ■ Camping, hiking, backpacking, guided walks, mountain biking, horseback riding, bird-watching, wildlife viewing, wildflower viewing ■ Adm. fee ■ Contact the park, 21600 Big Basin Way, Boulder Creek, CA 95006; phone 831-338-8861, 800-444-7275 (campground reservations). parks.ca.gov/central/santacruz/bbrsp406.htm

A CENTURY OF PARK LIFE is a short chapter in the story of trees 2,000 years old, but it's the difference between planks on someone's cabin porch and the 300-foot giants that shade the trails of this park. The campaign to preserve California's ancient coastal redwoods really began in this patch of the Santa Cruz Mountains. In 1899, Andrew P. Hill was tossed off the private land where he'd gone to photograph the giant trees. Anger at the denial of access and concern that the redwoods would soon fall to the lumberman's saw spurred Hill into action. With a 32-dollar bankroll, he started the Semervirens Club and began campaigning for a park. As a result, California's first state park—Big Basin—was created in 1902.

Information on the park can be found at the visitor center, located a few miles past the park's entrance (off US 9). It's an easy half-mile stroll from the center to the famous **Chimney Tree,** which was hollowed by fire. Step inside the tree and gaze up to the blue sky hundreds of feet above. Redwoods continue to grow through their outer layers even when their insides are gutted, which allows us the womblike experience of huddling inside a living tree. To see other awesome trees such as the 329-foot **Mother of the Forest** and the burl-covered **Animal Tree,** take the half-mile **Redwood Nature Trail** near the center. Markers and a brochure remind you that there are other things growing here, including Douglas-fir, madrone, azalea, and huckleberry. The cool forest also provides a rich habitat for animals from mountain lions to spotted owls to tree frogs.

There are many other trails of varying lengths in the park. For a view of **Sempervirens Falls,** a small, pretty, and ferny waterfall, take the 4-mile **Sequoia Trail** loop from the parking area. A more rigorous 8-mile hike, beginning across from the visitor center, combines parts of Skyline to the Sea Trail with **Hollow Tree Trail.** You will pass through old-growth forest, several creeks, and a chaparral plant community. For those wishing to ride, rather than walk, the fire roads in Big Basin are open to mountain biking, and there are several equestrian trails.

Big Basin is the largest of a string of state parks that virtually connect the ridgeline of the Santa Cruz Mountains to the rugged coast. At the northernmost point, right off Skyline Drive, is **Castle Rock State Park** *(408-867-2952).* The unusual rock formations in its steep canyons are popular with rock climbers. Below Castle Rock is Big Basin, which roughly follows the Waddell Creek drainage; and on the coast, just north of where a wedge of Big Basin reaches down to the ocean at Waddell Beach, is **Año Nuevo State Reserve** *(650-879-0227).*

A breeding colony of elephant seals (see sidebar below) are the big attraction at Año Nuevo State Reserve from December to May, when guided tours about three hours long take visitors to see the colonies. You must sign up in advance for walks with an interpreter, the only way you are allowed near the colony. Like the redwoods, the elephant seals get all the attention, so people forget there are sea lions, sea otters, gray whales, and many birds to be seen here, too.

If you are prepared to backpack and spend several nights in reserved backcountry camps *(Big Basin Redwoods SP, 831-338-8861),* take the **Skyline to the Sea Trail,** which begins in Castle Rock State Park and twists down the drainage 31 miles to the Pacific Ocean. Various species of hawks, owls, and woodpeckers can be seen in this area. You'll see 70-foot Berry Creek Falls along the way and find Waddell Beach at hike's end.

In addition to the trail camps, Big Basin has developed campsites. Because this area is close to the Bay Area and Santa Cruz, these sites fill quickly on weekends. You should call ahead for reservations. ∎

Elephant Seals

The world's largest mainland breeding colony for the northern elephant seal is found in Año Nuevo State Reserve. During the mating season, December to the end of March, 4,000-pound bulls battle for mates on the reserve's beaches.

As many as 600 pups are born from these matings. Although the adult seals depart the site in March to return to the Pacific to feed, the weaned pups don't venture out into the ocean for another six weeks, sometime around May.

Elkhorn Slough NERR

■ 4,000 acres (estuarine research reserve 1,300 acres) ■ Central California, 55 miles south of San Jose, off Calif. I ■ Season year-round ■ Hiking, walking, guided walks, boating, kayaking, canoeing, bird-watching, wildlife viewing ■ Adm. fee ■ Contact the reserve, 1700 Elkhorn Rd., Watsonville, CA 95076; phone 831-728-2822. www.elkhornslough.org

DISTRACTED BY THE QUAINT harbor village of Moss Landing or the 500-foot cement stacks of a power plant, it's possible to drive right by Elkhorn Slough (pronounced "slew") on your way around Monterey Bay on busy Calif. 1. If you do, you'll miss a peaceable kingdom inhabited by majestic great blue herons and double-crested cormorants, preening sea otters and harbor seals, leopard sharks and bat rays, and many other bird, mammal, and fish species. Elkhorn Slough also has hundreds of plant species and a variety of habitats. The latter include pickleweed salt marshes (pickleweed is a favorite food of California's endangered clapper rail), freshwater wetlands, salt ponds, grasslands, mudflats, and live oak woods.

To help protect this area, the 1,300-acre **Elkhorn Slough National Estuarine Research Reserve,** one of the nation's first estuarine research reserves, was established in 1979. Yet it's not strictly natural anymore. Levees have been built and water is pumped to restore salt marshes and

Harbor seals, Elkhorn Slough National Estuarine Research Reserve

provide habitat for the brown pelicans and snowy plover that nest here.

Coastal wetlands and salt marshes such as Elkhorn's are hard to find in modern California. Elkhorn Slough has had its own problems, endangered by actions such as the diversion of the Salinas River by farmers, the removal of a protective sand spit from the harbor, and, of much bigger impact, the Army Corps of Engineers' opening of an artificially deep and wide mouth to the slough in 1946. There also have been problems with DDT residue that reappears during rainy years. Yet the wildlife that depends on the marsh has adjusted, and the birds migrating along the Pacific flyway stop regularly. In 1992, the North American record for the most bird species sighted in a single day—more than 200—was set here.

To reach the reserve's visitor center, take Calif. 1 to Moss Landing and turn east onto Dolan Road to Elkhorn Road. Follow Elkhorn north to the reserve entry. The **visitor center** offers fine exhibits and is the starting point for several trails. Hike the 2.2-mile **South Marsh Loop Trail** and its offshoots to the Whistle Stop Lagoon and the North Marsh Overlook. On the return, you'll pass a heron and egret rookery, high in the pine trees above a pond. The 0.8-mile **Long Valley Loop** will lead you to a shady woodland of live oaks and grassy hillsides and quiet fingers of the slough.

If you prefer to see the sights by water, you can launch your own canoe or kayak at Kirby Park, located in the upper part of the slough or from Moss Landing Harbor, where kayaks are also available for rent. ■

Monterey Bay

■ Central California, south of Santa Cruz. ■ Best months late Feb.–mid-June
■ Hiking, boating, scuba diving, walking, fishing, biking, horseback riding, bird-watching, whale-watching, wildlife viewing ■ Contact Monterey Bay National Marine Sanctuary, 299 Foam St., Monterey, CA 93940, phone 831-647-4201; or Hollister Field Office, Bureau of Land Management, 20 Hamilton Ct., Hollister, CA 95023; phone 831-630-5000

LOCATED IN THE MONTEREY BAY area is a section of the enormous **Monterey Bay National Marine Sanctuary,** which follows 276 miles of shoreline from Rocky Point, 7 miles north of the Golden Gate Bridge, to Cambria Rock, in San Luis Obispo County, and extends an average of 30 miles offshore. Established in 1992 to keep the habitat healthy, the sanctuary forbids oil drilling and places some restrictions on the handling of marine life. But people are allowed to fish, as well as kayak, sail, scuba dive, and whale-watch in the waters. In fact, many of the visitors who come to play on Monterey Bay have no idea it's a part of a sanctuary.

One of the sanctuary's defining features is the **Monterey Bay Submarine Canyon.** Deeper than the Grand Canyon and one of the world's largest underwater gorges, it plunges to 10,663 feet and provides a home to a great diversity of species, including the file-tail cat shark and spiny king crab. From March through September, an upwelling of cold water from the depths brings a high level of nutrients to the surface. This causes plankton blooms that set off a chain of feeding, involving humpback and blue whales, large numbers of seabirds, and other creatures.

Onshore, a new nature sanctuary will be opening within the next five years. The stretch of beach extending north from Monterey and Seaside is being decommissioned from military base—28,000-acre Fort Ord, closed in the early 1990s—to parkland and wild habitat. The beachfront will be transferred to the California Department of Parks and Recreation; the inland dunes and hills will be overseen by the Bureau of Land Management, with a mandate to protect rare maritime chaparral habitat and native grasses. Bikers (there are currently 50 miles of trails on BLM lands) say it is the best place around the bay to see wildlife such as deer and bobcats. ■

Cannery Row's Sardines

When commercial fishing began in Monterey Bay in the early 1900s, the sardine supply seemed endless. By 1945, some 23 canneries stood on the shoreline—known as Cannery Row—and 250,000 tons of sardines were harvested annually. But then the catch began to decline, possibly due to overfishing, and by 1952, it had dwindled to nothing. Now the sardines may be returning, but they're unlikely to find their way to Cannery Row, today a fashionable place for art galleries, restaurants, and souvenir shops.

Monterey Bay Aquarium's three-story living kelp forest

Monterey Bay Aquarium

Beneath the placid surface of Monterey Bay—from the tide pools along the rocky beach of Point Lobos to the dark underwater world of the 2-mile-deep Monterey Bay Submarine Canyon—lies a vibrant, varied, and fecund world. To get a peek at it, you should stop in the city of Monterey and visit the splendid Monterey Bay Aquarium *(886 Cannery Row, Monterey, CA 93940-1085. 831-648-4800. www.mbayaq.org. Adm. fee).*

Philanthropist David Packard and his family are behind the aquarium, which was erected in 1984 on Monterey's famous Cannery Row (see sidebar opposite). In fact, the aquarium incorporates parts of one of the many abandoned canneries there.

What distinguishes the aquarium most is its intimacy with the bay itself, including the seawater that is pumped directly from the ocean into the exhibits. Among them are a three-story living kelp forest, a two-story sea otter exhibit, jellyfish galleries, the largest display of living deep-sea creatures in the world, and a new family gallery called Splash Zone. Featuring almost 60 species, Splash Zone explores life in coral reefs and rocky beaches through hands-on exhibits and special areas for infants and toddlers to facilitate learning through play.

The aquarium is actively involved in research, some of which it shares with the visitors—including many school groups—that throng through its exhibits. A deep-sea video feed, beamed to the aquarium via microwave technology six to eight times a day, allows students to look over the shoulders of scientists who are studying the canyon in submersibles.

To reach Monterey Bay Aquarium, take Calif. 1 to Calif. 68 west to Pacific Grove, then follow signs to Cannery Row.

Exploring the shoreline at Point Lobos State Reserve

Point Lobos State Reserve

■ 1,320 acres (770 acres underwater) ■ Central California, 3 miles south of Carmel on Calif. 1 ■ Hiking, walking, guided walks, sea kayaking, tide-pooling, scuba diving, bird-watching, whale-watching, wildlife viewing, wildflower viewing ■ Adm. fee for cars ■ Contact the reserve, Rte. 1, Box 62, Carmel, CA 93923; phone 831-624-4909. pointlobos.org

FROM ITS TIDE POOLS TO ITS rugged headlands to its wildflower meadows, Point Lobos is a microcosm of the central California coast, providing a compact and easily accessible classroom of coastal history and ecology, with a host of barking sea lions at the lectern. Point Lobos is home to hundreds of sea lions from August to June. The ancestors of these sea lions inspired the name borne by this jutting peninsula just south of the resort town of Carmel. During the late 1700s, Spanish residents christened the offshore rocks Punta de Los Lobos Marions (Point of the Sea Wolves) because the barking sea lions there sounded like wolves.

During the summer, sexually active males (it's unusual to see females here) head south to mate with females in the Channel Islands. Pups from these unions are born in spring. Back at Point Lobos, spring brings the birth of great blue herons, Brandt's cormorants, and sea otters. You may see a mother sea otter floating on her back, grooming a pup on her belly.

Point Lobos has a wide variety of plant communities. There are beautiful wildflower meadows as well as northern coastal scrub. The scrub—3-to-6-foot-tall, small-leaved evergreen shrubs with lush herbaceous undergrowth—provides good cover for small animals. You'll also find Monterey pines and the gnarled but hardy cypress trees that have become the symbol of the Monterey Bay area, including one of only two native stands of Monterey cypresses *(Cupressus macrocarpa)* on the coast.

Point Lobos has been home to the Ohlone Indians, a Chinese fishing community, a livestock pasture, a whaling station, and a cannery. In 1933 a state reserve was established here. Today you can hike the reserve's trails and watch the otters, seals, brown pelicans, cormorants, and other wildlife. In the 770-acre underwater preserve offshore, divers can explore towering trees of kelp and marine life sheltered in the seaweed understory.

What to See and Do

Only about 150 cars are allowed in the reserve at one time, so during busy seasons (especially summer), you may have to wait for someone to leave. (You can also park along Calif. 1 and walk in.)

Once inside the reserve, you can choose from three parking areas. (Tables in these areas are the only places you may picnic.) To the north is Whalers Cove; to the west, Sea Lion Point; to the south, China Cove. The trails from each are short and offer scenic rewards.

If you want to scuba dive, snorkel, or kayak, take a right turn toward Whalers Cove. (Divers and kayakers must register at the entrance station. Only a limited number are permitted each day.) Divers can explore the kelp forests in **Whalers Cove** and **Bluefish Cove**, just to the west. Kayakers need to check with rangers to be sure that they won't disturb great blue herons, harbor seals, and other creatures that bear young here.

California Condors

After an absence of more than 30 years, the 10-foot wingspan of the California condor is casting shadows over the Big Sur coast and the Santa Lucia Range. Once again the majestic condors can be spotted riding thermals along the ridges of the coastal mountains, or roosting among turkey vultures in Pfeiffer Big Sur State Park. This is one of the great wildlife recovery stories of recent history, but a happy ending is not yet assured.

Among those involved in recovery work is the Ventana Wilderness Society, a private nonprofit group that in 1997 began a reintroduction program to save the condor, which was on the verge of extinction after a drastic decline over the past century. For three years, the society released nearly two dozen young condors in the Big Sur area.

The birds seem to be doing well. But condors don't mature for seven years, so it will be a while before it's known if they can successfully mate and reproduce in the wild.

The Ventana Wilderness Society *(831-455-9514),* based at Andrew Molera State Park (see pp. 86 and 91), monitors the condors and other birds in the area. From March to November, bird-lovers can drop in at the sanctuary just after sunrise and spend a few hours helping with birdbanding and other work.

Weston Beach, Point Lobos State Reserve

Watching for sea lions and whales, Point Lobos State Reserve

If you prefer to get some information on the reserve first, follow the entry road straight ahead to **Sea Lion Point** and the reserve's information station. You can also access many of the trails here, such as the 0.6-mile **Sea Lion Point Trail** loop. It takes you out on a promontory for a view of sea lions on the offshore rocks. As you explore tide pools and watch the ocean smash against granite outcrops, don't forget to look beneath your feet. In the Carmelo formation exposed here, you'll find sculpted sandstone embedded with harder stones.

If you choose the 0.8-mile **Cypress Grove Trail,** you'll wind through a rare grove of Monterey cypresses to promontories above the kelp beds and offshore rocks.

The **North Shore Trail,** 1.4 miles long, connects Sea Lion Point to Whalers Cove and offers great views of the ocean and coves. One-mile **South Shore Trail,** with access to the rocky beaches, skirts the other side of the peninsula toward China Cove.

At China Cove, 1-mile loop **Bird Island Trail** takes you to Pelican Point. On the way, you pass a steep staircase down into **China Cove,** an emerald thumb of water lapping white sand. Pelican Point overlooks **Bird Island,** which is protected from mainland predators by a narrow channel. In spring, the island is packed with nesting Brandt's cormorants. Brown pelicans float in and out.

Over the next few years, the reserve will expand with the addition of the **Point Lobos Ranch,** bought by the Point Lobos Land Trust (831-625-5523). The ranch, which lies east of Calif. 1 from the reserve, will provide meadow displays of wildflowers and upland habitat to complement the seashore park. At present, the trust provides occasional weekend naturalist programs on the property. ∎

Driving the Coast

AMERICA WORSHIPS THE ROAD, and certain scenic routes are canonized— Montana's Going-to-the-Sun Road, for instance, or the Blue Ridge Parkway in Virginia and North Carolina. But few road trips can match Calif. 1, from Big Sur, between Monterey and San Luis Obispo. From this twisting, cliff-perched road, you'll see 90 miles of white-sand beaches, surf-carved rocks, and an occasional whale spout on the ocean horizon. The narrow road is not for the faint-hearted. But the reward of breathtaking views, seen from frequent pullouts, is enough to draw thousands of travelers in the summer.

Completed in 1937, the highway took 15 years of hard, risky labor, costing several lives. If you can forgive the builders for violating this wild landscape, you might admire their handiwork, particularly bridges such as the 260-foot-high Bixby Creek Bridge, between Garrapata State Park (for

Bixby Creek Bridge on Calif. 1

information call 831-667-2315) and
Andrew Molera State Park (see p. 86).

Not surprisingly, the highway is
sometimes closed for repair. The El
Niño rains of 1998 shut down travel
for months while landslides and road
collapses were fixed. Slides, of course,
are a natural occurrence. But man has
worsened nature's tendencies: Cut a
road into a steep slope, and the criti-
cal angle of that slope is heightened.
Cleaning up after a slide often involves bulldozing debris off the top
of a slide, dropping sediment into

the intertidal zone, and leaving big
scars above the road, ripe for more
erosion.

Whether due to roadwork or a glut
of summer tourists, slow traffic can
be frustrating. The best antidote is to
stop at one of the many pullouts,
clamber down to a beach, or just find
a quiet place to gaze. For instance,
south of Palo Colorado Road, a wide-
shoulder area on the ocean side of
the road at Notley's Landing has a
great ocean view. Or south of the
Bixby Creek Bridge you can pull over
for the 270-degree view from Hurri-
cane Point. Garrapata State Park,
northernmost of the Big Sur parks, is
accessed on the ocean side only by
roadside pullouts, from which you can
(carefully!) climb down to tide pools,
or hike a mile-long bluff trail looking
for whales.

The California Coastal Commission,
the state agency that works to protect the coast environment and public
access to it, has created the best
coastal cove-by-cove guide. *The California Coastal Access Guide (University of
California Press, 1997)* covers the coast
from Oregon to Mexico and has side-
bars on everything from tsunamis to
clamming. If you prefer listening to
reading, get the Big Sur Land Trust's
"Big Sur Unsurpassed" *(Big Sur Land
Trust, P.O. Box 221864, Carmel, CA
93922. 831-625-5523)*, a tape featuring historians, naturalists, and celebri-
ties who talk to you about the sights.

When you consider the population
pressures in the Golden State, the
preservation of the Big Sur coast is
one of the triumphs of American
conservation. There are pockets of
private land, both hippie hovels and
upscale luxury resorts, but there's
little to clutter the views, and that
hasn't changed in almost 50 years. ■

Big Sur Parks

■ Southern California, between Point Lobos and Lucia on Calif. 1 ■ Year-round
■ Camping, hiking, backpacking, walking, guided walks, fishing, biking, mountain
biking, horseback riding, bird-watching, whale-watching, wildlife viewing,
wildflower viewing ■ Contact Big Sur Station #1, Big Sur, CA 93920;
phone 831-667-2315

ALONG THE BIG SUR COASTAL REGION, you can travel from mountaintop
to ocean, from the ridgeline of the Santa Lucia Range, down through
canyons to sandy-beached coves, headland cliffs, and intertidal zones
teeming with life. The intersection of coastal mountains and pounding,
wind-whipped ocean creates a kind of coastal war zone on the continent's edge, awe-inspiring and beautiful.

　　Above the surf, the bluffs stair-step back in marine terraces cut by surf
at different stages of the mountains' uplift, which began five million years
ago, a mere minute of geological time. Winds from the northwest batter

Point Sur Light Station State Historic Park

moisture-laden air against the wall of shoreline, and 50 to 70 inches of rain fall annually here (but a short hike over the ridge and you're in dry chaparral country). Most of the rain falls in the winter, often washing out portions of legendary Calif. 1 (see pp. 82-83). In the dry summer, the cold ocean water brought down from the north by the California Current generates fogs that salve the coastal redwoods.

The beaches in Big Sur's coves and the intertidal zone—the space between high and low tide—are favorite stops for visitors and, in less accessible areas, pinnipeds such as sea lions and seals. From high atop the cliffs, you can see the kelp habitat just offshore, and down by the surf you will find mussels, anemones, and many other species amid the rocks and the sand. Coves are frequently the endpoint of deeply cut canyons, shadowy wet worlds of ferns and trillium and tall coastal red-woods. The country from Point Lobos south to San Simeon offers extra-ordinary views at every turn. On the following pages you will find a number of the many parks and beaches where you can experience the wonders of Big Sur.

What to See and Do

Although you can drive the length of the Big Sur coast in a single day, you won't really see it that way. It's better to wander for a few days, experiencing the many terrains—such as redwood groves along trickling streams, white-sand beaches, and wild mountains—and choosing among an abundance of places where you can stop to hike, swim, fish, horseback ride, or simply enjoy the vistas. At night you can camp on a bluff, bunk in a rustic lodge, or even soak in luxury at a cliff-hugging resort.

Information on all the state parks along the coast, advice about trail conditions, as well as guide and naturalist books for the Big Sur area are available at Big Sur Station, which is located on the east side of Calif. 1, just half a mile south of the entrance to Pfeiffer Big Sur State Park.

Make sure when you plan your trip that you understand the mix of private, state, and federal lands along the coast, so you won't find yourself at the gate to Pfeiffer Beach with a state pass in hand (it's federal). Call 805-995-1976 for information.

Andrew Molera State Park

Relatively undeveloped, 4,800-acre Andrew Molera State Park (831-667-2315. Fee), located 20 miles south of Carmel off Calif. 1, is a

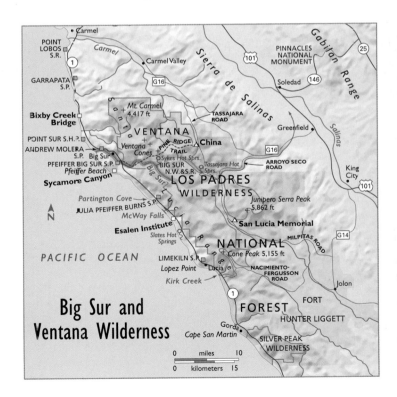

Big Sur and Ventana Wilderness

Sea otter swimming among kelp

The Otter Survives

Hunted vigorously through the 19th century, the California sea otter was considered extinct by the 1920s. But the small community of Big Sur residents knew better. The Pfeiffer family, ranchers whose name now graces several places in Big Sur, decided it was wiser to keep the remaining otters a secret.

Margaret Owings, the late founder of the Friends of the Sea Otter, related a story that epitomizes the family's attitude about the animals: One day in 1929, John Pfeiffer took his son-in-law fishing on a Big Sur beach. Spotting the little heads of some animals swimming in the kelp, the young man asked his father-in-law what they were. Pfeiffer shushed him, "They're considered extinct, and we want to protect them. Somebody would come down and shoot them."

The tight-knit community of Big Sur kept their secret until 1938, when sections of Calif. I first opened and more people began coming to the area. Though the truth was out, with the help of activists such as Owings, the otters were protected. Hunting was outlawed by international treaty and state regulations.

The otter has made a significant comeback, with a population that is now close to 2,000. This pleases travelers but it's even more important for the coastal ecosystem because the sea otters help keep other marine life, such as abalone, from destroying important habitat.

Sea otters are big eaters, consuming 25 percent of their weight daily. Shellfish are a favorite food. Abalone, on the other hand, dine on kelp. When there are no otters preying on abalone, the abalone flourish and consume large amounts of kelp. That reduces the kelp forests, where so many coastal creatures find shelter and food. During the 1920s, the kelp forests were greatly reduced; when the otters began to recover, kelp, too, made a comeback.

Following pages: Big Sur coast

Pfeiffer Falls, Pfeiffer Big Sur State Park

great place for walking, biking, and horseback riding. You can bike or hike the 2-mile round-trip to the beach and headlands where the Big Sur River enters the ocean. Or take the 9-mile **Bluff and Ridge Trail,** which begins at the south side of the river's outlet and offers great views of the ocean. It also goes inland through oak and redwood forests. If you prefer another mode of travel, see the concessionaire (831-625-5486) in the park about horseback rides to the beach.

For those who would like to spend the night and don't mind hauling their equipment, a third of a mile from the parking lot, there is a secluded, primitive trail camp (831-667-2315. Fee).

Pfeiffer Big Sur State Park

Those travelers wishing for more comfortable sleeping accommodations in an equally impressive setting should continue south on Calif. 1 for another few miles to Pfeiffer Big Sur State Park (831-667-2315. Fee) and Big Sur Lodge. Cottage-style guest rooms, some with fireplaces, snuggle beneath the shade of California laurels, live oaks, and redwoods.

The lodge sits on a site once occupied by a much more rustic resort, run by members of the Pfeiffer family, which settled in the area in 1869. One of Big Sur's earliest non-Indian families, the Pfeiffers logged, raised bees, and ranched on their isolated homesteads here. In 1908, John Pfeiffer and his wife, Florence, decided to establish a resort. Twenty-five years later, they sold their land to the state, and the park and lodge were established.

Hot Springs

There are several hot springs in the Big Sur area, so soak lovers have a range of options. The most famous mineral-spring retreat is the **Esalen Institute** (Highway 1, Big Sur, CA 93920; 831-667-3005), where New Age gurus dispense wisdom and massages and guests soak in tubs overlooking the ocean. Far inland, on the Carmel Valley side of the Santa Lucia Range, is **Tassajara** (831-659-2229), where you can combine your soaks with Zen meditation as guests of monks who know very well how to run a resort. Free spirits, though, don backpacks and hike into **Sykes Hot Springs,** 10 miles up the Pine Ridge Trail from Big Sur Station, where hand-built rock pools alongside the Big Sur River give you a variety of temperature options. Bathing at all three of these places is, as they say, "clothing optional."

This park, located about midway along the coastal journey, is often considered the centerpiece of a Big Sur visit. Although it has no ocean-front real estate, Pfeiffer Big Sur State Park offers peaceful, shady settings beneath redwoods, conifers, cottonwoods, and willows, lovely meadows, and access to the Big Sur River.

The **Big Sur River,** which runs right next to a campground and all through the park, is large enough to carve a pretty gorge and to sustain populations of crawdads, steelhead, and rainbow trout.

Begin your visit by acquainting yourself with the fauna of Big Sur along the 0.7-mile **Nature Trail,** which begins its loop at the Redwood Grove on the east side of the river, a quarter mile from the park entrance. Another mile down the road, you come to the trailhead of **Gorge Trail,** a 0.2-mile amble to the river at the bottom of the gorge. You can wade, swim, or sunbathe on the pebbly beach; you'll find more pools if you clamber upstream. This is also a starting point for the **Mount Manuel Trail,** which covers 4 steep miles to the peak, and then, in the national forest, continues into Ventana Wilderness (see pp. 93-94).

At the north end of the park, the **Pfeiffer Falls Trail** starts among big redwoods and crisscrosses the creek upstream to 60-foot Pfeiffer Falls. From here, head west to the **Valley View Trail,** and loop back to the nature center, a total trip of less than 2 miles.

Pfeiffer Beach

This beach is simply one of the most beautiful places in the world. But there's no sign, and if you don't know where to turn, you'll miss it. Just south of Pfeiffer Big Sur State Park, but north of the Big Sur post office, little Sycamore Canyon Road turns off to the west and drops down for 2 winding miles to the beach *(permit required for beach access; 805-995-1976).*

From the parking area, follow the short trail along Sycamore Creek to the beach, a mile-long strip of white sand with dramatic rocks, which are some three or four stories in height and pummeled and tunneled by the waves.

You may see sea otters, brown pelicans and cormorants here. Hikers and climbers can make their way over Cooper's Point at the beach's north end to Andrew Molera State Park (see pp. 86 and 91). Other visitors prefer simply to watch the beautiful sunset for which Pfeiffer Beach is renowned.

Julia Pfeiffer Burns State Park

About 10 miles south of Pfeiffer Big Sur State Park is Julia Pfeiffer Burns State Park *(831-667-2315)* and a beautiful cove where **McWay Falls** plummets 80 feet to the beach—or, during high tide, the ocean. To view the falls, hike the quarter-mile **Waterfall Trail** *(Wheelchair accessible)* to an overlook, where the view down through blue gum trees, cypresses, and other exotic plants make it feel like a Caribbean hideaway. You are not allowed down on the beach.

The park also has inland trails that climb among the redwoods. The **Ewoldsen Trail** begins near the picnic area above the parking lot along McWay Creek and winds up along the stream through redwoods and oak and tanoak groves. Here you might see goldfinches and black-headed grosbeaks. Eventually the trail tops grassy open ridges where your view of the ocean horizon is unimpeded.

Experienced divers with permits can explore the granite-bottomed beauty and underwater caves in **Partington Cove** at the northern end of the park.

There's plenty of wildlife to see here, including sea lions, seals, and sea otters. In December and January and March and April, you may spot migrating gray whales. ∎

Spending the night at Santa Lucia Memorial Campground, Los Padres NF

Ventana Wilderness

■ 205,323 acres ■ Southern California, San Lucia Range, between Monterey and Cambria ■ Year-round ■ Hiking, fishing, wildlife viewing ■ Contact Monterey Ranger District, Los Padres National Forest, 406 S. Mildred Ave., King City, CA 93930; phone 831-385-5434

SINCE MOST TRAVELERS TO Big Sur come to comb the beaches and look out to ocean, they often turn their backs on the Santa Lucia Range that fences the rugged coastline from the rest of California and thus miss some steep, beautiful wilderness. The Santa Lucias are a mere 100 million years old. Once an island, the range has been forced upward by the clash between the San Andreas Fault and the Pacific plate. At present, the Santa Lucias have reached a height of some 6,000 feet and are still rising.

Hikers delving into the Ventana will discover redwood forests, wildflower meadows, challenging vertical terrain, and now and then a sighting of rare wildlife such as California condors and exotic wild boars. Compared to the number of travelers who roam the ocean's edge, however, hikers in this backcountry are few. Steep trails and hot summers account for this discrepancy in part, but many people hardly know the wilderness is here.

The western edges of the wilderness get a great deal of fog and rain—up to 100 inches per year in certain places—while inland areas are much drier. Most of the rain falls between the months of November and April, when wildflowers such as sage and buckwheat begin putting on a show. Hikers will notice the scars of large forest fires that burned through here in 1977 and 1999. Look for wildlife, too. Boars with long, curved tusks, introduced here by sport hunters in the 1930s, are seen on very rare occasions. Steelhead and rainbow trout swim in the Big Sur River. While hiking the ridges, keep an eye out for California condors (see sidebar p. 79) riding the thermal currents—once facing extinction, now nearly two dozen make their home in the Big Sur area.

What to See and Do

Two trails begin at Pfeiffer Big Sur State Park (see pp. 91-92) and several more along Calif. 1. One of the most popular routes into the backcountry is the **Pine Ridge Trail,** which heads east from Pfeiffer Big Sur State Park to Sykes Hot Springs (see sidebar p. 91), 9 miles away. The 100-degree F spring collects in several man-made river-rock soaking tubs above the Big Sur River.

Most visitors choose to go no farther. But the trail actually continues on for another 15 miles across the Santa Lucia mountains amid the grand looking peaks known as the Ventana Cones and down the east slope to China camp (a developed campground). This is a backpacking trip of three or more days. So you don't have to backtrack, you can shuttle a car up Carmel Valley to China camp.

From China camp, you can also hike north along the **Carmel River Trail** or **Miller Trail,** which form an overnight loop, with waterfalls and wildflowers such as lupine and shooting stars along the way. At the southern end of the wilderness, a steep 2.3-mile hike up from Kirk Creek will take you to the top of **Cone Peak** (5,155 feet) for a 360-degree view of ocean and wilderness.

Then hike **Cone Peak Road** (a dirt road) back to **Nacimiento-Fergusson Road** (paved, but little used) east to Calif. 1 and Kirk Creek. This area offers spectacular coastal views. There's a campground (805-995-1976. Fee) and two trails leading to the beach. ∎

Nipomo Dunes

■ 15,900 acres ■ Southern California, north of Guadalupe off Calif. I ■ Best
seasons fall and winter ■ Hiking, walking bird-watching, wildflower viewing
■ Adm. fee ■ Contact the Dunes Center, 1055 Guadalupe St., Guadalupe, CA
93434; phone 805-343-2455. www.dunescenter.org

IT'S AN ODD JUXTAPOSITION: a trail
by a quiet lake, a quiet stretch of
beach backed by scalloped sand
dunes, and 1,200 fenced acres
where helmeted pilots roar over
the dunes in their beach buggies.
Each is an aspect of an 18-mile
national natural landmark called
the Nipomo Dunes, comprising
two state parks, several natural
area preserves, and acres of dune
lakes and native habitat.

The Nipomo Dunes have been
building grain by grain for 18,000
years, forming from eroded mountain sediment carried by rivers and
creeks into the ocean. From there,
the sand washed up on the beach,
and the wind distributed it, creat-

Nipomo Dunes

ing maginificent sculpted dunes, some reaching 500 feet in height.

The dunes are covered with anchoring masses of some 240 native
plants—more than a dozen of them endangered species such as the La
Graciosa thistle, the beach spectacle pod, and the crisp dune mint. In
the spring, you'll see a rainbow of brilliant flowers, including blue dune
lupine and yellow Hooker's primrose. Because the younger dunes near
the beach are unstable and vegetation is delicate, and because the area
between the foredunes and ocean provides criticial habitat for the endangered snowy plover, visitors should stay on the boardwalks.

A 4,500-acre area of the dunes, **Guadalupe-Nipomo Dunes National
Wildlife Refuge** is managed by the U.S. Fish and Wildlife Service. It
includes 500-foot high **Mussel Rock Dune** and **Oso Flaco Lake,** a great
birding spot. The endangered California least tern and the brown pelican
are among the species seen here. To reach the refuge, go north from Guadalupe on Calif. 1 for 2.5 miles, then west on Oso Flaco Road for 3 miles.

Pieces of the past can be found among the dunes. Here and there are
shell middens left by Chumash Indians, and some even stranger artifacts:
parts of a movie set. In 1923, Cecil B. DeMille shot *The Ten Command-
ments* here, then buried pieces of the set, "the City of the Pharaoh," in the
sands. A local effort to save the movie set is underway. ■

Santa Monica Mountains NRA

■ 150,000 acres ■ Southern California, north of Santa Monica on Calif. 1 or US 101 ■ Best seasons winter and spring ■ Camping, hiking, backpacking, kayaking, canoeing, fishing, mountain biking, horseback riding, bird-watching, wildflower viewing ■ Contact the National Park Service visitor center, 401 W. Hillcrest Dr., Thousand Oaks, CA 91360; phone 805-370-2301. www.nps.gov/samo

THOUGH THE SANTA MONICA MOUNTAINS split their city into two parts, a lot of people in Los Angeles don't know about the protected open spaces that range from the knobby dry ridges of the mountains to the coastal beaches crammed with surfers. The Santa Monica Mountains are unique in several ways: A transverse mountain range, the Santa Monicas run east-west, instead of the north-south configuration of most North

Riding through Topanga State Park, Santa Monica Mountains NRA

American mountain ranges; and the climate is a Mediterranean ecosystem, unique in the United States and rare the world over.

If you follow the direction of this range from the Los Angeles River west toward the Oxnard Plain, it points toward the Channel Islands, which are believed to be additional peaks in the range extending out into the ocean. It's a young mountain range (the most recent uplift was 5 million years ago) and, like other east-west ranges around the Los Angeles Basin, is part of the geological turmoil caused by the San Andreas Fault.

The mountains are sandwiched by the thoroughfares of southern California, US 101 to the north and Calif. 1, also known as the Pacific Coast Highway, to the south. Yet the roads and traffic detract only slightly from the beauty of the deep canyons that pour from the mountains into the ocean, from Mugu Lagoon at the northwest end to Topanga and Malibu Canyons to the east. The lagoons are busy with grebes, herons, egrets, sea ducks, sandpipers, and plovers, the adjacent beaches are busy with sunbathers and surfers. The canyons, ridges, and hills provide essential corridors for wildlife, including mountain lions, deer, and bobcats.

Santa Monica Mountains National Recreation Area was created in 1978 to care for this important region. It comprises state parks, private lands, and reserves managed by dozens of state, federal, and private agencies, all working together to protect the area's special features. In this case, those special features include not only lagoons, beaches, and canyons, but remnants of movie sets, ranches, and trophy houses on private inholdings as well. Like Golden Gate NRA (see pp. 60-65), there are historic sites here, fingers of urban development, and a host of recreational activities from horseback riding to mountain biking. Hikers in Solstice Canyon can one minute be enthralled by an array of red penstomen and yellow monkey flower, then find themselves gazing up at futuristic mansions cantilevered off the ridges above.

The National Park Service has aggressively sought to acquire key chunks of the private land within the system, and work continues to complete links such as the Backbone Trail, which will ultimately thread 60 miles through the mountains. The trail is one way of stitching together the scattered elements of Santa Monica Mountains NRA.

What to See and Do

If you need advice and maps to find your way around this jumble of relatively undeveloped lands, stop at the National Park Service headquarters and visitor center in Thousand Oaks (see p. 96).

US 101 runs along the northern boundary of the mountains, while Calif. 1 runs along the southern, shoreline side. Calif. 1 will give you access to the Santa Monica Mountains NRA's many

Malibu Lagoon State Beach

beaches—such as **Malibu Lagoon State Beach** or **El Matador State Beach**—and both highways will intersect with roads leading into the various individual parks. Or take Mulholland Highway, which cuts through the center of the area.

You can pick up Mulholland on the oceanside from Calif.1 at Leo Carrillo State Park *(818-880-0350)*. The road twists all the way east to the hills behind West Hollywood, where it connects to **Franklin** and **Runyon Canyons.**

Some 500 miles of trails run through SMMNRA's state and federal lands. **Topanga State Park** *(Topanga Canyon Rd. to Entrada Rd.; 818-880-0350)* has 36 miles of hiking, riding, and biking trails. Some, such as 5.3-mile **Rogers Road Trail,** wander through grasslands colored by wildflowers, including golden stars, blue-eyed grass, and mariposa lilies.

Many visitors to **Malibu Creek State Park** *(Off Virgines Rd.; 818-880-0350)* choose to hike or bike the 2.4-mile **Crags Road,** a relatively flat trail following the creek beneath large sycamores and oaks. The trail goes to **Century Lake** (good fishing there) then to the old set of the *M.A.S.H.* television show. A rusting jeep and ambulance rest along the trailside.

Farther west is **Solstice Canyon** *(Off Corral Canyon Rd.),* considered one of the most beautiful canyons in the mountains. For a short, moderately steep hike, take 1.8-mile **Rising Sun Trail,** which switchbacks up the canyon's west-facing slope before gradually descending to the Solstice Canyon Visitor Center. It leads you to an old house site with a series of

Grunions

Walking the moonlit sand of a southern California beach near the high-tide line on a summer night, you find yourself tiptoeing among thousands of wiggling silvery fish.

Those silver fish are grunions. From March through August, they ride the highest tides of the lunar cycle to the beach. As the surf retreats, the females work their tails into the sand and lay thousands of eggs. The males curl around the females to fertilize the eggs, which remain buried until the next high tide, in about two weeks. The babies then hatch and slip into the ocean.

beautiful pools and small waterfalls. Although you'll notice some rather spectacular houses built into the mountainside above, you get a sense of unconfined nature here that you might not have thought possible in L.A.

The last piece of SMMNRA on the western edge is 15,000-acre **Point Mugu State Park** *(818-880-0350),* one of the few places where no roads penetrate. At the park's heart is **Boney Mountain State Wilderness Area,** which includes Sandstone Peak, 3,111 feet above sea level. The park has 75 miles of trails and fire roads as well as 5 miles of beach, both rocky and sandy, and the **Great Sand Dune** at the mouth of Big Sycamore Canyon. To reach the canyon's headwaters, take the 7-mile **Old Boney Trail** from the northern entrance of the park. ∎

Channel Islands National Park

■ 250,000 acres (125,000 acres underwater) ■ Southern California from Point Conception to north of Los Angeles ■ Year-round ■ Primitive camping, hiking, backpacking, guided walks, boating, kayaking, sailing, swimming, scuba diving, fishing, bird-watching, whale-watching, wildlife viewing, wildflower viewing ■ Contact the park, 1901 Spinnaker Dr., Ventura, CA 93001; phone 805-658-5730. www.nps.gov/chis

AS ROUGH-EDGED AND ISOLATED as the Channel Islands are, there is a Bali Ha'i quality to this small chain found in the battering seas off the southern California coast. On a clear day, the arches and spires and smooth hills of the islands loom out of the flat ocean horizon. Live-forever plants and yellow-blooming coreopsis blanket the land; gulls and pelicans by the thousands nest there, and unique animals such as island foxes hunt for rodents and insects.

Richer still is the life in the surrounding waters. Huge kelp forests,

Seabirds perching atop Arch Rock, on the northern side of Anacapa Island

deep ocean trenches, and even old shipwrecks provide living quarters for all sorts of fish and invertebrates from elephant seals to humpback whales to sea urchins.

The eight Channel Islands lie west of Santa Barbara and Ventura. Channel Islands National Park, created in 1980, comprises five of them: Anacapa—actually three islets joined at the lowest tides—closest to the mainland; Santa Cruz, a favorite camping site that mostly belongs to the Nature Conservancy; Santa Rosa, where important archaeological sites show early evidence of humans; San Miguel, at the weatherbeaten western extreme; and little Santa Barbara, far to the south. (Santa Catalina, San Clemente, and San Nicolas are not part of the park.)

The Chumash Indians once inhabited the four northern islands—San Miguel, Santa Cruz, Santa Rosa, and Anacapa—paddling to the mainland to trade in their tomols, canoes made of driftwood planks. (About 10,000 years ago, during the last ice age, when the ocean level was lower, the four islands formed one large body, dubbed Santaros by geologists.) A different tribe, the Gabrielino, lived on Santa Barbara Island.

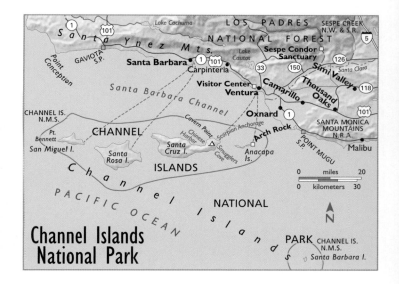

Channel Islands National Park

Scientists love the islands because they are largely cut off from the rest of the world and can be studied like a large petri dish. Isolated species, such as certain forms of buckwheat dudleya, chicory, and cream cups, or the island fox (a cousin to the mainland's gray fox), sometimes evolve in unique ways. This fox, for instance, is no bigger than a house cat.

A national marine sanctuary, established in 1980, makes the protection of marine life a priority in the waters 6 miles out from each island. Many changes in the underwater world, though, are far from simple, and we know much less about ocean life than we do about terrestrial doings. Park managers know at least that the areas completely closed to fishing, such as the deep landing cove at Anacapa, are important as study sites for species monitoring and comparison with areas that are fished.

The commercial fishery around and in the park waters is huge, particularly for squid and sea urchins. It accounts for 15 percent of California's fishing industry. Protecting the millions earned harvesting urchins is one reason this remains essentially a "sea otter free" area—otters eat sea urchins. Some people, however, would like to reintroduce the otters for ecological balance (see sidebar p. 107). The demand for some delicacies, such as white abalone, has all but wiped out those species here.

The struggle between conservation and economic issues continues here, and there are some serious underwater problems. Yet great strides have been made on land to heal the scars from years of ranching (from the mid-1800s to 1998) and the introduction of non-native species of plants—such as the South African ice plant, which leaches salt into the soil to the detriment of native plants—and animals. The NPS has successfully removed mules, rabbits, sheep, and cattle from the islands. In addition, the park service removed pigs from Santa Rosa and will be removing the last of the pigs from Santa Cruz soon. Removal of these animals has allowed the native plants and animals to flourish.

A popular recreation destination, the Channel Islands National Park annually draws some 330,000 people to its **visitor center** in Ventura. Among the attractions are an indoor marine life exhibit, a native plant garden, and Chumash artifacts. During the summer, divers with cameras and microphones drop into the landing cove to give people on the dock and in the center's auditorium a close-up video tour of the underwater world, pointing out sea snails and fish such as garibaldi, and taking hold of an octopus, which squirts ink.

About 290,000 recreational visitors, including those who come to fish, venture out to the islands themselves. Commercial boats and aircraft transport most of the people to Anacapa Island, the closest to Ventura, or to Santa Cruz, an excellent base for sea kayaking. But all five islands are worth visiting.

Channel Island: For the Birds!

Some 99 percent of California's seabirds find nesting and roosting accommodations in Channel Islands NP. In fact, like some land birds, including the Santa Cruz Island scrubjay, certain seabirds—such as the California brown pelican—nest only on these islands.

The western gull seems especially partial to Anacapa, which is the largest breeding area in the United States for that bird. In May, thousands of western gulls give birth to two or three brown-striped chicks. Their nests are often right next to the path on the easternmost islet, and when you walk by, they will sass you. If they think their chicks are in real danger, they'll take wing and dive-bomb your head.

East Anacapa Island   *Following pages:* Dolphins gliding through Channel Island waters

What to See and Do

The **visitor center** at the marina in Ventura has displays and information about the islands. Right next door in Santa Barbara, you can hitch a ride to the islands with concessionaire boats *(805-642-1393, from Ventura; 805-962-1127, from Santa Barbara).* Or you can fly to Santa Rosa Island from Camarillo *(805-987-1301).*

While traveling by boat, keep alert for marine life. January through March, gray whales pass close during their annual migrations between Baja and Alaska, and in recent years blue and humpback whales have reappeared here. And you can expect to have dolphins show up for a little race with your boat or to frolic about the bow. Orcas (killer whales) and great white sharks may also be seen.

Anacapa Island

Anacapa Island is only 11 miles from Oxnard on the mainland, making it the most popular destination. Anacapa comprises three islets; visitors land in a cove on the northern side of the easternmost one, near the dramatic 40-foot-high **Arch Rock.** You then climb steep stairs to the tableland. Follow the 1.5-mile trail to the island's top, which sports yellow-flowered coreopsis and the live-forever plants, with their purplish flowers.

Brown pelicans will wing by in neat formation, and gulls will be everywhere, especially during May and June, when they nest here by the thousands (see sidebar p. 103). The prohibition against fishing (this is one of the park-protected areas) makes this a great place to dive. You'll swim by soft coral stands of red and golden Gorgonians and see such fish as opaleyes, blacksmiths, and bat rays.

Santa Cruz Island

The eastern end of 60,000-acre Santa Cruz Island is open to the public and can keep you busy for days. When the boat docks at **Scorpion Anchorage,** passengers disembark with coolers, camping gear, and even kayaks. The camp-

Boating around Santa Cruz Island

Channel Island Choices

In the Channel Islands, as elsewhere, economic concerns sometimes clash with ecosystem needs.

Roughly 15 percent of California's ocean harvest comes from within the park, including red sea urchins (the purple are too small to harvest profitably), which are popular in Japan. The sea urchins eat kelp, which grows off the coast. But the kelp forests, which many other marine species need to survive, are fast diminishing, in part because of the proliferation of sea urchins.

A possible solution to this problem would be to reintroduce sea otters into the area. (In the 19th century, sea otters were hunted and removed from the Channel Islands.) Though they thrive in the kelp fields, sea otters don't eat the plant, but they do eat shellfish—including sea urchins.

It would seem logical to return sea otters to restore ecological balance. But the fishing industry will resist any attempt to put sea otters back in these waters.

---

ground is just up the creek bed and the launching point for kayaks, Cavern Point, is on the north side. Kayakers can head out around Cavern Point to deep sea caves beneath dramatic cliffs.

You can hike the headlands east on a trail overlooking **Chinese Harbor** or climb a 1,500-foot peak, then descend to **Smugglers Cove,** a pretty beach.

Of the five, this island has the greatest diversity of habitat. The largest part of it, the western end, belongs to the Nature Conservancy. To take a tour call the conservancy (805-962-9111).

Santa Rosa Island

Santa Rosa Island offers dramatic topography: tall ridges and deep canyons, with a northern "wall" that drops steeply off into the channel. Some 195 species of birds may be seen on the island and several animal species, including island foxes and elk.

Santa Rosa's also an archaeological treasure trove, with many Chumash sites. The remains of one human inhabitant are dated 13,000 years ago. Site visitors must be accompanied by rangers.

San Miguel Island

San Miguel Island bears the brunt of Pacific Ocean weather, and its windswept landscape gets fewer visitors than the other islands. Fewer humans, that is. Seals and sea lions crowd its 27 miles of beach to breed and raise pups, and birds are everywhere, including reintroduced peregrine falcons.

A 14-mile (round-trip) hiking trail leads to **Point Bennett,** the pinniped-viewing area. Visitors must be escorted by a park ranger on all hikes. There's boat service from the city of Santa Barbara.

Santa Barbara Island

Santa Barbara Island, to the south, is a small (640 acres) haven for nesting birds, including the rare Xantus's murrelets. There are nature walks with a ranger, or you may explore the trails yourself. ■

Enjoying Torrey Pines State Reserve

Torrey Pines State Reserve

■ 1,500 acres ■ Southern California, 15 miles north of San Diego off I-5
■ Best seasons spring and summer; whale-watching in winter ■ Hiking, guided
walks, kayaking, scuba diving, biking, bird-watching, whale-watching, wildlife
viewing ■ Adm. fee for cars ■ Contact California Department of Parks and
Recreation, 9609 Waples St., Suite 200, San Diego, CA 92121; phone 858-755-
2063. www.torreypine.org

THE RAREST TREE in the United States grows on the craggy coast of southern California just north of San Diego. Here and on Santa Rosa Island
grow the few thousand surviving Torrey pines, a gnarly coastal tree with
needles long enough to use in knitting. Growing amid greasewood, cactuses and other low-slung shrubbery, the trees dominate the landscape.
But they live a precarious existence on the bluffs of this reserve, hemmed
by the Pacific Ocean on one side and suburban sprawl on the other.

There are three distinct parts to this park. The state reserve includes
the bluffs and steep, eroded canyons cutting down to the beach; Torrey
Pines State Beach runs about 5 miles south from Del Mar beneath the
bluffs; and just north of the reserve lies **Los Peñasquitos Lagoon Natural
Preserve,** a tidal-charged marsh much valued by migrating birds and
bird-watchers.

What to See and Do

To reach **Torrey Pines State
Reserve,** take I-5 north from San
Diego to the Carmel Valley Rd.
exit. Go west 1.5 miles, then take a
left on Camino Del Mar. Continue
a mile to the entrance.

What was once a little pueblo-
style inn atop the bluffs is now an
informative visitor center with

helpful docents. From this high
vantage, trails radiate out on the
cliff edge and down to the beach.
The most popular is **Guy Fleming
Trail,** a 0.7-mile loop that gives a
great overview of the park: pines,
cliffs, beach, and lagoon.

Or try the half-mile **Parry
Grove Trail,** which winds through

the **Whitaker Memorial Native Plant Garden** (signs help identify plants such as coast cholla and toyon). The trail then descends to a bench overlooking the ocean, where you'll notice how the pines grow more stunted and twisted as they get pummeled by ocean weather. In January, the bluffs are a good place to scan for migrating gray whales. To reach the surf, most visitors take the mile-long **Beach Trail.**

Torrey Pines State Beach is a great walking beach. You'll see surfers and darting bottle-nosed dolphins. As you hike south the beach becomes less crowded, in part because there are spots where passage is difficult at high tide. (Be alert to tide times.) Cliffs rise

above you, and if you look up, you may see hang gliders taking off from Glider Port. A few miles south, you round a promontory and arrive at **Black Beach,** which is remote enough that many of the regulars see no need for clothing.

Los Peñasquitos Lagoon is a tidal marsh, rather mucky and bland when you look down on it from the backside of Torrey Pines reserve, around which it curves. It is a valuable piece of habitat, however, one that birders will recognize as a treasure chest of species rarely viewed in this urbanized stretch of the coastline. Snowy egrets stilt walk in the mudflats, and rare birds such as the light-footed clapper rail nest here amid the pickleweed. ■

Cabrillo National Monument

■ 144 acres ■ Southern California, San Diego, via I-5 or I-8 to Calif. 209 south to Point Loma ■ Best season winter ■ Hiking, guided walks, tide-pooling, bird-watching, whale-watching ■ Adm. fee ■ Contact the monument, 1800 Cabrillo Memorial Dr., San Diego, CA 92106; phone 619-557-5450. www.nps.gov/cabr

HIGH ATOP POINT LOMA, which guards the entrance to San Diego harbor, this popular spot is a great place to spend a sunny, sea-breeze day. Visits generally start at the **visitor center,** where you'll learn about tide pools, gray whales, and other marine subjects.

Next you may want to see the **Old Point Loma Lighthouse,** an 1854 tower that was replaced in 1891 by a beacon nearer the ocean below. Near the lighthouse is a whale overlook with telescopes for watching the 40-ton gray whales. The best viewing months are December and January.

Take the 2-mile (round-trip) **Bayside Trail,** which drops down along the east flank of the point. Walking amid coastal sage scrub, your chances are good of spotting red-tailed hawks, great horned owls, Anna's hummingbirds, and brown pelicans.

To get closer to the ocean, drive down a steep road to the tide pools on the west side of the point. The mild waves that wash this intertidal zone make it a great place to get a closer look at sea stars, sea hares, green anemones, and feather boa kelp. (The animal and plant life may be fragile and should not be handled.) ■

Great blue heron, Tijuana River NERR

Tijuana River National Estuarine Research Reserve

■ 2,500 acres ■ Southern California, 15 miles south of San Diego off I-5
■ Walking, guided walks, fishing, horseback riding, wildlife viewing ■ Contact
the reserve, California State Parks, 301 Caspian Way, Imperial Beach, CA 91932;
phone 619-575-3613. parks.ca.gov/south/sandiego/trnerr.html

RIDING HORSEBACK THROUGH THE BRUSH in Tijuana River National Estuarine Research Reserve, you can explore the river valley, salt marsh, and dune beach of a key stopover on the Pacific flyway, perhaps spotting such endangered species as the light-footed clapper rail. There are 27 miles of riding trails in the **Tijuana Valley,** including paths to the top of **Spooners Mesa** for panoramic ocean views (you can see the Coronado Islands offshore) and a route through **Smugglers Gulch,** once used by Native Americans and rumrunners. Numerous recreational riders use the wildlife refuge, including commercial outfitters who lead trail rides.

There are also trails for walkers. Those from the visitor center take you out into prime birding areas around the mouth of the **Tijuana River.** You can explore the creek beds—watch out for quicksand—and then along the beach from the river's outlet to the Mexican border, where a tall fence has been erected in an attempt to keep out illegal immigrants. On the beach, be careful to stay near the water to avoid disturbing seabirds nesting on the dry sands and dunes.

This wetland habitat supports a wealth of birds and other wildlife, including the endangered least Bell's vireo. It is a haven for birds on the Pacific flyway, with 370 migratory species recorded. In addition to several endangered birds, the refuge is also home to an endangered flower, the salt marsh bird's beak.

At the reserve's north entrance *(west off I-5 at Coronado Ave. in Imperial Beach),* near the visitor center—where 20 years ago car bodies and other trash littered the area—2 acres have been planted with coastal plateau plants of southern California. Today upland shrubs such as buckwheat and black sage, as well as dune plants such as sand verbena and evening primrose, line the reserve's paths. ∎

Tijuana River Estuary

On the southern California coast, the Tijuana River estuary is one of only two relatively undisturbed salt marshes, where freshwater streamflows and saltwater tides mix to create an extraordinarily productive habitat. It is also one of 25 estuarine research reserves nationwide. At this reserve, scientists monitor and study fish, invertebrates, birds, and water quality, provide information for management planning in the drainage, and undertake restoration efforts such as a recent project to plant cordgrass. Scientists and naturalists at the reserve also provide educational programs and environmental workshops on wetlands for U.S. and Mexican educators, school groups, and visitors.

Early morning bird-watching, Tijuana River NERR

California Deserts

Sunset in Anza-Borrego Desert State Park

IT MAY TAKE AWHILE but the desert will win you over. True, it is a hot, dry, unforgiving environment, although it is not as unfriendly to life as it may appear at first glance. A closer look reveals many plants, animals, and insects, all of which have learned hard lessons of survival by adapting to their harsh surroundings. Many are found nowhere else. The charms of the desert are not unlike the prickly pear cactus—a coarse, dangerous surface that suddenly produces a gorgeous purple flower. Protecting this huge area of desert—25 percent of the entire state of California—is in itself a monumental task. In 1976, Congress set aside more than 25 million acres as the California Desert Conservation Area. It includes all of this arid region's national and state parks, private reserves, military training sites, and almost 10 million acres under the auspices of the Bureau of Land Management.

While we tend to think of wildlands as forested and mountainous, some of the most remote wilderness in the Far West is treeless and flat except for a few sculpted sand dunes. In fact, a majority of federal wilderness in California is in the arid south, found within three big desert parks—Death Valley National Park, Joshua Tree National Park, and Mojave National Preserve—and on the BLM's huge holdings.

In some respects, deserts are the endgame of many of the Earth's geological processes. Erosion has reduced much of the rock in deserts from solid slabs to the finest grains of sand. Regions that were once wet and jungly and densely populated with life are now becoming ever drier, a trend that may have something to do with the way tectonic plates move and continents evolve. After completing a hydrological cycle of evaporation and rainfall around the Equator, air currents almost totally devoid of moisture flow to subtropical desert regions.

That lack of precipitation—less than 10 inches annually—defines the ecosystem. But within that definition there is much room for variety, and in fact the California

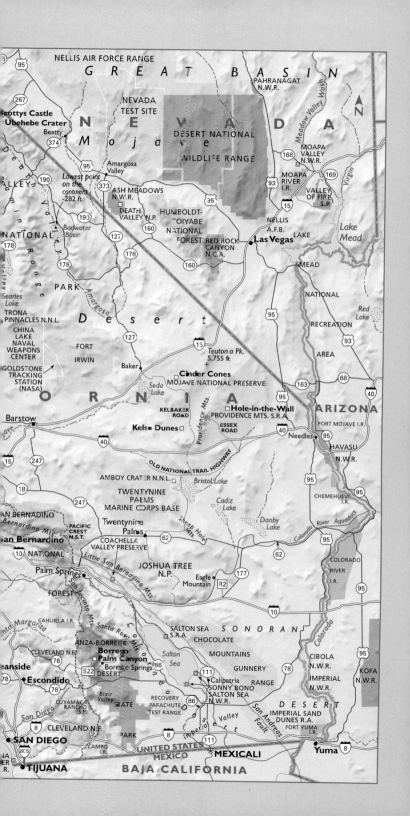

California fan palms, Coachella Valley Preserve

desert includes portions of three quite different types of deserts, the Colorado, the Mojave, and a small portion of the Great Basin Desert.

All three of California's deserts are blocked from receiving moist, Pacific Ocean air currents by mountain ranges: the Coast Ranges, the Sierra Nevada, and the Peninsular and Transverse Ranges of southern California. Now and then, though, comes a year of unusually heavy precipitation, like 1998, and suddenly the spring desert explodes with blossoms that haven't opened in ages. Drier years can be fairly dull.

The Colorado Desert, a subdivision of the much larger Sonoran Desert, is especially dry, low elevation terrain that stretches into California from northwest Mexico, just east of the Peninsular Ranges that extend northward from Baja California. It is shaped by two great forces: the San Andreas Fault, which runs through it, and the Colorado River, which these days rather feebly makes its way toward the Gulf of California. At the center of this desert —and in the trough of the fault—is the Salton Sea, a huge lake that first formed more than 500 years ago, dried up, and

Devils Golf Course, Death Valley National Park

then was re-created in 1906 by a break in an irrigation dike on the Colorado River near the Mexican border.

To the north, running up the east side of the Sierra Nevada, the Mojave is more varied in its terrain. There is a spot in Death Valley National Park that lies 282 feet below sea level, and a peak immediately to the west that rises to 11,049 feet. The Mojave's credentials as a true desert are impeccable—Death Valley averages less than 2 inches of rain a year. It is a forbidding landscape, yet it attracts many visitors, who come undaunted by the bleak terrain and the torrid sun.

What is the lure of the desert? Actually there are many. Cool nights under clear skies where every star is a diamond pinhead. Who can resist the contorted beauty of plants like the ancient Joshua Tree or the soft white petals of the evening primrose? The miraculous lush setting of a palm-shrouded desert hot spring appears like magic. The pastel sculpture of windblown dunes presents an irresistible picture. Finally, the splendid isolation one can experience in this outsized land is hard to beat. ■

Anza-Borrego Desert State Park

■ 600,000 acres ■ Southern California, west of the Salton Sea and east of Escondido on Calif. 73 ■ Best months Oct.-May ■ Camping, hiking, mountain biking, horseback riding, wildflower viewing, natural hot springs, pictographs ■ Day-use fee for some areas ■ Contact the park, 200 Palm Canyon Dr., Borrego Springs, CA 92004; phone 760-767-5311. http://parks.ca.gov

THE DESERT BLOOMS OF spring bring thousands of visitors to this state park, one of the largest in the entire United States and arguably one of the nicest. It's at the upper end of the Sonoran Desert, tucked against the slopes of the Santa Rosa, Volcan, and Laguna Mountains west of the Salton Trough. It's wetter than desert parks farther east, sometimes struck by summer thundershowers big enough to bring flash floods.

Six million years ago the eastern part of Anza-Borrego was underwater—an extension of the Sea of Cortés. Three million years ago it was a relatively lush land where birds, camels, and sabertooths roamed. Two great forces have worked to dry out this region around the Salton Sea: vertical shifts along the San Andreas Fault system lifted ridges that block moist ocean air, and the Colorado River built up a delta that gradually redirected water that once flowed into the Salton Basin.

Several springs, including those at Borrego Palm Canyon and Yaqui Well, bubble from the hilly west side of the park, watering shady palm oases. Borrego Valley in the north-central part of the park is a high, dry basin, cut by arroyos that drop off toward the Salton Sea (see p. 121). Life seems informal and unhurried in this area, though it's only an hour's drive from San Diego.

The park sprawls around the town of Borrego Springs, the kind of small town where now and then a Boston string quartet appears. There are developed and primitive campgrounds, or you can camp anywhere you want along 500 miles of backcountry roads, as many desert rats prefer to do. Visitors also can stay at historic resorts such as La Casa del Zorro (*3845 Yaqui Pass Rd., Borrego Springs, CA 92004. 760-767-5323 or 800-824-1884*). The Borrego Springs Chamber of Commerce (*760-767-5555*) can provide a complete list of resorts.

The park is named for Juan Bautista de Anza, a Spanish explorer who first passed through here in 1774, and for the desert bighorn sheep (*borrego*) that roam the higher country. An endangered species struggling to survive despite loss of habitat, disease, and predation by mountain lions, about 170 of these animals live in the park vicinity.

The most striking aspects of Anza-Borrego are not evident at every moment—the wildflowers only bloom for a few months a year, the bighorn sheep are elusive, and the oases and other pockets of life are tucked away in remote corners. This can be frustrating for photographers, but it makes a treasure hunt for the rest of us.

Ocotillo plant

What to See and Do

You can get an idea of what's in store at the **visitor center,** located at the western end of Palm Canyon Drive in Borrego Springs. Here you'll find exhibits, an outdoor garden with helpful signs identifying plants of the desert, and a man-made pond where you can observe the tiny, silver desert pupfish, an endangered species.

From the visitor center, take the easy 3-mile round-trip **Borrego Palm Canyon Trail** to a grove of big California fan palms. The only palms native to California, they create a beautiful oasis around the cool, sandy-bottomed stream. The springs that feed the stream are farther up the canyon, beyond where the developed trail ends. Downstream the water tumbles over a small waterfall of sculpted rock. The oasis world is busy with the sights and sounds of California quails, canyon wrens, verdins and a variety of hummingbirds, lizards, and other desert wildlife. Two other short trails that begin at the visitor center are the **All Access Trail,** which is wheelchair accessible, and the 1.2-mile **Borrego Springs Trail** to the campground.

In the Tamarisk Grove area, roughly 20 miles south of Borrego Springs, the **Yaqui Well Nature Trail,** a 1.6-mile trek through tamarisk trees and creosote bushes, leads to a desert water hole where birds gather despite the mildly sulfurous odor. The **Kenyon Overlook Trail** is an easy 1-mile loop that winds through cactuses and agaves and eventually rewards you with a view of the Salton Sea to the east. At Mountain Palm Springs in the southern corner of the park, you'll find the **Pygmy Grove** and **Southwest Grove Trails;** the former is a 1-mile round-trip, the latter, 2 miles.

At Blair Valley, the **Pictograph Trail** climbs gently 2 miles to one of the pictograph sites left by ancient inhabitants of the valley. Continue for another mile and you'll drop into a little box canyon where a dry waterfall provides an opening in the rock overlooking the Vallecito Valley. In most cases you drive over unpaved roads to reach the trailheads.

For real variety in landscape, visit the **Borrego Palm Canyon** area and then contrast it with a trip to either the stark Borrego badlands or the rugged Split Mountain area. There are many dirt roads in the park, leading far off the beaten track. A 4WD vehicle is advisable, but park rangers can tell you where you can safely travel with a regular vehicle. Numerous naturalist programs and guided hikes are offered throughout the year.

Spring is the time of year to see this desert at its showy best. But good timing is vital when it comes to catching the primroses, sand verbenas, and ocotillos in bloom. Between February and April, the blossoms start to open, depending on elevation, rainfall, and weather. They usually peak in March.

To receive a personal alert about the wildflower season, send a self-addressed, stamped postcard to the park. Naturalists will mail it back about two weeks before the desert bursts into full flower. ∎

Salton Sea

■ 380 square miles ■ Southern California near the Mexican border, north of I-8; Calif. 111 follows the eastern shore; Calif. 78 and 86 skirt the western shore ■ Best months Oct.-June ■ Camping, hiking, boating, fishing, bird-watching ■ Contact Sonny Bono Salton Sea National Wildlife Refuge, 906 W. Sinclair Rd., Calipatria, CA 92233; phone 760-348-5278

THE SALTON SEA is the product of a colossal accident: In 1905 an irrigation dike on the Colorado River gave way and, over the course of two years, poured water into the arid Imperial Valley creating the largest lake in California.

Centuries ago, the Colorado River fed into a much larger lake that reached to the base of the Santa Rosa Mountains in the west.

Fishermen, Salton Sea State Recreation Area

When the Colorado changed course around 1500, rerouting itself to the Gulf of California, the lake dried up and disappeared. Four hundred years later, the water was back, and birds came with it. The rich habitat around the southern end of the lake harbors Canada geese, American avocets, black-necked stilts, pintail, marbled godwits, Caspian terns, Yuma clapper rail, and great blue herons. A 1,785-acre **wildlife refuge** created here in 1930 is now an important stop on the Pacific flyway.

But there are problems here, and they underline how unnatural is this desert lake that sits on the San Andreas Fault 232 feet below sea level. With no outlet the lake's water evaporates in the broiling heat and leaves its minerals behind. It is saltier now than the Pacific Ocean and is growing more so all the time. Water still flows into the Salton Sea, but not directly from the Colorado; rather, it filters through farm fields and arrives loaded with impurities. There is so much agricultural runoff that the lake has risen, gradually drowning the marshes of the refuge where birds feed. Refuge managers have been forced to plant crops for the birds.

The pale blue lake stretches north for 35 miles into a treeless desert landscape, which seems not to discourage boaters, anglers, or swimmers. Generally, the water at the north end of the lake is cleaner. All of the fish in the lake are introduced species, including sargo, orangemouth, corvina, and Gulf croaker from the Gulf of California and the popular sport fish tilapia, which was brought in from the neighboring irrigation canals.

Check with officials at the refuge or Salton Sea State Recreation Area (*North Shore. 760-393-3052. http://parks.ca.gov. Adm. fee*) on the northeast side of the lake for health advisories regarding swimming or eating fish. Various bacteria and viruses, including avian botulism, have affected fish and bird health in recent years. ■

Coachella Valley Preserve

■ 20,000 acres ■ Southern California, near Palm Springs off I-10 ■ Best months Nov.-April ■ Hiking, guided walks, horseback riding, bird-watching ■ Contact the preserve, P.O. Box 188, Thousand Palms, CA 92276; phone 760-343-1234

Interpretation at Coachella Valley Preserve

IN THE HEART OF the Coachella Valley, best known for tony Palm Springs, lies an unblemished cluster of sand dunes and oases straddling the Indio Hills. Coachella Valley Preserve, where rare creatures such as the desert pupfish survive, was primarily set aside to protect habitat for the threatened Coachella Valley fringe-toed lizard. It is jointly managed by six partners: two federal agencies, two California departments, and two private groups; the Center for Natural Lands Management and the Nature Conservancy.

The valley lies between the Santa Rosa and San Jacinto Mountains and the Little San Bernadino Mountains. Like so much of the topography in this part of California, the basin was widened by the shifts and extension of the San Andreas Fault, which runs through it. The preserve protects an expanse of the valley floor; the terrain is characterized by alluvial fans—the result of erosion and sediment deposition from the mountains—dunes, and hammocky blow-sand fields. These fields provide the raw material that the wind eventually piles up into slip-faced dunes.

In this drifting landscape, the Coachella Valley fringe-toed lizard "swims" beneath the sand surface, out of reach of predators and the baking heat of the sun. The dunes and blow-sand areas are only accessible by guided tour, offered sporadically in the spring or by prearrangement with the preserve manager.

There are six trails in the preserve, covering some 20 miles. All but one begin at the visitor center. The trails provide access to the preserve's 11 oases. If you're pressed for time take the three-quarter-mile-long **McCallum Trail** that winds among fan palms and ponds of cool water in **Thousand Palms Canyon** near the center of the preserve. Between June and September temperatures are almost always over 100°F, which makes the canyon's shady **Thousand Palms Oasis**—the second largest concentration of fan palms in California—all the more valuable.

Water rises through the subterranean faults to form pools among the lush, green palms. Here you will find the threatened desert pupfish. The shady oasis also provides a valuable habitat for a number of resident and migratory birds, including turkey vultures, red-tailed hawks, greater roadrunners, Gambel's quails, and verdins. ■

Joshua trees at sunset

Joshua Tree National Park

■ 794,000 acres ■ Southern California, 140 miles east of Los Angeles, 50 miles north of Palm Springs ■ Best seasons fall and spring ■ Camping, hiking, rock climbing, mountain biking, bird-watching, wildflower viewing, auto tour ■ Adm. fee ■ Contact the park, 74485 National Park Dr., Twentynine Palms, CA 92277; phone 760-367-5525. www.nps.gov/jotr

A HIGH DESERT SCATTERED WITH Joshua trees is a stunning sight. It looks like an army of spindly green soldiers, frozen in place as they raised their arms in delirium under the hot sun. The Joshua tree is the star of this relatively new national park, which was established to protect the unique desert ecosystems found within its borders.

Joshua Tree National Park actually encompasses two different kinds of desert. To the south lies the Colorado Desert, stretching through the Salton Trough from Mexico. It is characterized by lower elevation and less precipitation, and is dotted with cactuses, smoke trees, and spindly ocotillo. To the north is the Mojave—the comfort zone for the Joshua trees—with higher elevation and cold winters in which the sparse rainfall is concentrated. The Mojave is situated between the Colorado Desert and

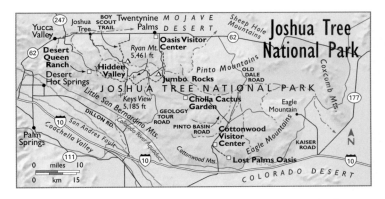

Joshua Tree National Park

the barren Great Basin Desert, and has some characteristics of both.

The park lies on the eastern edge of the Transverse mountains that run eastward from the Pacific Coast, and all through it lie geological faults. Now and then the earth gives a big shake as the faults' edges grind against each other. On October 14, 1999, the Hector Mine Earthquake centered 30 miles north of Joshua Tree registered 7.1 on the Richter scale.

Desert Tortoise

A generation ago, you'd see the distinctive, yellowish rectangular shields of the desert tortoise shell all over the Mojave Desert. But the tortoises' diet of desert grasses has been curtailed by the continuing disappearance of habitat. Many have fallen prey to an upper respiratory tract infection and young turtles are hunted down by ravens. They are now listed as a threatened species.

It is against the law to handle these creatures. Under dire circumstances, such as a tortoise on a highway, you may move it just off the road. Approach the tortoise slowly; if you spook one, it may void its essential water. For advice, call Joshua Tree Tortoise Rescue at 760-369-1235.

Along with the Joshua trees, one of the most arresting sights in the park is the piles of rocks that emerge from the desert floor. In squared columns and rectangular chunks like the toy blocks of a giant, they sit atop and against each other at places like Jumbo Rocks. They began as molten rock called monzogranite, which rose through the Earth's crust and hardened beneath the surface.

Vertical and horizontal fractures called joints formed, and when sediments eroded and exposed the rock, the joints were weathered smooth and widened by temperature, water, and wind. Later, more molten rock pushed into some of these cracks, forming lighter colored dikes among the boulders. These big rocks and cracks make Joshua Tree a hot climbing spot.

For most people, though, Joshua trees are the lure. Their trunks are actually dense bundles of fibers, with no rings to indicate age, but they can live up to 300 years, dropping seeds or extending rhizomes through the soil to sprout new trees. Most years, they produce dense clusters of white blossoms in the late winter to early spring, which attract cactus wrens and Scott's orioles. Female yucca moths invade the blossoms, carrying the nectar to other trees and leaving it with their eggs, pollinating another tree; nothing is wasted in the desert.

Because Joshua trees thrive at altitudes of 2,500 to 5,000 feet above sea level, most are found in the northwestern section of the park. The south end of the park has its own stark beauty, a lower altitude desert dominated by creosote bushes and a few hardy trees such as ironwood. At various places throughout the park short nature trails with interpretive signs help you identify plants such as the paloverde, the indigo, and the ocotillo, a spindly plant that survives in the desert by shedding its leaves whenever things get too dry and then producing them again when moisture returns.

What to See and Do

The desert feels like an alien world to many people, so they tour the park without ever venturing too far from the car. But Joshua Tree is a wonderful place to hike, especially in the morning or late afternoon, and the cool evenings make camping under a desert sky crammed with stars a deeply renewing experience.

Park Boulevard

Get oriented at the Oasis Visitor Center in Twentynine Palms, then drive south into the park. You will find yourself on Park Boulevard, which from this entrance to the town of Joshua Tree is one of the most scenic drives in the park. Campgrounds, a road tour, jutting peaks, and jumbled blocks of

Rock climber in Hidden Valley, Joshua Tree National Park

Nature's Warehouse

When naturalist Dar Spearing of Joshua Tree National Park tours the high desert, he likes to say he's "going shopping out there." He looks at a juniper, for instance, and imagines the bark made into diapers and the berries fermented to make gin.

Yucca plant roots produce oils for soaps, and the leaf fibers are woven into baskets, clothing, and sandals. The pulpy, pear-shaped fruit of the prickly pear cactus makes a sugary candy.

Ephedra is a nasal decongestant and pinyon pine nuts can make a tasty trail snack. Lichen is even used in a deodorant. Not surprisingly, many of these unconventional uses were discovered first by Native Americans.

monzogranite where rock climbers practice their moves can all be reached off Park Boulevard. Just off the road are popular areas like **Jumbo Rocks,** and Hidden Valley and the Wonderland of Rocks.

There are worthwhile hiking trails throughout this area, including the scenic 16-mile **Boy Scout Trail**—the trailhead is just west of Hidden Valley Campground—and **Ryan Mountain Trail,** a steep but rewarding 3-mile trek to the top of this 5,461-foot peak. From the top of Ryan, you can see the valleys of the park, and also see the murky edges of smog creeping over the mountains to the west.

The encroaching human presence can also be seen by driving up to 5,185-foot **Keys View,** also in the western corner of the park. It's a spectacular vista of the mountains to the west, the Coachella Valley below, and the Salton Sea to the south.

Rock climbers love the big slabs of rough granite here, but they don't much love the new regulations restricting fixed anchors in most of the park. Free climbing permits are available at the visitor center. **Hidden Valley and the Wonderland of Rocks** is the most popular area, especially in the spring and fall, when the temperature is perfectly comfortable. There are close to 6,000 separate routes; the Joshua Tree Rock Climbing School *(760-366-4745. www.joshuatreerockclimbing.com)* will provide guides and lessons.

There are numerous unpaved roads for mountain bikers and vehicles with high clearance or 4WD, among them the 18-mile (round-trip) **Geology Tour Road,** which turns south off Park Boulevard just west of Jumbo Rocks and explores Pleasant Valley. Stops are numbered at intervals along the route; you can pick up a brochure at the visitor center or at the head of the road.

Desert Queen Ranch

The Desert Queen Ranch, also in the park's northwest section, is a great stop for families; kids can see what it was like to homestead in America's outback, where you shared bathwater once a week. William Keys, born in Russia, arrived in 1910 and acquired the Desert Queen Mine as payment for back wages. His ranchhouse, schoolhouse, and collection of memorabilia can be visited on an interesting 90-minute guided tour *(760-367-5555. Fee; reservations recommended).*

Southern Joshua Tree

You can drive across the park from north to south on the Pinto Basin Road, which takes you into the drier Colorado Desert. Though it lacks Joshua trees, it offers compensations: Along the road is the beautiful **Cholla Cactus Garden Trail,** where a quarter-mile loop takes you among teddybear cholla, calico cactus, and the odoriferous creosote bush that dominate at this sunbaked lower elevation. You can begin a 4-mile hike through desert arroyos to **Lost Palms Oasis,** the largest grove of California fan palms in the park, at the Cottonwood Visitor Center near the south entrance.

Much of the little-visited east side of the park is designated wilderness, added when the national monument became a park in 1994. Parts of this backcountry can be explored on 4WD tracks, such as Old Dale Road and Eagle Mountain Road, left behind by historic mining operations. ■

Barrel cactus

Trail into Amboy Crater

Amboy Crater National Natural Landmark

■ 640 acres ■ Southern California, west of Needles on Old National Trail Hwy.
■ Best months Oct.-May ■ Primitive camping, hiking, mountain biking
■ Contact Needles Field Office, Bureau of Land Management, 101 W. Spikes
Rd., Needles, CA 92363; phone 760-326-7000

FROM A DISTANCE, it looks like a blackened bundt cake in the pale desert. **Amboy Crater** is a basalt cinder cone that sits alone in the Mojave in the desert country between Barstow and Needles. At 1,500 feet across and 250 feet tall, it's an inviting landmark; once visitors are lured closer, they often end up hiking to the rim.

Amboy is the result of a fairly recent eruption, possibly only 500 years ago. There are others of a similar nature in the desert stretching east from Barstow, but this one has an almost perfect shape, and a flat floor. Cinder cones are formed during a fairly weak explosion that throws lava fragments in the air. The cones usually discharge lava from vents around the base, and indeed around Amboy there is an extensive lava field around the crater, pocked with lava tubes, tunnels, spatter cones, and fissures.

A mile-long road *(no cars allowed)* from the parking area leads to the base of the cone. From here a 1-mile trail heads up the side and circles the rim. What appear from a distance to be dried-up lakes within the cone are actually the remnants of lava dammed within the crater. A spur of the rim trail leads to the floor of the crater through an opening on the west side where lava breached and crumbled the cone's rim.

There's no shade and the summer heat can get to you. But between March and May a purple, white, and yellow display of sand verbenas, marigolds, desert primroses, and desert lilies carpets the crater area. ■

Soda Lake, Mojave National Preserve

Mojave National Preserve

■ 1.6 million acres ■ Southern California, southeast of Barstow off I-15 or I-40 ■ Best months Oct.-March ■ Camping, hiking, wildlife viewing, spelunking ■ Contact the preserve's Desert Information Center, 72157 Baker Blvd., Baker, CA 92309; phone 760-733-4040. www.nps.gov/moja

OF THE THREE GREAT DESERT PARKS in California, only Mojave National Preserve encompasses parts of all the region's desert ecosystems; the Colorado Desert from the south, the Mojave Desert's high country, and the Great Basin Desert that stretches across Nevada to the east.

Mojave National Preserve, one of the largest units administered by the National Park Service, was created under the 1994 California Desert Protection Act. Like most parks set aside in modern times, there are conflicting uses within its borders such as mining and hunting. Private land holdings dot the area and roads and power lines cut through the preserve, giving it a cobbled together look. There are few amenities for tourists, but the elements lying within its boundaries—sculpted dunes that seem lit from within, volcanic rock formations, desert mountain ranges, and unique limestone caves—make a visit well worth the effort.

Like Death Valley to the north, this is Basin and Range country, where the Earth's surface reflects the process of tectonic plates colliding and overriding one another. As the Pacific plate pushes under North America, chunks of surface have split and tilted up to form several small mountain ranges here. Hot spots and bulges have occurred where magma pushed toward the surface, creating features such as the Cinder Cones and the Hole-in-the Wall.

Park officials are hatching plans to turn the old Spanish-style Kelso Depot into a visitor center; some private interests have plans, too, including possibly a golf course and an airport for Las Vegas not far from the park's eastern boundary. For now, and for the best, this park is the province of wanderers who are happy finding their own way.

What to See and Do

Park officials at the Mojave National Preserve Desert Information Center in Baker will be glad to give you maps and offer suggestions, but there is little in the way of assistance once you move on into the preserve.

Among the few developed trails in the park is the **Cima Dome Trail,** a 4-mile round-trip tramp to the top of 5,755-foot **Teutonia Peak,** which is crowned with a crowded stand of Joshua trees. The trailhead is on Cima Road, 6 miles north of Cima.

Head east from Baker on Kelbaker Road and make your first stop the **Cinder Cones,** just 12 miles from Baker. Visible from the road, the cones are smooth, symmetrical hills of accumulated debris around a vent hole. The oldest cones began forming about 7.5 million years ago. Around the cones you'll find black basalt lava-flow beds.

If you have a 4WD vehicle, there are roads back into these

Bladderpod flower

volcanic beds. Kelbaker Road skirts one of the youngest flows. Continue along Kelbaker Road to Kelso and you'll see tall, white dunes to your right. A little over 7 miles past the town of Kelso, a dirt road on the right has a sign for **Kelso Dunes.** Three miles down this road is a parking area from which you can hike into one of the largest dune systems in the country. These are "living" dunes, moving east from an area called Devil's Playground, but also living in the sense that there are colorful spring blooms, coyotes, mice, and sidewinder rattlesnakes.

Hole-in-the-Wall

Back at Kelso, take Kelso Cima Road northwest to Cedar Canyon Road, then continue 6 miles east to Black Canyon Road. Head south through **Gold Valley,** one of the most beautiful areas of the preserve. This is pinyon-pine forest country, with cliff walls favored by raptors and some strange rock formations shaped by volcanism.

The Hole-in-the-Wall, about 6 miles down Black Canyon Road, is a pile of rubble on a monumental scale. The material was expelled some 18 million years ago in a huge volcanic belch by the Woods Mountains just to the east.

A 2-mile (round-trip) trail leads through an opening in the cliff wall down into the wildly pocketed **Banshee Canyon.** This is a relatively easy hike except for the beginning: You climb down through the hole using metal rings imbedded in the rock. A 7-mile connecting trail winds through a landscape of mesas and boulders to the Mid-Hills Campground.

Rattlesnakes

A few rules for exploring rattlesnake country: First, watch your step. Second, look for rattlers in the open, particularly during times of moderate temperature (twilight and daybreak during the summer). Third, never hike alone in snake country. If you are bitten, keep the bite lower than your heart, and remain calm.

That last part may be easier if you know that rattlers are shy, not aggressive, and don't strike every time they rattle— the noise is just a defensive warning. Nor can they strike very far, about half their length and no more than a foot off the ground. You should also know that rattlesnake bites rarely kill though they can make you very sick.

Providence Mountains SRA

In the midst of this new reserve is an old one, Providence Mountains State Recreation Area (760-928-2586), where **Mitchell Caverns** offer some of the state's most interesting cave formations. An ancient seafloor provided the limestone; several million years ago, water saturated this rock and slowly dissolved it to form big water-filled underground chambers that later dried out.

Guided tours (fee) are held daily (Sept.-May) to look at the stalactites and stalagmites, draperies, helictites, and popcorn. In today's desert conditions, no moisture percolates in to create new formations. ■

Death Valley National Park

■ 3.4 million acres ■ Southern California, west of Beatty, Nev. on Nev. 374; from the west, Calif. 190 off US 395 ■ Best seasons fall, winter, and spring ■ Camping, primitive camping, hiking, auto tour ■ Adm. fee ■ Contact the park, P.O. Box 579, Death Valley, CA 92328; phone 760-736-2331. www.nps.gov/deva

THERE ARE PEOPLE, otherwise sane, who go to Death Valley during the summer. They've heard about the highest recorded temperature in the country, 134°F, and they think killer heat and desolation are the hallmarks of the park. Extremity of environment is indeed what makes Death Valley special, but to experience its beauty and the ingenious ways that flora and fauna have adapted here, you should visit in the winter, or, best of all, the spring.

In those seasons you will find temperatures cool enough early and late in the day to linger at Dantes View and hike along the ridge to the south for views of the alluvial fans on the valley below. A scramble up beautiful Mosaic Canyon will be fun, not grueling, and if you're in shape you can tackle 11,049-foot Telescope Peak. In the cooler months, it's less risky to steer your 4WD vehicle into the remote wildlands of the park to visit wonders such as the Eureka Dunes or the Saline Valley's hot springs.

It's a shame Death Valley is saddled with its name, because what strikes you here is the tenacity of the survivors, like the sweet-smelling turtleback leaves, or the desert iguana in the sand dunes. The story goes that the valley's name was bequeathed by Julia Brier, a pioneer woman who got stuck in the valley on her way to the California goldfields in 1849. She had to abandon her wagon and oxen as rescuers led her up the west side of the valley, the beginning of a 260-mile trek back to civilization. She looked back and said ruefully, "Goodbye, Death Valley."

When you look down at the valley from some of the highest overlooks, such as Zabriskie Point, you may be able to see that the valley is distinctly demarked by the geological faults that surround it, including the Garlock Fault to the south; in fact, the valley has been formed by those faults, pulled apart, and subsided by what geologists call "extension," rather than eroded by rivers. Bare-shouldered mountain ranges and valleys alternate in typical Basin and Range topography here, as the Earth's surface stretches and tilts. Since Death Valley National Park was designated in 1994—and became the largest national park in the contiguous United States—it has included parts of neighboring basins as well, such as the Saline and Panamint Valleys.

There was a time, about 30 million years ago, when you would have seen a very different world here. Then, about 25 million years ago as the coastal ranges of California began to rise and the faults stretched and deepened, Death Valley took its present form. Fossils indicate that some seven million years ago it was a dripping woodland, populated with deer,

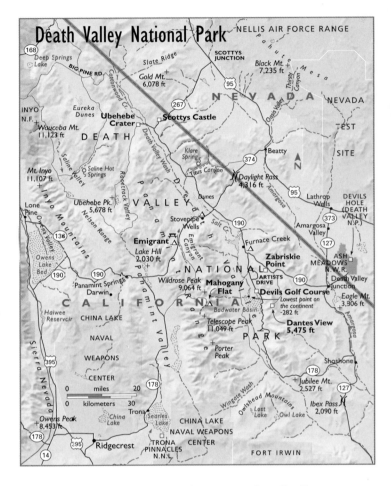

dwarf horses, tapirs, and rhinos. Lakes covering the valley floor as recently as 2,000 years ago left behind salt deposits—the white salt flats and the pinnacles of the Devils Golf Course—as they evaporated.

Indian tribes, most recently the Shoshone, found ways to adapt and live in this country, and there are rock art and artifacts indicating a presence 9,000 years ago. Stories of gold strikes brought prospectors late in the 1850s, but the only big mining success after decades of digging was borax. Mining remains an issue in the modern park, where old mining claims may still be pursued, and plans are afoot to dig talc and iron ore.

Development, including the park's two resorts, puts a strain on resources such as water, and the Shoshone tribe, which has historic claims within the park, has plans to develop its own resort on tribal lands at Furnace Creek. The additions of 1994 brought more problems: Burros, an exotic species, roam these lands, destroying vegetation, trampling springs, and competing with native bighorn sheep for forage.

What to See and Do

A conventional visit to the park includes obligatory stops at well-known places such as **Badwater Basin,** where the lowest point on the continent, at 282 feet below sea level, is found, and Dantes View, a panoramic overlook at an elevation of 5,475 feet.

But there are great opportunities for solitary adventures in the 95 percent of the park that is designated wilderness, as long as you have a sturdy vehicle, good hiking boots, and a lot of water. Over 400 miles of dirt roads provide access to these areas; for the most part all you'll need is a high-clearance vehicle.

In addition to Death Valley's seven campgrounds, backcountry camping is allowed in much of the park. Note that certain guidelines must be followed and some areas are off-limits. Check with park officials before setting off.

Few places in the world can provide such consistently beautiful sunsets and sunrises, when the soft light draws out the color of the sand and rock, and silhouettes badlands and dunes. If you want to get the most out of Death Valley, make like the local wildlife and pursue your outdoor activities at dawn or twilight.

Furnace Creek Area

Take Calif. 190 to Furnace Creek. There you'll find a visitor center and a museum, where you can get maps and advice. In this area is the Furnace Creek Inn and Ranch Resort *(760-786-2345)*. The ranch offers a more rustic experience down in the valley; the inn that sits high above on a hillside is far more upscale. But why seek a roof when you can camp under one of the cleanest skies in the world—and probably not get rained on?

Golden Canyon near Furnace Creek   *Following pages:* Dunes near Stovepipe Wells

From here, your choices will depend on how much time you have. Many visitors drive through in only a day or two, and have a satisfying time with some short hikes, great views, and perhaps a little natural history lesson from a park interpreter.

On a short visit you'll have time to follow the twists up the dry bed of **Mosaic Canyon** near Stovepipe Wells, north of Furnace Creek; south of it, off the Badwater Road, you can visit Badwater and the **Devils Golf Course,** a salt lake bed that has broken into jagged crystalline chunks, like the chaotic icing on a very large cake. You can also take the 9-mile **Artists Drive Loop** and stop to soak in the pastel pinks, yellows, greens and reds of the **Artists Palette,** created by oxides and minerals in the rocks.

Not to be missed is a drive up a twisting road to **Dantes View,** where you'll see the lay of the land better than any map can show you. From a vantage point above Badwater Basin, the valley's lowest point, you can see across to the peaks of the Panamint Range. Now and then in a wet spring, there will be standing water in the valley. You will see dark fans flaring at the base of the mountains on both sides of the valley, the alluvial sand and gravel washed down through the canyons and spread on the floor. These materials tend to be darker than the tan muds and sands and white salts of the old lake bed. You can hike down along the ridge south of Dantes View to stretch your legs and see it from different angles.

Back in your car, on the way into the valley, stop at **Zabriskie Point,** a colorful mixture of volcanic and sedimentary rock that once fronted a lake, with long yellow fingers of eroded material gripping the earth. In the soft sandstone are prints left by camels, mastodons, and horses.

Northern Death Valley NP

North of Furnace Creek, one of the biggest attractions is the Death Valley **sand dunes,** 2 miles east of Stovepipe Wells off Calif. 190. Like frozen waves, these tan dunes rise and fall on a shoreless ocean all around you when you climb to the top of one. There are 14 square miles of sand in this dune field. Most of the sand is made of quartz fragments, forged deep in the earth, uplifted, then eroded off a mountain range and pushed about by the wind until they drifted here. The deep roots of mesquite trees can get a grip in the dunes, and they attract insects, kangaroo rats, lizards, and larger predators like coyotes, most of which do their work at night.

For a little history, you can tour **Scottys Castle** (*53 miles N of Furnace Creek. Fee),* a mansion built by prospector and local character, Death Valley Scotty, between 1922 and 1933. The only gold Scotty ever found was in the pocket of a wealthy Chicago backer, who paid for the Moorish castle, which is now part of the park. Eight miles west of the castle is **Ubehebe Crater,** a 600-foot-deep indentation that blew cinder and ash about 2,000 years ago. From the parking lot at its rim, there is a short trail to the rim of the smaller, newer **Little Hebe Crater.**

If you have the vehicle and

Sunrise at Death Valley National Park

Water hole in the Badwater Basin, near the lowest point in the United States

Survival in the Desert

Treat any trip into the desert— even by vehicle—as a wilderness journey. Plan your route thoroughly, and make sure friends know your schedule. People have survived in the desert since time immemorial by following some simple rules: Carry and conserve water, avoid the heat and sun of midday, and don't panic, whatever happens.

You lose a quart of water per hour walking in 100-degree heat, so drink *at least* a gallon a day. If you're carrying it, know that water weighs about eight pounds per gallon. Bring more than you think you'll need, and turn back before you've consumed half of it. If you're counting on finding water, bring purifying tablets or a pump to avoid intestinal parasites, and check with rangers to make sure sources you see on the map are really there.

Wear a wide-brimmed hat and sunglasses and lather on the high SPF sunscreen to protect your skin. You'll conserve moisture if you wear loose-fitting long pants and long-sleeved shirts. Plan for cold nights, too. Cotton is best for day-time; wool or synthetic fleece that wick away moisture, plus a wind shell, for wet weather and nights.

There are several conditions that can affect desert travelers and it helps to know the signs. Irritability, muscle cramps, and dark urine signal dehydration. Find some shade, drink water, take salt tablets, breath through your nose, and eat only lightly until you've rehydrated.

If you feel sweaty, cool, fatigued, light-headed, perhaps nauseated, you may have heat exhaustion. Get out of the sun, keep still, and drink liquids in small but frequent doses.

Heat stroke is more serious; your skin is dry and hot, you suffer vomiting and headaches, your mind is confused. Your sweat glands have shut down, and your temperature is rising to potentially fatal levels. Remove clothing and cool off if possible by immersing in water or wet towels. Massage arms and legs and drink slowly. Don't take aspirin. The greatest danger of all is panic. If you get lost or hurt, calm yourself down, find shelter, keep drinking water, and be patient. That's the way denizens of the desert survive.

some savvy about traveling safely in desert wilderness, visit **Eureka Dunes** at the north end of the park. Wake in the morning to see the light moving down the banded minerals in the surrounding hills, then rapidly sliding down this huge mound of sand. Or you can drive the Saline Valley Road, a very rough track with dramatic views along the west side of the park, down from the Nelson Range into the Saline Valley, where there are large hot springs that have been delightfully "fixed up" with rock grottos and a desert garden by a group of informal, and often unclothed, vagabonds.

Hiking

With a little more time in the park, you can drive up Emigrant Canyon to the charcoal kilns on Wildrose Canyon Road. From the kilns parking lot take the 4.2-mile **Wildrose Peak Trail**, hiking through pinyon and juniper forest, to the summit of 9,064-foot Wildrose Peak. Back at the car, follow Wildrose Canyon Road to its terminus at the Mahogany Flat Campground, where you'll find the trailhead for the **Telescope Peak Trail**. It's a strenuous 7-mile climb up to the highest point in the park at 11,049 feet.

Ask at the visitor center for directions to some of the lesser known trails, including a hike into Titus Canyon to **Klare Spring,** a 6.5-mile one-way trek from the Titus Canyon Mouth parking area.

There are numerous backcountry loops into beautiful areas of the park where few people venture, such as the 26-mile **Cottonwood-Marble Canyon Loop.** This is a difficult cross-country route that is not maintained; you'll need a high-clearance vehicle just to reach the trailhead at the end of Cottonwood Canyon Road. Remember that you have to drink at least a gallon of water a day, and many of the springs in this country have been contaminated by burros.

The most enticing season in the park is spring, when a profusion of color refutes the notion that this valley is dead. Some years, the bloom is spectacular; in low water years, it can be subdued. In February and March, poppies, verbenas, evening primroses, and cactuses found at lower elevations flower; in April and May the alpine wildflowers—Indian paintbrushes, lupines, and others—as well as the high desert Joshua trees, open their showy blossoms. Some years there are carpets of desert goldflowers. When planning a wildflower trip, check with the park to see how much rain fell over the previous winter. ■

Erosion patterns, Death Valley National Park

Burro in Red Rock Canyon State Park

Red Rock Canyon State Park

■ 27,500 acres ■ Southern California, 25 miles north of Mojave on Calif. 14
■ Best months late Feb.-May, late Sept.-Nov. ■ Camping, hiking, rock climbing,
mountain biking, horseback riding, wildflower viewing ■ Adm. fee ■ Contact
Mojave Desert Information Center, 43779 15th St. W., Lancaster, CA 93534;
phone 661-942-0662. http://parks.ca.gov

ON THE NORTHWEST EDGE OF THE Mojave Desert where the Sierra Nevada
foothills rise from the plains, runoff has cut through sedimentary and
volcanic rock to form canyons, leaving colorful traces of red, white, and
brown. The layering of different types of rock contributes to the sometimes bizarre formations. Erosion-resistant volcanic rock and softer
sedimentary rock filled an ancient valley in succeeding layers. They were
raised adjacent to the uplift of the Sierra Nevada by two prominent faults.
Erosion resulted in dark pillows of igneous rock atop fluted colonnades
of sedimentary rock, with distinct colors to accent the differences. Fossils
found in the park suggest there were wetter, lusher times 13 million to
7.5 million years ago when saber-toothed tigers, horses, rhinoceroses,
and camels roamed grassy slopes and forests around an ancient lake.

Much of the colorful rock can be seen from a car, even along Calif. 14,
and there are several possibilities for scenic drives in the park. In many
cases you'll need a 4WD vehicle and a map; talk to the park staff about
road conditions. The two natural preserves within the park, **Hagan
Canyon** and **Red Cliffs,** are closed to automobiles, but along their trails
you'll find spring wildflower blooms and rarities such as the Red Rock
tarweed. Pick up a brochure at the park's visitor center and hike the half-
mile **Desert View Nature Trail.** From this trail a feeder trail climbs up to
the ridge above the White House Cliffs. The 1.5-mile loop **Hagan Canyon
Nature Trail** visits the dry falls in the canyon, where there are bright red
bands of mineral in the cliffs. The trail begins at Abbott Drive near its
intersection with Calif. 14. ■

Antelope Valley California Poppy Reserve

■ 1,745 acres ■ Southern California, near Lancaster ■ Best months Feb.-May
■ Wildlife viewing, wildflower viewing ■ Adm. fee ■ Contact Mojave Desert
Information Center, 43779 15th St. West, Lancaster, CA 93534; phone 661-942-
0662. http://parks.ca.gov

EVERY SPRING Antelope Valley explodes with color, dominated by the brilliant orange of the California poppy. The desert grassland here also welcomes yellow coreopsis, gold fields, and lupine. All of them provide food and cover for mice and kangaroo rats; these creatures, in turn, attract predators such as coyotes, bobcats, and even the occasional mountain lion.

California poppy

Generally, flowers begin appearing in February, and the bloom can run until May, sometimes into June. Though the reserve ecologists attempt to enhance the blooms through prescribed burns to decrease the impact of non-native grasses, they admit it isn't clear what makes for springtime profusion: It's a guessing game each year. Call the reserve hotline *(661-724-1180)* for the most up-to-date information.

The excellent **Jane S. Pinheiro Interpretive Center,** open only during the blooming season *(mid-March–May),* can give you maps and orientation. Seven miles of trails loop around the valley to several higher viewpoints. The 1.5-mile **Lightening Bolt Trail** begins near the interpretive center, passing Kitanmuk Vista Point and leading to Antelope Butte Vista Point. The 1.4-mile **South Loop Poppy** and 1.8-mile **North Loop Poppy Trails** both begin at the center and lead you through fields of poppies.

American antelope, also called pronghorns, are the valley's namesake. Today these animals can be found mostly on the Tejon Ranch Company's private ranch *(661-248-3000. Adm. fee),* which sprawls across the Tehachapi Mountains northwest of the reserve. During the spring wildflower season it is possible to visit the ranch but you may also be lucky enough to catch a glimpse of the pronghorn along the ranch's borders. ■

CentralValley

LIKE A PAIR OF WINGS unfolding from the Sacramento River Delta, long, wide valleys fan out in two directions. The Sacramento Valley to the north and the San Joaquin Valley to the south both lie between the Sierra Nevada and the Coast Ranges of California. They are known collectively as the Central Valley, or, if you ask local farmers, the world's breadbasket. Only a century ago, it could have been called the American Serengeti, a broad prairie of grasslands, marshes, and open thickets where pronghorn,

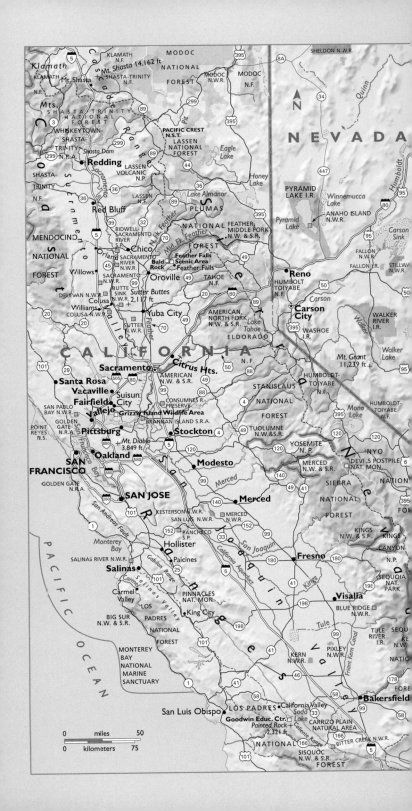

grizzly bears, and enormous flocks of birds roamed.

Much has changed: Wetlands have been drained, woods cleared, and rivers diverted to turn the valley into a crop machine neatly organized into geometric fields of rice, grapes, and cotton The teeming ecosystem that once covered 22 million acres and supported a wealth of wildlife has been reduced over the last 2 centuries to less than 1 million acres. When you find a surviving pocket of natural habitat—a grassy savanna or buggy marsh—it's like stumbling on a rare, hidden treasure.

The Central Valley stretches over 400 miles from north to south, and averages 40 miles in width, much of it near sea level despite its distance from the ocean. It was the bottom of a sea 24 million years ago, which is why fossils can be found at high altitude in the mountain ranges that border it today. When the Coast Ranges began to rise about ten million years ago, they formed a dam between the ocean and inland California. The Central Valley became a deep catchall basin for the sediments erod- ing from the growing mountains on both sides. The uplift caused by the collision of the Pacific and North American tectonic plates has created a deep fault system under the western side of the valley, where erosion sediments run as deep as 40,000 feet. That enormous bed of sediment deserves considerable credit for the success of farming in the valley.

Streams draining the valley join the Sacramento River at its delta east of San Francisco Bay to create a huge maze of meandering water now

Mossy rocks near Feather Falls, Plumas National Forest

Browsing deer

shaped by human hands. Seventy years ago, the semiarid valley represented an irresistible opportunity to farmers and a formidable challenge to water engineers. They envisioned an extensive network of dams to collect spring runoff from the mountains and canals to distribute it to farms. The massive Central Valley Project was launched in the 1930s by the U.S. Bureau of Reclamation, and today the natural flow of the valley has been turned into an artificial system of basins, spigots, and drains.

For now, many of the southern San Joaquin Valley's rivers that once flowed from the Sierras into a vast, shallow lake near Visalia are diverted into fields. What's left of them sometimes peters out before your eyes as you drive the highways beside vast orchards of orange trees, where once there were riverside groves of valley oaks. Not far from the dried-out streambeds, big canals like the California Aqueduct brim with water.

Visitors who hope to see the Central Valley as it once was must settle for glimpses. Typical is the Kaweah Oaks Reserve on the eastern outskirts of Visalia just off Calif. 198, where about 325 acres of valley oak woodlands are protected by a local land trust. Blink as you drive by and you'll miss it, but if you stop, get out, and walk around you're bound to find herons, songbirds, and the California legless lizard, all creatures with precious few places to call home in the valley these days.

Large mammals such as the pronghorn and tule elk, which once lived along the rivers of the valley, are mostly gone, along with the gray wolves and grizzly bears that preyed on them. Deer have survived by moving up into the foothills and mountains. But a visitor with an interest in nature can still find subtle beauty to observe and some outdoor recreational fun

Paddling on the Upper Sacramento River

in the Central Valley. Plenty of birds migrating along the Pacific flyway still find places to rest, particularly along the wide, slow-moving Sacramento River, where efforts have been made to restore habitat and provide forage in cultivated fields. You might never think to look for elk roaming the flatlands of California's interior, but they can be found on the grassy Carrizo Plain, at the southern end of the San Joaquin Valley.

Included in this chapter on the Central Valley are some fringe areas, where the valley floor bends up into oak-covered foothills and canyon mouths. Pinnacles National Monument sits at the edge of the Coast Ranges near Salinas, and on the east side near Oroville is beautiful, delicate Feather Falls. Places like these highlight the intimate link between valley, foothills, and mountains. The Sierra Nevada may seem distant and aloof, but it has a considerable impact on the valley world. Cold air from the mountains sweeps down into the valley, where it generates low-lying, thick fog—a serious driving hazard—and traps polluted air from coastal and valley cities. The ozone in this mix appears to be hurting both pine forests and amphibian populations in neighboring foothills.

Since the mid-1990s, state and federal water officials under pressure from environmental groups have been exploring ways to enhance habitat and protect wildlife while still delivering the water demanded by politically powerful agriculture and urban areas. The solutions under consideration for reviving the San Joaquin River are typical of the way nature is manipulated in the valley: Water would be pumped from the Sacramento Delta up the southern valley and dumped into the riverbed, where it would flow back downstream to the delta. ∎

Bare hills of the Carrizo Plain

Carrizo Plain Natural Area

■ 250,000 acres ■ South-central California near Bakersfield ■ Best months Dec.-May ■ Hiking, biking, wildlife viewing, wildflower viewing ■ Many dirt roads are impassable in wet weather. There are few services in the area; start your trip with a full tank ■ Contact U.S. Bureau of Land Management, 3801 Pegasus Dr., Bakersfield, CA 93308; phone 805-391-6000 or 805-475-2131. www.ca.blm.gov/bakersfield/carrizoplain.html

AT THE SOUTHERN END OF THE San Joaquin Valley you can get a glimpse of life at an earlier time, life that includes giant kangaroo rats and coyotes, as well as reintroduced pronghorn and tule elk wandering their native tallgrass prairie. Once, this kind of habitat was as common as, well, grass. Now two million acres has been reduced to less than 100,000 acres.

The diminutive and little-known Caliente and Temblor Ranges that cradle this preserve were pushed up as the prairie lands between them sank along the San Andreas Fault, forming a basin where all moisture drains inward to Soda Lake. Once much larger, the lake today covers about 3,000 acres, surrounded by white alkali and mudflats. Humans may not find it attractive, but migrating birds love it. A large percentage of California's sandhill crane population winters here from October until late February. Wildflower displays of rare California jewel flower, violet jimsonweed, brownish yellow tarweed, and orange, white, or yellow milkweed blanket the slopes until May with a blaze of color.

The birds and flowers are more easily seen than some of the endangered species that make their home here. Keep a sharp eye out for the little, fawn-colored San Joaquin kit fox or the oddly named giant kangaroo rat (all of a few inches long). When you look across the plain for tule elk or pronghorn, don't be fooled by cattle; they're allowed in during the early spring to graze on exotic grasses from Europe and Asia, thus clearing space on the prairie for native plants that bloom later in the spring.

The **Goodwin Education Center** (*Open to visitors Dec.-May*) on Soda Lake Road at Painted Rock Road is a good place to get oriented, with displays about the area and guided walks and scheduled tours. Look for signs marking the 0.67-mile trail to U-shaped **Painted Rock.** This sandstone outcropping rises from the plain and is decorated with numerous prehistoric Native American pictographs.

Tragically, the site was vandalized in the 1920s, but you can still make out some of the colorful artwork associated with the Chumash. General access to the site is limited from mid-July through February. Then from March to mid-July Pointed Rock can be visited by guided tour only (*no fee*) in order to protect nesting prairie falcons.

The **Selby Campground** near the base of the Caliente Mountains, offers easy access to the oak and juniper woodlands of Caliente Ridge as well as the sandstone Selby Rocks. Another hiking opportunity, the quarter-mile **Soda Lake Trail** begins at the overlook along Soda Lake Road and leads to the lake's edge. Visitors also enjoy biking around the sprawling preserve on existing roads.

This delightful enclave is jointly administered by federal, state, and private agencies. Not surprisingly, the Carrizo Plain is being studied for possible designation as a federal national monument. ∎

San Joaquin Kit Fox

The San Joaquin kit fox, with its big ears and delicate little body, looks more like a chihuahua or a cute stuffed animal than a wild predator. Kit foxes at Carrizo Plain are sometimes mistaken for small coyotes when they dash in front of headlights at night, but they are actually half the size of a house cat.

Though the kit fox makes few daylight appearances, it's become something of a poster child for the campaign to protect Carrizo Plain as an irreplaceable habitat. There are more endangered species here than anywhere else in California; as open space in the valley disappeared, wildlife concentrated at Carrizo.

Pinnacles National Monument

■ 24,182 acres ■ Central California, 35 miles south of Hollister via Calif. 25 and Pinnacle Hwy. ■ Best seasons fall–spring ■ Hiking, rock climbing, bird-watching, wildflower viewing ■ Day use only ■ Contact the monument, 5000 Calif. 146, Paicines, CA 95043; phone 831-389-4485. www.nps.gov/pinn

PERCHED IN THE GABILAN RANGE between the Salinas Valley and the Central Valley, the vertical slabs of Pinnacles National Monument have been protected since 1908. This status has largely prevented the invasion of grazing livestock and exotic species, and allowed native plants and animals to flourish. Recently, the monument was enlarged by the addition of adjacent Bureau of Land Management property.

Now park officials are working with Congress to purchase an additional 2,000 acres of lower elevation private ranchland that lies to the east. This annex, if approved, would include a creekside campground. It would also fend off the residential development creeping down from the Bay Area, and provide more habitat for some of the unique wildlife that make the area home, including mountain lions, peregrine falcons, and over 400 species of bees (see p. 154).

Volcanic dome at Pinnacles National Monument

The craggy elevations at the heart of this preserve provide a welcome contrast amid the smooth, oak-covered hills of central California. They are the remnants of a volcano that erupted 23 million years ago, split apart, and moved north along the San Andreas Fault to its present location in the dry hills above the Salinas Valley southeast of Monterey Bay.

Steep canyons, caves, sheer walls and spires make Pinnacles National Monument a heavenly place for raptors and rock climbers. The latter group prizes the technical challenges of sheer rock faces, some jutting 700 feet straight up. Easily accessible routes—not so easy to climb—are part of the attraction for the ropes-and-helmets crowd, but there are many other delights to be found here. Casual hikers prefer the less vertical High Peaks Trail with its spectacular views. Or you can descend into lightless caves, which are actually passages under old rockslides. Because of the drastic changes in elevation within the monument, you'll find several distinct climatic zones: dry chaparral hills cloaked in toyon, chamise, and manzanita; oak- and pine-covered woodlands; and, above all, the bare rock world of lichen and mosses.

Because of the Pinnacles' proximity to the Bay Area and Silicon Valley, weekends are crowded. If you're climbing and hiking, avoid the hottest months of summer; bring a good supply of water anytime of year.

What to See and Do

The two entrances to the monument aren't connected by road; you can enter from the west and get information at the Chaparral Ranger Station, or come in from the east, where the **Bear Gulch Visitor Center** and park headquarters are located. Trails through the tall rocks at the center of the monument link the halves. Though the going is steep in places, it's possible to circumnavigate the pinnacles in half a day.

You can pick up maps and find information on ranger-led activities at the visitor center. This is also the starting point for numerous trails, none of them terribly long,

that range from strenuous to fairly level. The steep climbs are most rewarding: Try the 5-mile (one way) **High Peaks Trail.** After a series of switchbacks, you'll wander the ridgeline among the highest knobs with stunning views of the valley before descending to the picnic area at Chalone Creek.

From here, you can hike the easier 2.3-mile (one way) **Old Pinnacles Trail** beneath canyon walls to the red-rock Balconies area. Follow the **Balconies Cliffs Trail** west another 1.4 miles to reach the Chaparral Ranger Station.

An interesting shortcut through the pinnacles for those with a flashlight is the 0.4-mile **Balconies Caves Trail.** Be careful of the low ceilings, drop-offs, and slippery rocks. Another cave experience lies south of the visitor center on the easy 0.7-mile (one way) **Bear Gulch Caves Trail.** You can then take the **Chalone Peak Trail** another 3.5 miles to a fire lookout on the 3,303 foot peak.

The crumbly volcanic rock at Pinnacles is not the best for handholds or bolts, but the climbs are so challenging that they attract a crowd. Many established routes have the bolts already in place on faces with names like **Discovery Wall,** the **Balconies,** the **Frog,** and **Cortadera Wall.**

Be sure to check with the visitor center before setting out; during raptor nesting season, some areas of the park are closed. Several guides to climbing routes are available at the park, or you can visit the Friends of the Pinnacles website (*www.pinnacles.org*). ∎

Bees Among the Spires

"When California was wild," John Muir wrote, "it was one sweet bee-garden." Even today he would be happy with Pinnacles National Monument. Over 400 species of wild bees live here, more variety than you'll find anywhere else in the United States. But in an area with charismatic creatures such as hawks and mountain lions, these tiny denizens get little attention. A recent survey of bees at Pinnacles revealed 13 previously undescribed species, including some with unique characteristics, such as a mouthpiece to force open flower buds. Naturalists at the monument occasionally give slide talks about the bees.

Climbing in the Balconies, Pinnacles National Monument

Grizzly Island Wildlife Area

■ 15,300 acres ■ Central California, 15 miles southeast of Fairfield via Calif. 12 and Grizzly Island Rd. ■ Open for hiking Feb.–mid-July ■ Hiking, canoeing, fishing, biking, bird-watching ■ Adm. fee ■ Contact the complex, California Department of Fish and Game, 2548 Grizzly Island Rd., Suisun, CA 94585; phone 707-425-3828

THE MEANDERING RIVER SYSTEMS OF THE Central Valley converge in the 738,000-acre Sacramento Delta, forming the largest estuary in California, a slow-moving swamp beloved by birds and other wildlife. That, at least, is what it used to be; the look, shape, and very nature of this huge, rich drainage area has been dramatically altered by human design.

Deltas grow because the water slows as it nears sea level, spreading out and piling up the sediments and sodden vegetation brought downstream by tributaries. Around the time of the 1849 gold rush, would-be farmers began building levees in the Sacramento Delta so they could drain the water that covered the rich peat soil. Now, a maze of canals and levees sunders the delta, holding back the river from cultivated "islands" that are

Tule elk at sunrise, Grizzly Island Wildlife Area

actually sinking below the level of the surrounding water. Like the Central Valley that drains through here, the delta country has been altered radically to supply land to local farmers and water to the rest of California. The vegetation and dirt-laden floods that built up these delta lands have been absent since the levees were built, and the result is subsidence. As drained land has sunk beneath sea level, the 1,000 miles of levees have been built higher, some as tall as 30 feet, raising fears that they may give way. That could cut off water that's now piped to southern California, and upset the delicate balance of salt and fresh water that makes the best delta habitat.

If you want to see the delta country in all its former glory, your destination should be Grizzly Island, one of those sunken, levee-protected pieces of land that has now been given over to wildlife. Grizzly Island is surrounded by the 84,000-acre Suisun Marsh, the largest contiguous estuarine marsh in the United States.

When there were still grizzly bears roaming Mount Diablo to the south, the bruins used to come down to the island for its fall blackberries and rosehips. The bears are gone, but at Grizzly Island today you'll find tule elk and river otters foraging, ducks and geese on the fly, and egrets wading. In the brackish tidal currents swim striped bass and sturgeon. And all of this can be found less than an hour from a busy freeway.

Stop first at the visitor center on Grizzly Island Road to pick up a map of Grizzly Island. Then you can drive or bike the levees and service roads or get out of your vehicle to hike trails along the sloughs and marshes. Particularly in the winter and spring, wear boots, because the weather is often drizzly, and there's a lot of mud on the trails and unpaved roads. Waterfowl such as ducks and pelicans are abundant during the winter. In the spring you may spot wobbly tule elk calves—but do not approach them under any circumstances, as the mother may attack. At any time of the year you may see river otters, great blue herons, or bald eagles. You can also explore the area on fat-tired bikes or put a canoe or kayak in the water *(rentals at Suisun City Marina, 800 Kellogg St., Suisun City, CA 94585. 707-429-2628)*. The tides bring salty water up the channels, though ponds of fresh water are maintained by pumps.

Though the larger delta that surrounds Suisun Marsh is hardly a "natural" landscape anymore, its intricate canals and channels still provide useful habitat to fish and fowl. They also attract a large number of boaters from the San Francisco Bay area who journey up these waterways and park at small resort areas like the Suisun City Marina. There are other resorts and marinas tucked back among the delta islands, some of which can only be reached by water.

In open areas near the bay, windsurfers frolic; farther inland, summer water-skiers can crowd the open water. You can also explore by car on roads that crisscross the waterways between Pittsburg and Stockton. Take Calif. 12 to get to **Brannan Island State Recreation Area** *(916-777-6671)*, with its countless islands that shelter more than 75 bird species; Calif. 4 follows a more southerly route along the bay; and Calif. 160 winds through sleepy delta towns and across numerous drawbridges. ■

Fishing for sturgeon, Grizzly Island Wildlife Area

Snow geese at Sacramento NWR

Sacramento National Wildlife Refuge Complex

■ 69,510 acres ■ North-central California, 10 miles south of Willows via I-5 and Road 62 ■ Best bird-watching Nov.-March. Visitor center closed weekends April-Sept. ■ Hiking, kayaking, canoeing, bird-watching, auto tours ■ Adm. fee ■ Contact the refuge, 752 Cty. Rd. 99W, Willows, CA 95988; phone 530-934-2801. www.rl.fws.gov/sacnwrc

AS THE HUMAN IMPACT ON THE Central Valley grew, snow geese found it increasingly hard to find a place to stop overnight on their migration flights. The subdivisions, farms, highways, and commercial development that have robbed them of wetlands and streams continue apace, but efforts are underway to re-create habitat along the Pacific flyway, and there are some modest success stories.

Visitors to the Sacramento Wildlife Refuge Complex can drive, hike, and even paddle along the Sacramento River and through some stunning scenery. This chain of precious sanctuaries is bringing back the wetlands, woodlands, and grasslands that blanketed the valley before farms took over. Sacramento National Wildlife Refuge Complex comprises six separate units—Sacramento, Colusa, Delevan, Sacramento River, Sutter, and Butte Sink—on both sides of the Sacramento River. Wildlife officers have worked with local farmers to reduce stubble burning and restore bird habitat, resulting in a resurgence of bird populations, including species such as the white-faced ibis, as well as hundreds of thousands of migrating geese and many mammals.

From the entrance, follow the signs 1 mile to the refuge complex headquarters and informative visitor center, where you can get directions to the other units of the refuge. There are short wetland walking trails at three of the refuges: Sacramento, Colusa, and Sacramento River.

Out here you'll discover butterflies, frogs, and muskrat amid the cattails and other marsh vegetation. But wildlife biologists suggest you'll see more and spook less if you drive the 6-mile auto tour at **Sacramento NWR,** with a stop at the viewing platform along the route. **Colusa NWR** has a similar, but shorter (3 miles), driving tour. Visit between November and March for the busiest bird season, and do your touring in the morning. Limited areas are open to pheasant and duck hunting between October and January.

Boaters also pass through parts of the **Sacramento River NWR,** often as part of longer excursions. There are no rentals available in or around the refuge, so come prepared. This section of the river is smooth and slow moving. Refuge managers note that it's hot and buggy, but that's part of their way of discouraging all but the most ardent bird lovers; they don't want great crowds of visitors. Not unless they have feathers. ■

Bird-watcher at Sacramento NWR Complex

Sunset at Sutter Buttes

Sutter Buttes

They are called the "smallest mountain range in the world." The highest peak stands only 2,117 feet above sea level. You might spot it as you drive north of Sacramento on I-5 toward Williams; a bump on the flat floor of the Sacramento Valley, a cat under the rug. The dark, leathery rock is andesite, a form of lava that burst through a dome of sedimentary rock pushed up by magma during the last ice age. Today, the cluster of peaks is castle-like, with high valleys surrounded by moats of eroded rock.

So, what are the Sutter Buttes doing out here? Some geologists suggest they are the southernmost link of the Cascade chain, though they are thought to have been extinct for over a million years, unlike some of the taller volcanoes, such as Lassen Peak to the northeast. The Maidu Indians suggested that "Histum Yani," as they called it, was the spot where man and woman were created, and where

spirits went to rest after death.

It's a good place for rattlesnakes, raptors, and reflection. But it's private land; your options are either to drive or bicycle around the buttes, a 39-mile trip that you can do on county roads via West Butte, North Butte, East Butte, and Pass Roads, or get permission from landowners to hike.

Most owners are fairly cooperative, particularly with the Middle Mountain Foundation (1000 Lincoln Rd., #H, Yuba City, CA 95991. 530-634-6387), a nonprofit group dedicated to preserving the buttes. The foundation guides hikes in the fall and spring and conducts educational programs about the buttes.

To drive to Sutter Buttes, first head north from Sacramento on Calif. 99 to Yuba City, then go west 15 miles on Calif. 20. Alternatively, you can travel east from I-5 at Williams on Calif. 20. You'll see the buttes from a distance through the valley haze, standing alone at the heart of the valley.

Feather River

■ 80 miles long ■ North-central California north of Oroville via Calif. 70 and Pevitz Road ■ Feather Falls is best viewed during the spring runoff ■ Camping, hiking, boating, canoeing, waterskiing, mountain biking, horseback riding, fishing ■ Contact Feather River Ranger District, Plumas National Forest, 875 Mitchell Ave., Oroville, CA 95965; phone 916-534-6500

A COUPLE OF CENTURIES AGO, the west-flowing rivers of the Sierra Nevada surged with snowmelt in the spring and spread huge fans of alluvial material across the Central Valley. Today, dams line the canyons that emerge from the foothills along the basin's edge, and the water is stored in reservoirs for irrigation and power generation.

The various forks of the Feather River flow into the largest of these reservoirs, 16,000-acre **Lake Oroville.** On hot weekends people rush here from the valley floor to fish, water-ski, and camp; many others boycott the lake, deploring the loss of salmon spawning runs and the diversion of streamflows that sometimes reduces the North Fork Feather River from one of the finest trout-fishing streams in the West to a mere trickle.

But there are still beautiful drives and hikes along the Feather River tributaries above the dam. And if you don't object to dams, you can canoe, houseboat, and fish in the deep lake *(rentals at Bidwell Canyon Marina, 801 Bidwell Canyon Rd., Oroville, CA 95966. 530-589-3165),* where populations of bass and rainbow trout thrive, as well as kokonee salmon and catfish. Speed restrictions keep the upper reaches peaceful.

The dam is well out of view of hikers who trek to **Feather Falls,** the great wonder of this river system. The 640-foot drop is the sixth highest in the United States. The falls thins to a delicate ribbon as the summer progresses and the snowpack that feeds it declines; it is best viewed in the spring or early summer.

You can reach the trailhead via Calif. 162, and Forbestown and Lumpkin Roads; the nearly 8-mile round-trip hike on the **Feather Falls Trail** is an up-and-down workout around steep, wooded ridges and canyons. Horses and mountain bikes are also allowed on this trail, though it's not overused. Along the way, you'll see **Bald Rock** to the west, a granite dome that bulged into the Earth's crust 140 million years ago and has withstood the erosion of softer rocks around it. An easy 1-mile (round-trip) trail leads to Bald Rock from another trailhead off the Oroville-Quincy Highway on Bald Rock Road. From the top you will enjoy splendid views of Lake Oroville and the Sutter Buttes (see p. 161).

You can also see some beautiful country from the car windows on the 130-mile **Feather River Scenic Byway,** which follows Calif. 70 up the North Fork Feather River through its steep canyon just above the reservoir, and then goes through some of the Sierras' most productive goldfields and over the Pacific Crest to Quincy. ■

Feather Falls, Plumas National Forest

Sacramento River

■ 380 miles long ■ North-central California, access off I-5 from Mount Shasta south to Shasta Lake, and below Shasta Dam at Redding or near Corning ■ Camping, white-water rafting and kayaking, canoeing, swimming, tubing, fishing, wildlife viewing ■ Contact Contara Trustee Council, 2440 Athens Ave., Redding, CA 96001, phone 530-225-2269; or Shasta Cascade Wonderland Association, 1699 Calif. 273, Anderson, CA 96007, phone 530-365-7500 or 800-474-2782

THE SACRAMENTO RIVER TIES THE volcanic peaks of northern California to the flat expanse of the Central Valley. It begins in the high country near Mount Shasta as a lively, forest-shrouded mountain stream, then gradually changes into a meandering lazy river as it flows down toward the delta. Largely unappreciated by those living in its watershed, the Sacramento is the aquatic artery that keeps California's lifeblood circulating.

The tumbling, entrancing river above Shasta Dam got noticed in the worst way in 1991, when a railroad car filled with pesticide spilled into the stream, killing fish and vegetation over a 40-mile stretch. The worst

Fly-fishing, Sacramento River

inland ecological disaster in California history gained the river much needed attention—and 14 million dollars to rejuvenate it.

Today, fishermen are once more hooking trout, and rafters and kayakers are bouncing through white-water rapids with Mount Shasta looming above. Meanwhile, education efforts are proceeding apace, led by community environmental groups along the river.

Below the dam is another sort of river; wider, smoother, darker, and lined in places with the sort of habitat once typical of valley rivers. Cottonwoods and oaks lean over the water, and ospreys swoop for fish. People float by in kayaks, canoes, rafts, and inner tubes, often spending days on the river, camping on sandbars as they make their leisurely way down the valley. An extended overnight float might put in at **Bidwell-Sacramento River State Park** *(530-342-5185)* near Chico, and pull out at **Colusa-Sacramento River State Recreation Area** *(530-458-4927)* near the town of Colusa.

It's fine to swim in the water—particularly in the clear pools above Shasta Dam—but be sure to bring plenty of bottled water to drink; runoff from agriculture and other operations crowding close to the banks makes it unsafe to drink from the river. ▪

Sierra Nevada

Bridalveil Fall, Yosemite National Park

FOR ALL ITS STUNNING DIVERSITY of terrain, California is defined first and foremost by mountain ranges. From the deep, verdant canyons of the Klamath Mountains to the snowcapped volcanoes of the Cascades, all the way south to the sun-scorched chaparral ridges along the Mexican border, it's the eye-catching presence of these burly, new-fledged mountains that gives the Far West its youthful character. But the range that exemplifies the region like no other is the mighty Sierra Nevada, the mountains

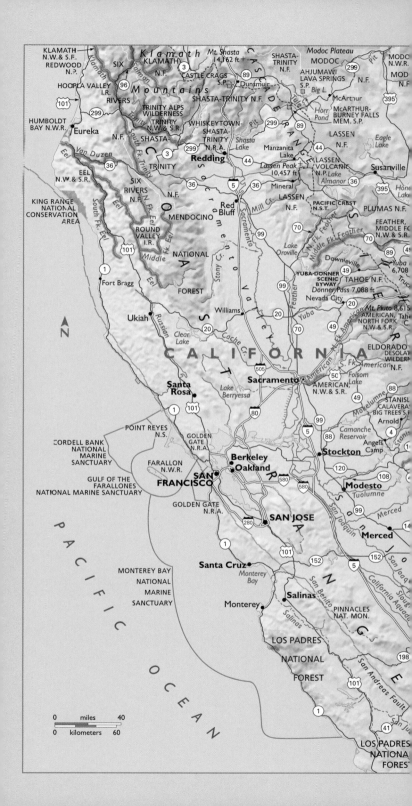

John Muir lovingly christened the "Range of Light." When the Sierra Nevada's shimmering peaks are viewed at twilight—the sharp glint of exposed granite and the soft rose-glow of powdery snow-fields—they almost appear to be illuminated from within.

This range is the great engine that drives the Far West and its people. The water that falls as rain and snow on its western ramparts flows down steep slopes in rushing torrents to power hydroelectric turbines. Reaching lower altitude, the ample flow irrigates some of the world's most productive farm-land and slakes the thirst of ever expanding metropolitan areas. From the ground itself came gold and silver that lured countless thousands of fortune-hunting emigrants to California. Although the mountains yielded fabulous riches to only a handful, the rest stayed and found other pursuits.

The Sierra Nevada is the barri-cade that divides California from Nevada and the bulk of the coun-try lying to the east. Unscalable by moisture-laden clouds from the Pacific, its soaring peaks are responsible for Nevada's bone-dry climate. With large tracts of road-less, unspoiled high country, these mountains also serve as a reminder of the region's frontier heritage. The grandeur of the landscape still offers respite from the civilized world as well as an opportunity for elemental chal-lenge, whether you are a climber reaching for a handhold or a poet grasping for an adjective.

The high country also provides a refuge for species of flora and fauna that are fast disappearing

Agave plant in bloom, Kings Canyon National Park

from more populated quarters at lower altitude. These irreplaceable treasures include groves of thousand-year-old giant sequoias that pierce the sky, bighorn sheep defying gravity as they negotiate near vertical grades, and native golden trout purling through frigid, crystal-clear lakes. Not all of the mountain denizens are so charismatic, but lungless salamanders and even lowly snow algae have equally important roles to play in the complex symbiosis that ties the health of these mountains to the well-being of the valleys and coastal habitat far below.

The Sierra Nevada is one of the largest mountain ranges in the world, 400 miles long and 50 miles wide in places, with 13 individual peaks over 14,000 feet above sea level. It is also one of the world's youngest ranges: The rock that comprises these mountains is called the Sierra batholith, volcanic magma that was hardened into granite underground by tremendous pressure and thrust upward from the collision of tectonic plates, it rose to its present dominating elevation only in the last three million years—the blink of an eye in geological terms. The great earthquakes that periodically rock California indicate that the Pacific plate is still grinding against North America, and still pushing the range ever upward. The slow but inexorable effects of wind and water have not had sufficient time to soften the Sierra Nevada's profile. Its peaks remain distinctively sharp and irregular, sculpted only by the action of glaciers at higher altitude.

In this chapter California's other northern mountains have been lumped together with the Sierra Nevada, and "lumped" seems the right word for the peaks of the Klamath Mountains and the Cascade Range. All three converge in a mountainous traffic jam near the head of the Sacramento Valley, offering some of the state's most spectacular scenery.

The Klamath Mountains, geologists believe, are actually an extension of the Sierra that broke off about 130 million years ago when both were significantly smaller and surrounded by the waters of an ancient sea. By the time these ranges began to lift in earnest, tectonic action had pushed the Klamath section about 60 miles west of the northern Sierra. They didn't continue to rise like their larger cousin to the south. As a result they present a more weathered appearance today, although the wet coastal climate also created fast-flowing white-water rivers that have cut deep, rugged canyons. Sandwiched between the dramatic northern California coast and the loftier grandeur of the Sierra Nevada, the Klamaths are sometimes overlooked. But their rich habitat is key to the survival of many species, from the steelhead trout and salmon that spawn in its rivers to older conifer species that have died out elsewhere in the state.

The last piece of the Far West's mountainous topographic puzzle is the Cascade Range. Into the gap that had opened between the Sierra Nevada and the Klamaths poured lava from the volcanic Modoc Plateau to the northeast. The molten rock drove out the last remnants of ocean and eventually formed the towering symmetrical cones we see today. The Cascades are still a hot spot, as evidenced by the eruption of Lassen Peak in 1914 and Mount St. Helens in 1980—another sign that the mountains of the Far West, like any youngsters, still hold many surprises. ∎

Sunset at Emerald Bay, Lake Tahoe

Sequoia and Kings Canyon National Parks

■ 863,741 acres ■ Eastern California, Sequoia via Calif. 198 from Visalia; Kings Canyon via Calif. 180 from Fresno ■ Best months May–Sept. ■ Camping, hiking, backpacking, guided walks, mountain climbing, fishing, horseback riding, cross-country skiing, snowshoeing, wildlife viewing, cave tours ■ Adm. fee. State fishing license required; climbing permit for Mt. Whitney required ■ Automobiles may enter parks from west only ■ Contact the parks, 47050 Generals Hwy., Three Rivers, CA 93271; phone 559-565-3341. www.nps.gov/seki/

THE SURVIVAL OF CALIFORNIA'S ancient sequoias is one of the conservation movement's greatest triumphs. The trees themselves have been coveted by loggers since the 1800s, and the area in which they grow has faced other threats. Many of the region's rivers have been dammed and diverted by farmers in the valley below. More ominously, 40 years ago the beautiful mountain setting was eyed by the Walt Disney Corporation for a Tyrolean-style ski resort at the town of Mineral King.

Fortunately, thanks to federal protection, bighorn sheep still roam the cliffs, California condors still soar on thermal air currents, and visiting humans can still gaze up the ramrod straight trunks of 270-foot-tall trees that have stood sentinel in these mountains for more than two millennia.

Some sequoia groves are safeguarded by the Forest Service in Sequoia National Forest (559-784-1500). Within the forest is another 20,000 acres of old-growth trees that stand as part of the new Giant Sequoia National Monument. Created on April 15, 2000, this preserve is another piece in a jigsaw puzzle of public land that has been taking shape for over a century, since a campaign began in nearby farm town Visalia to protect the big trees and the watershed of the central Sierra Nevada.

Today, the protected areas come close to encompassing a complete cross-section of the western Sierra ecosystem: chaparral country, oak and grass hills, precipitous glacial canyons, wild white-water rivers, granite monoliths, and soaring peaks along the Sierra Crest. Within Sequoia and Kings Canyon National Parks are some of the largest and longest living things on Earth, giant sequoias, and the tallest peak in the continental United States, Mount Whitney. Huge parcels of rugged wilderness, including a canyon that John Muir thought rivaled Yosemite's, beckon adventurous backpackers.

Sequoia and Kings Canyon are managed together, and both have sequoia groves, dramatic rock formations, and untamed rivers. The former is more accessible to the casual visitor; Kings Canyon, on the other hand, is primarily a wilderness park, although some of the most thrilling sections of the canyon actually lie outside the boundaries of the park in Sequoia National Forest.

Old-growth sequoia

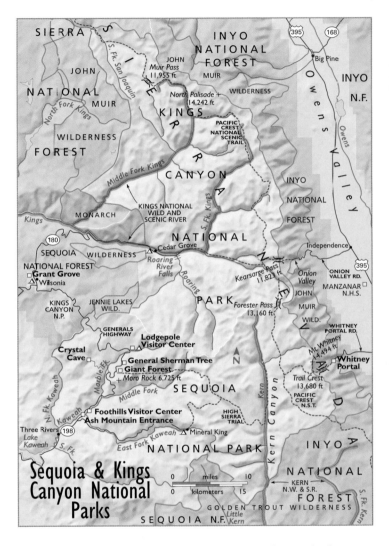

Sequoia & Kings Canyon National Parks

With less than half as many visitors as Yosemite, these parks share some of the same problems: traffic on narrow roads, for instance, and black bears that take a liking to human food. The most serious danger is visible when you climb Moro Rock and look toward the Coast Ranges: air pollution from the valley below and the San Francisco Bay area, which is affecting pines, amphibians, and may damage young sequoias.

The Park Service is conducting an extensive air-quality-monitoring program to pinpoint the damage to vegetation and wildlife. Efforts are also underway to return some developed areas to their natural state. In one instance, a hundred-year-old lodge has been torn down and the area around it replanted with sequoia seedlings.

What to See and Do

If you have only one day to spend in Sequoia, plan to visit **Giant Forest** and **Grant Grove,** the two most accessible—and the most breathtaking—stands of giant sequoias. They are located along twisty **Generals Highway** *(vehicles longer than 22 feet not recommended)*, which connects the Ash Mountain Entrance with the Big Stump Entrance. Upon entering the park at Ash Mountain, stop at the **Foothills Visitor Center** for displays describing the area's ecology.

Before reaching Giant Forest, the highway passes a parking area below **Moro Rock,** a big dome of granite overhanging the Middle Fork Kaweah River. You can climb the 400 stone steps—carved by the Civilian Conservation Corps in the 1930s—to the top for an awe-inspiring view down into the canyon and up to the peaks of the Great Western Divide.

Just east of Moro Rock you'll find the 1.8-mile **Crescent Meadow Trail,** a pleasant 3-hour hike through level "wet meadow" habitat filled with corn lilies. In the early spring you might see black bears and deer feeding on fresh shoots of vegetation.

Visitors with plenty of time and backcountry experience can take the 61.5-mile **High Sierra Trail** from the meadow, across the Great Western Divide, along the Kern River Canyon, and up the Sierra Crest to the summit of Mount Whitney.

Farther down Generals Highway, you'll find another parking area on the south side of the road at the head of the **Hazelwood Nature Trail,** a 1-mile self-guided walk with informative signs about the area's nature and history.

Nearby you'll find **Crystal Cave,** one of the many marble-solutions caves in the park. The cave is a maze of rooms

Sequoia Reproduction

Giant sequoias—sometimes called Sierra redwoods—are ancient forest survivors, resistant to fire and disease. Tree fossils indicate their ancestors grew in Nevada and California millions of years ago. But climate changes in modern times have limited these magnificent giants to a narrow band of elevation on the western slope of the Sierra, and they need certain conditions in order to reproduce.

A sequoia can weigh 1,000 tons and rise 250 feet tall, but the seeds that drop from its cones are so small that 90,000 of them weigh a pound. Squirrels and beetles gnaw at the cones, releasing the seeds. Heat from fire does the same thing.

But to take root, the seeds need to fall on bare ground. Fire, which clears away underbrush, has generally been suppressed for the last century in American forests to preserve commercial timber. Current park policy allowing natural and prescribed fires in the Sierra Nevada, controversial though it is, does lead to a healthier forest and more young sequoias sprouting in the shadows of their huge relatives.

Black bear at Giant Forest, Sequoia National Park

and passageways decorated with stalactites and flowstones. Open from mid-May through September, the cave is accessible only by a guided tour, which is well worth your time. Get tickets in advance at either Lodgepole or Foothills Visitor Center. For more information contact the Sequoia Natural History Association *(559-565-3759)*.

At **Giant Forest** numerous paths weave among the huge sequoias. The 275-foot-tall **General Sherman Tree** is found at the beginning of the 2.5-mile **Congress Trail.** This is a good spot to observe the somewhat peculiar growing habits of these leviathans. Sequoias have the greatest trunk circumference of any tree species—up to 102 feet around—but their tops are often stumpy and jagged from lightning strikes. The trees attain their full height after about 800 years; after that they only grow stouter, much like aging humans.

Backpacking

The parks provide wilderness routes for ambitious backpackers who want to cross the Sierra Nevada from one side to the other. Maps can be obtained at all park visitor centers. A popular trail leads from the Owens Valley at Onion Valley to Cedar Grove, a 23-mile journey one way. You'll cross the Sierra Crest at Kearsarge Pass and see some incredible vistas of wilderness, as well as yellow-bellied marmots, golden eagles, pikas, deer, and voles in and around meadows of lupine, columbine, monkeyflowers, and Indian paintbrushes. Be aware that park regulations require you to carry all food in bear resistant storage containers. It's always a good idea to check in with park rangers before venturing into the backcountry.

At the southern end of Sequoia National Park off Calif. 168 *(road open in summer only)* is **Mineral King,** the area once slated for development as a ski resort, and another access point for hikes and backpacking trips.

Climbing Mount Whitney

Although Mount Whitney lies within Sequoia National Park, it's generally climbed from the east side, through Inyo National Forest (see pp. 183-84). A permit is required to tackle the 14,494-foot summit. *(Eastern Sierra Inter-Agency Visitor Center 760-876-6222).* Note that from mid-May through October there is a daily quota of 50 overnight climbers and 150 day-hikers.

The journey begins at the Whitney Portal, 13 miles west of the town of Lone Pine, in Owens Valley on US 395. From there, a trail winds nearly 11 miles through high-elevation pine forest, into alpine areas with exposed rock, and finally to the summit. In the process, hikers will gain over 6,000 feet in elevation. Six miles up the trail, you'll reach **Trail Camp,** your last chance to pitch a tent; at 8 miles you'll meet **Trail Crest,** the "spine" of the Sierra Nevada, where you cross from Inyo National Forest into Sequoia National Park. Then it's on to the flat, rock-strewn summit—if you haven't run out of water or stamina. It's not a technical climb: The first known summiteers were three fishermen from Inyo County, in 1871. John Muir wrote, "Almost anyone able to cross a cobble-stoned street in a crowd may climb Mt. Whitney."

Still, of the 10,000 people who obtain permits to climb the peak each year, only about half sign the summit register. That's enough traffic to make this somewhat less than a solitary experience. Once you're on top, however, especially at sunrise or sunset, the scale and beauty of surrounding peaks makes the effort worthwhile. Look at the archipelago of peaks and deep valleys stretching north and east, then refocus for more subtle sights. Keep an eye out for pikas, eagles, and gray-crowned rosy-finches, which nest above timber-line and like to tag along with human food sources. Look, too, for the tiny blue flowers called sky pilots in the rock crevices. ■

Executive Action

Historically, the executive branch has used whatever laws it could find to protect lands without a congressional vote. At Sequoia, developers were first blocked by the General Land Office in 1880. Three years later the U.S. Army set aside Mount Whitney for scientific study. Congress didn't get around to creating a park until 1890.

Like Theodore Roosevelt before him, President Bill Clinton used the 1906 Lacey Antiquities Act to establish new parks and monuments and expand others, including Sequoia and Kings Canyon and Pinnacles National Monument. These unilateral moves have angered some locals and congressmen who feared logging and recreation opportunities would be lost.

Following pages: Horse packers in Kings Canyon National Park

Kern Wild and Scenic River

■ 151 miles long ■ Eastern California, rises in northeast corner of Sequoia NP,
flows through Inyo and Sequoia NF, then southwest through Isabella Lake
reservoir to San Joaquin Valley ■ Best months June–Sept. ■ Camping, hiking,
boating, white-water rafting and kayaking, canoeing, fishing, bird-watching,
wildlife viewing, river boat tours ■ Fee for boat tours ■ Contact Kern River,
Cannell Ranger District, Sequoia National Forest, P.O. Box 9, Kernville, CA
93238; phone 760-376-3781. www.r5.fs.fed.us/sequoia/Kernriver

IN SEQUOIA NATIONAL PARK, the southern end of the Sierra massif splits,
forming two lines of peaks running on either side of the Kern River's dramatic gorge. The Sierra Nevada has many rivers tumbling down its steep
sides, but only the Kern runs in a southerly direction. Along its banks are
some of the finest remaining virgin riparian woodlands in California,
and the river itself boasts some great white-water runs.

The Kern begins among alpine lakes along the Kings-Kern Divide,
surrounded by huge peaks, including Mount Whitney. Over the eons,
rainwater dug into a "soft" spot here, where a long geological fault had
fragmented the underlying rock. Glaciers gouged the U-shaped upper
valley, which becomes more V-shaped as the river makes its wild descent.

On its journey south, the Kern offers lengthy sections of rough-and-
tumble river in the deepest of valleys, becoming only somewhat gentler as
it leaves the park and flows through Sequoia National Forest into Isabella
Lake. There it suffers the fate of most west-slope Sierra Nevada rivers; the
water is impounded and parceled out to power producers and irrigators.

Only the most intrepid hikers and paddlers make it to the upper section of the Kern's **North Fork.** It isn't just the unremitting Class V and VI
rapids, it's the long wilderness trek, 21 miles carrying boats and gear.
Capable kayakers can get plenty of challenges downstream near Kernville,
often putting in at the **Forks,** where the Little Kern joins the main river.
They have to be careful lest the beauty of the granite slabs and waterfalls
distract them from the tough rapids. Easier paddling is found downstream on the short and popular **Powerhouse Run.**

Just upstream from Isabella Lake, the National Audubon Society's
Kern River Preserve *(760-378-3044)* protects crucial riverbank woodlands of red willow, Fremont cottonwood, and the largest contiguous
stand of Great Valley cottonwood in the country. The 1,283-acre preserve
sits at the intersection of three distinct ecosystems: the Sierra Nevada,
the Mojave Desert, and the Central Valley.

The preserve has a wealth of songbirds, including the endangered
willow flycatcher and the yellowbilled cuckoo. Other avian highlights
include the bright red summer tanager and a fantastic seasonal migration
of turkey vultures. Every fall 25,000 to 30,000 vultures—the largest
documented sightings north of Mexico—gather over a six-week period.
You're also likely to see many species of mammals such as deer, black
bears, mountain lions, bobcats, and kangaroo rats. ■

Bristlecone pines in Shulman Grove, Inyo National Forest

Ancient Bristlecone Pine Forest

■ 28,000 acres ■ East central California, south of Bishop via US 395, Calif. 168, and White Mountain Rd. ■ Best months mid-May–Oct. ■ Camping, hiking, mountain biking, cross-country skiing ■ Adm. fee ■ Contact White Mountain Ranger Station, Inyo National Forest, 798 N. Main St., Bishop, CA 93514; phone 760-873-2503. www.r5.fs.fed.us/inyo

THE OLDEST LIVING THING on the planet looks like a giant, gnarled piece of driftwood that somehow got cast ashore high in the White Mountains of the Inyo National Forest along the California-Nevada border. It's an ancient bristlecone pine called Methuselah, after the Old Testament patriarch who lived to be nearly a thousand. In fact, the Methuselah tree is much older, about 4,700 years, meaning it was already more than two centuries old when the Great Pyramid of Khufu was built at Giza.

Bristlecones grow stunted and twisted in harsh environments at over 9,500 feet above sea level. Hammered by wind, scorched by lightning, they survive freezing winters and prolonged drought. Their thick, resinous wood grows as little as an inch in diameter over the course of a century. Parts of the treetops will die off, but a thin band of bark keeps alive just as much of the tree as the available moisture and nutrients from the meager soil can support. In the course of their incredibly long life span these magnificent trees become living sculptures, with crazily warped grain and hues of brown, gray, and red in the trunk and limbs.

What to See and Do

Forest rangers claim that this area has the best view of the Sierra Nevada anywhere. To see this stunning vista take White Mountain Road 8 miles north of Calif. 168. Here you will also find **Schulman Grove,** the best place to see the trees and learn about the forest at a seasonal visitor center. Then hike the 4.5-mile loop **Methuselah Trail,** which drops down into a canyon full of wildflowers, including green gentians, lupines, buckwheats, and Indian paintbrushes, and passes through the Schulman Grove. Or you could take the shorter **Discovery Trail,** which climbs through another ancient grove on a 0.75-mile loop. Interpretive signs describe the scientific investigation that determined the trees' age in the 1950s.

In early June, a good gravel road opens to **Patriarch Grove,** 12 miles beyond Schulman Grove. Turn right on leaving the visitor center parking lot, then continue straight ahead. Overlooking Nevada and the Sierra Nevada, this landscape features the largest known bristlecone pine, called the Patriarch Tree. The road closes after the first major snowfall.

Most Nevadans and Californians couldn't tell you where the White Mountains are. It's hard to get respect when you sit in the shadow—in this case, literally the rain shadow—of the mighty Sierra Nevada. The White Mountains are much drier and show little of the granite outcropping common to the Sierra Nevada. Their softer, sedimentary rock surface is also much older, about 500 million years. Cold and thin-soiled, these mountains sustain less forest and wildlife than their neighbors to the west across the Owens Valley.

It would surprise many to know that the third highest peak in California is 14,246-foot **White Mountain Peak.** You can hike the strenuous 14-mile (round-trip) trail in a day. To get to the trailhead, continue on the gravel road 4 miles past Patriarch Grove to a parking lot 2 miles below the University of California's Barcroft Laboratory. There is a locked gate here to prevent cars from going any farther, but hikers can pass through.

On the way to the peak, you'll pass through fields of lupine and buckwheat, and, if you're lucky, you may see bighorn sheep, although not in great numbers. More numerous are the birds, including golden eagles, mountain bluebirds, sage grouse, red-tailed hawks, Steller's jays, and mockingbirds. Near the top the terrain becomes a stark moonscape of alpine tundra. ■

Cross-country skier, Mammoth Lakes area

Mammoth Lakes Area

■ 35 square miles ■ East central California, near Mammoth Mountain Ski Area on US 395 ■ Year-round ■ Hiking, backpacking, fishing, cross-country skiing, bird-watching, wildlife viewing ■ Contact Mammoth Lakes Visitor Center, 2500 Main St., Mammoth Lakes, CA 93546; phone 760-924-5500. www.r5.fs.fed.us/inyo/vvc/mammoth

THE BEAUTIFUL LAKES AND PEAKS of the Mammoth region and the Inyo National Forest lie just around the corner of the eastern Sierra foothills from the dry floor of Owens Valley and the sagebrush ranges that edge the Great Basin. Though somewhat compromised by resort development, the area is still an alluring portal to the wilderness along the Sierra Crest.

Mammoth Mountain—a dormant volcano that harbors a bustling ski resort—is on the western edge of the huge Long Valley Caldera. In May 1980 four major tremors in the Mammoth area prompted geologists to take a closer look at the caldera, which is almost unnoticeable from ground level because of its tremendous size, 20 miles long by 10 miles wide. Small earthquakes in the valley and the mountains to the west continue, but there's no indication an eruption is imminent.

That should leave you plenty of time to hike around and above the glacier-carved **Mammoth Lakes Basin.** You can hang around the five lakes in the basin, surrounded by pine forest and some private development, or take day hikes from Lake George to the **Crystal Crags,** which rise abruptly above Crystal Lake, or from Lake Mary up over **Duck Pass.** On the other side of the Sierra Crest you'll join the **John Muir Trail**— a good way to begin a much longer backcountry wilderness trip.

If the traffic around Mammoth is too much, drive 20 miles north on US 395 to the **June Lake Loop,** which takes you around lakes and creeks as stunning as the Mammoth Basin, but with smaller crowds. Several wilderness trailheads are along this loop road, including those for the **Yost Lake, Fern/Yost, Rush Creek, Parker Lake,** and **Walker Lake Trails.** Information about these and other trails within Inyo National Forest can be obtained at the Mammoth Lakes Visitor Center. Except for Rush Creek, these trails are less that 5 miles with moderate-to-steep elevation gain. The Rush Creek Trail provides access farther into the wilderness and eventually connects with the **Pacific Coast Trail** and the John Muir Trail.

Many mountain bike trails throughout the Inyo offer long cross-country rides through Jeffrey pines and along ridgetops. One popular route, the rugged 5.5-mile (one way) **Mountain View Trail,** is a single-track descent from Minaret Summit. Bike rentals are available from many sporting goods stores in the town of Mammoth Lakes and at the Adventure Center at Mammoth Mountain Ski Area *(800-626-6684).*

Many species of mammals can be found around Mammoth, including black bears, mule deer, coyotes, red and gray foxes, and pine marten. Bighorn sheep spend the majority of the year on precipitous slopes at high elevations and are harder to spot. Avian species range from song-birds such as the colorful western tanager to large raptors including red-tail hawks, northern goshawks, and ospreys. Inyo National Forest has dry sagebrush plains along the western edge of the Great Basin, but is most prized for its stands of red fir, lodgepole pines, and quaking aspens. It also contains the nation's largest grove of old-growth Jeffrey pines; some magnificent 200-foot-tall specimens are several feet in diameter. ■

Hot-spring bathers, Mammoth Lakes area

Devils Postpile National Monument

■ 798 acres ■ East central California, 11 miles west of US 395 via Calif. 203
■ Best season summer; closed winter ■ Camping, hiking, backpacking, guided walks, mountain climbing, fishing ■ Shuttle required (fee) except for campers and hikers with reservations. State fishing license required ■ Contact the monument, P.O. Box 501, Mammoth Lakes, CA 93546; phone 760-934-2289 (summer); or Sequoia/Kings Canyon NP (fall-spring; see p.173). www.nps.gov/depo

A HALF-MAD ARTIST might have hallucinated the Devils Postpile as a comment on modern urban design; the close-packed vertical staves of gray stone are reminiscent of a cubist cityscape. This sculpture, though, hangs on the high crest of the Sierra, at the portal to Ansel Adams Wilderness, and you'll find lush meadows and a beautiful waterfall close by.

It took a tricky combination of lava, glaciers, and time to make this rampart of vertical columns. About 100,000 years ago, basalt lava flowed from a vent on the side of the Mammoth volcano into the San Joaquin Valley, where it cooled, shrank, and cracked verti-

Basalt columns, Devils Postpile NM

cally. During the last ice age, 10,000 years ago, a glacier flowed over the postpile, smoothing the tops and sheering off a wall 60 feet high.

To get there, pass through the resort area of Mammoth Lakes and take a shuttle bus from the Mammoth Inn on Minaret Road to the monument's visitor center. Due to snow—the monument is at 7,600 feet—the road is open only from mid-June to Labor Day. A loop trail takes visitors atop the postpile to examine the smooth, tile floor look of the sheared hexagonal rocks; note that climbing the face is prohibited. There is a huge talus field at the base, evidence that these pillars now and then break off.

The 2-mile **Rainbow Falls Trail,** which starts downstream from the postpile, leads to the spot where the Middle Fork San Joaquin tumbles 101 feet over a wall of volcanic rock. The falls are actually dropping over what was once a canyon bank cut at an earlier time by the river when it followed a different course. There are also mineral springs and two other falls within the monument; a trailhead at the visitor center accesses the wilderness to the west. ■

Mono Basin National Forest Scenic Area

■ 120,000 acres ■ East central California ■ Best months April-Aug. ■ Camping, hiking, boating, kayaking, canoeing, swimming, fishing, mountain biking, birdwatching ■ Adm. fee to South Tufa area of Mono Lake ■ Contact the national forest scenic area, P.O. Box 429, Lee Vining, CA 93541, phone 760-647-3044; or Mono Lake Tufa State Reserve, P.O. Box 99, Lee Vining, CA 93541, phone 760-647-6331. http://parks.ca.gov

AFTER YOU'VE VISITED MONO LAKE, you may never again take a sip of water in Los Angeles without feeling a twinge of guilt. Once much larger than its current size of 70 square miles, Mono Lake began dropping in 1941 when the Los Angeles Department of Water and Power diverted its feeder

Tufa towers along the shore of Mono Lake

streams to slake the thirst of southern California. The shoreline marshes and stream habitats vital to wildlife began to disappear; the salinity of the lake doubled, from about 5 to 10 percent.

One unanticipated side effect as the lake level fell was the appearance of unusual, gnarly white rock formations above the surface. These are called tufa towers, and they form underwater as mineral-rich springs rise into the lake carrying calcium carbonate, or limestone. The material is carried up through the porous rock toward the surface, adding layers to the top of the towers, which are in effect petrified springs.

The Mono Basin is a dry, still world of sagebrush desert, but it lies at the foot of the Sierra's steep eastern scarp, only a short climb from forested, stream-riven mountains. While the surface of the basin is placid, there is a lot of activity underground: Black Point, on the lake's northern

A Conservation Success Story

Anyone who has seen the movie *Chinatown* knows it's not healthy to mess with Los Angeles when it comes to water. But David Gaines, an ecology graduate student who fell in love with Mono Lake in 1978, worked extremely hard to draw attention to its plight. In 1983—a year of heavy rains—the state legislature responded by directing water back into the streams that feed Mono Lake. The fish population grew, and Gaines found a new ally in the private organization, CALTrout. With grassroots pressure increasing, the Dept. of Fish and Game declared that future diversions from the lake would hurt Mono's rebounding fishery and, therefore, violate state law. Sadly, Gaines died in 1988 before seeing the full effect of his campaign.

perimeter, was once an underwater volcano. The Mono Craters to the south of the lake and the islands at its center only popped up recently, geologically speaking; Paoha Island is less than four centuries old. There is no volcanic activity at the present time, but seismic records indicate that these newborn mountains have not yet finished growing.

Mark Twain called Mono the "Dead Sea of California," but nothing could be further from the truth. The lake is beloved of ospreys, avocets, Wilson's phalaropes, eared grebes, snowy plover, and particularly California gulls, which nest in enormous numbers on Paoha Island. The food chain begins with the algae that shift the lake's color between green and blue; brine shrimp and alkali flies consume the algae; birds feed on the "shrimp soup." Almost one hundred species of waterbirds make an annual pilgrimage to the lake, and there were probably many more before L.A. began siphoning its water.

But now the creeks are running again, and the lake has begun to rise (see sidebar left). It will take several years to bring the lake back to a court-mandated level—not so high that it will cover the tufa completely. But in the meantime, fish have reinhabited the streams. The lake will never be as large as it was when there were still glaciers around this valley, feeding an enormous lake that spilled south into Owens Valley. Now the water never leaves the basin, and the salts concentrate the way they do in the Great Salt Lake, making it a buoyant swimming hole. And, the swimming hole is filling up again.

What to See and Do

Start with a visit to the small town of Lee Vining on the west shore, where there is a national forest visitor center as well as the informative displays at the the Mono Lake Committee Information Center (760-647-6595), an advocacy group that defended the lake against L.A.'s water grab. Begin a tour of Mono Lake at the south end, where a veritable city of tufa towers rises both onshore and in the water. Ospreys, great horned owls, and violet-green swallows sometimes nest in the formations.

Five miles east of US 395 on Calif. 120 lies a dirt road to the South Tufa Area on the southern lakeshore, where there is a 1-mile **interpretive nature trail.** In the summer rangers lead hikes here twice a day. Also at this end of the lake is **Navy Beach,** a good place to launch canoes or take a dip. You'll be surprised at how high in the water a boat rides—or a body floats, for that matter.

In nonmotorized boats you can explore the offshore tufa, and more energetic paddlers can journey 3 miles across the lake to its islands, either to visit or camp. But note that from April through July, the islands and the waters within 1 mile are closed to visitors. Some swimmers find that Mono's water irritates the eyes; others find it healing. In any case, it does leave a chalky residue on the skin.

Just south of the lake near Calif. 120 are the **Mono Craters,** considered the youngest mountain range in North America because they began forming only 40,000 years ago. **Panum,** the one closest to the lake, erupted only 640 years ago. You can hike up and around its plug dome. Take Panum Crater Road from Calif. 120 to the parking area at the road's end where the **Panum Crater Trail** begins. Be warned that the sharp-edged rock is tough on the soles of shoes.

You can escape into one of the creek canyons along the lake's west shore. The mile-long **Lee Vining Creek Nature Trail** starts at the Mono Basin Visitor Center just north of Lee Vining on US 395. The trail drops down along the shady banks of the tumbling creek. Seven miles north of Lee Vining you can drive up to Lundy Canyon and hike the 5.4-mile steep switchback trail to the **Hoover Wilderness.** The canyon explodes with wildflowers in the early to midsummer. The aspens put on a spectacular show of color in the fall. Several beaver ponds have active lodges, and you may also see deer, bears, coyotes, and lots of birds. ■

Aerial view of Mono Lake

Yosemite National Park

■ 747,956 acres ■ East central California, east of Modesto via Calif. 120; north of Fresno via Calif. 41; west of Mono Lake via Calif 120 ■ Visit year-round ■ Camping, hiking, backpacking. guided walks, rock climbing, white-water rafting and kayaking, swimming, fishing, downhill skiing, cross-country skiing ■ Adm. fee. Backcountry camping permit required ■ Contact the park, P.O. Box 577, Yosemite, CA 95389; phone 209-372-0200. www.nps.gov/yose

NO NUMBER OF SUPERLATIVES can do justice to the natural wonders of the Yosemite Valley. The highest waterfall in North America; the tallest uninterrupted granite monolith in the world; and mountains that Ralph Waldo Emerson dubbed "unmatched in the globe."

Most visitors to Yosemite National Park have a checklist of easily accessible must-see sights—lacy Bridalveil Fall, the sequoias in Mariposa Grove, the sheer face of El Capitan, Tuolumne Meadows, and the huge granite bulge of Half Dome. But with more time and a little leg power, the more adventurous visitor can enter Yosemite's extensive backcountry; few places on Earth offer monumental landscapes so concentrated and accessible. Here you'll find more extraordinary wonders, such as the potholes of Chilnualna Creek or the rock formations around Royal Arch Lake. Just as invigorating as the scenery is the sharp contrast you're bound to notice between this quiet, empty wilderness and the crowded valley floor far below.

The most dominating feature of Yosemite Valley, its granite rocks, were forged deep in Earth's furnace, then thrust upward about 100 million years ago, shucking off the softer layers of sediment above them to stand exposed at close to their present height. The distinctive U-shape of the valley is unmistakable evidence of glaciers at work. These bulldozers of ice have expanded and retreated countless times over the eons as climates shifted. Their most recent handiwork dates from a mere 300 years ago, during a "mini" ice age. In fact, small relict glaciers still survive on Mount Lyell and Mount Maclure.

The domes and sheer faces of Yosemite are also shaped by the way the protruding granite fractured, forming vertical "joints" where chunks broke away leaving freestanding monoliths like El Capitan. There is some debate over whether this process, called jointing, or the scouring action of glaciers really deserves the artistic credit, but no one will argue that the result is an extraordinary piece of natural sculpture.

Just as jointing creates steep vertical faces, another geological activity, called sheeting, produces bald, rounded heads like Half Dome. Granite which was once compressed deep in the Earth tends to expand as it reaches the surface and the weight upon it lightens. Moisture can work its way under the expanded surface, causing the outer layers to break away in sheets that follow the curve of the rock.

Not all of Yosemite's imposing giants are made of rock; the sequoias

Early morning sun on El Capitan, Yosemite National Park

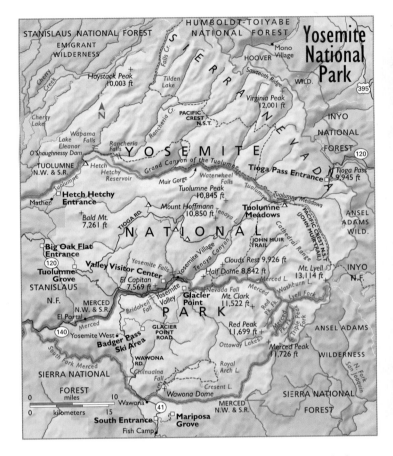

of Mariposa Grove are among the greatest attractions. Along with the rest of the parks, this grove was saved from development or exploitation in 1864, when the federal government granted Yosemite to California for public recreation. The United States got it back in June 1906—thanks to John Muir's impassioned campaign to stop livestock grazing in the high country—with the establishment of a national park. In the years since, an additional 704,624 acres of the park's backcountry have been given wilderness designation.

Muir was not so successful in another attempt to protect his beloved Yosemite. Early in the 20th century, the city of San Francisco began a campaign to dam the Tuolumne River for city drinking water. The reservoir, completed in 1923, drowned a beautiful valley in the park's northwest corner, though it spared the Grand Canyon of the Tuolumne above. Muir's successors at the Sierra Club have begun a campaign to decommission the dam and restore the free-flowing river.

The name Yosemite is derived from the language of the Miwok, a tribe that once built its villages along the Merced River, which runs through the valley. Today it is not only the Miwok who no longer call the valley home. The majestic—and sometimes notorious—grizzly bear has not been found in the park since 1895. Likewise gone are the bighorn sheep that once roamed the valley's crags and the high country above.

The black bears that remain have developed a definite hankering for human food and now constitute a major problem for park personnel and tourists—or maybe it's the other way around. More bear-human conflicts occur here than anywhere else on public lands. "This is like a big three-ring circus," said one camper in the summer of 2000, packing to leave.

What to See and Do

Like almost all of the park's roughly four million annual visitors, you should begin your visit in the valley. To avoid adding to the congestion of the park's narrow roads, take the free Yosemite Valley Shuttle Bus from any of numerous parking areas. The shuttle stops at all the major points of interest in the valley.

Make your first stop the **Valley** **Visitor Center** for a useful orientation of the attractions to be found in and around Yosemite Village. There are also many interesting exhibits in the center. Outside, be sure to visit the **Yosemite Museum**, where you will find historical paintings, displays on the Native Americans who once called Yosemite home, and even occasional demonstrations of basket-

Aspen leaves in autumn   *Following pages:* Hikers on the Mist Trail at Vernal Fall

weaving, beadwork, and other handicrafts. Also nearby are the re-created **Indian Village of Ahwahneechee,** a gallery featuring the work of Ansel Adams, and the **Wilderness Center,** where you can obtain backcountry trip planning materials, permits, and maps.

From here you can choose among hiking trails, paved bike-ways, or shuttle buses to explore the valley's wildflower meadows, deep forests, and incredible cliffs and waterfalls.

Hiking

Several easy hikes begin from the valley floor. The 0.5-mile **Lower Yosemite Fall Trail,** the 1-mile **Mirror Lake Trail,** and the 0.5-mile **Bridalveil Fall Trail** are among the most popular.

Harder to hike but commen-surately more rewarding is the 2-mile round-trip on **Upper Yosemite Fall Trail** to Columbia Rock, where awaits a beautiful view of the valley. Those looking for a greater challenge can continue another 2.5 miles to the top of Upper Yosemite Fall.

A journey up the **Mist Trail,** accessible from the Happy Isles shuttle stop, first leads you to **Vernal Fall.** In 2.8 more miles you'll come to the top of **Nevada Fall,** and after another 5 miles and 4,800 feet of elevation gain you'll reach the summit of **Half Dome.** The last stretch is a dizzying climb on a steep natural "stairway" bordered by waist-high cables anchored in the rock.

Biking

A great way to avoid driving your car from place to place in the val-ley is to bicycle. Bike rentals are available at the Yosemite Lodge bike stand *(209-372-1208)* or in Curry Village *(closed in winter).*

There's a paved, 12-mile loop bike trail that you can pick up at the Valley Visitor Center. The path gains very little elevation en route to Mirror Lake in the east and goes downgrade to the swinging bridge in the west. Cyclists can then share

Basket-weaving demonstration

Painting in Yosemite Valley

park roads—cautiously—with other vehicles to visit sights farther afield, such as **El Capitan.** This extraordinary monolith rising 3,593 feet from the valley floor is the largest single piece granite wall in the world.

Rock Climbing

El Capitan acts as a big magnet for rock climbers from all over the country and around the world. This ascent, which begins from the valley floor, is not for the inexperienced. The granite and its cracks are smooth and slippery, many routes are not bolted, and much of the climbing is very exposed. On El Capitan, climbers can choose among more than 200 different routes, some with colorful names like Manure Pile Buttress, Brail Book, and Central Pillar of Frenzy.

Regardless of your skill level, it is always a good idea to consult climbers who have experience with Yosemite's challenging routes. From April through November beginners can get guidance and instruction from the Yosemite Mountaineering School and Guide Service (209-372-8344). For climbing lessons during the winter months, contact the Badger Pass Ski Area (209-372-8444).

Other Activities

Experienced hang gliders can take flight from **Glacier Point,** a promontory directly above Curry Village. There are no glider rentals available in the park, and permission is required. Call the park to obtain more information.

Most Yosemite visitors are not here to risk life and limb. They might be happy just to ride the open tram for a narrated tour around the valley. They're content to walk through a meadow, or maybe have a swim in the **Merced River** in its lazy stretches around Happy Isles at the east end of the valley. The river gets livelier downstream past El Capitan, where the rapids reach Class III.

Cross-country skiers visit the valley in January and February, or go south to **Badger Pass Ski Area,** on the Glacier Point Road. The snow lasts longer at Badger, and you can follow the unplowed road up to Glacier Point for an overnight camp, led by a guide from the Yosemite Cross-Country Ski School, if you prefer. There's a small downhill ski operation at Badger Pass, too.

Mariposa Grove

Take the shuttle from the South Entrance or the Wawona Store rather than trying to squeeze into the always brimming Mariposa Grove parking lot. From there you can hike through the grove on a 3-mile (one way) trail leading to **Wawona Point.** Another option is to take a tram that stops at various places in the grove.

Among the highlights is the **Grizzly Giant,** which stands over 200 feet tall and may be nearly 3,000 years old. You'll also pass the **California Tree,** which has a tunnel through it where stages once drove, and the **Telescope Tree,** hollowed out by fire, allowing you to stand inside and look up at the sky. These shallow-rooted behemoths weigh as much as 300 tons. Consequently, healthy specimens sometimes topple (see sidebar p. 201), as you'll see at the **Fallen**

John Muir

JOHN MUIR WAS A VIGOROUS advocate for the preservation of the Sierra Nevada. He was also a tireless back-country explorer whose methods were decidedly low tech. If you tire of carrying a 75-pound pack in the mountains, try it Muir's way: "the free mountaineer with a sack of bread on his shoulder and an ax to cut steps in the ice." At 11,000 feet in Yosemite, Muir made his bed without bag or blanket in a pine thicket, crawling out now and then to warm by a fire. He rarely seemed to consume anything but bread and tea, and welcomed the solitude of the wilderness. "Few places in the world are more dangerous than home. Fear not, therefore, to try the mountain-passes. They will kill care, save you from apathy, set you free."

The Scotland-born, Wisconsin-raised Muir planned to study medicine at the University of Michigan until the outbreak of the Civil War convinced him to move to Canada. There he invented a machine to mill broom handles that would have made him rich but for a fire in 1866 that burned the Canadian factory to the ground. He then lit out on a vagabond botanical expedition south to Florida and Cuba. A bout of malaria finally led him to abandon the tropics for the cooler climes of the American West.

Though his name is now forever linked to the Sierra Nevada, his early love of the outdoors was rambunctious and indiscriminate: When he arrived in San Francisco by steamer and was asked where he wanted to go, he replied, "Any place that is wild." He fell in love with the entire state of California. Looking from Pacheco Pass "one shining morning" for the first time at the Central Valley—so tamed by human ingenuity today—he dubbed it "flowery, like a lake of pure sunshine." Then he gazed upward and saw a towering mountain range "so gloriously colored and so radiant, it seemed not clothed with light, but wholly composed of it. like the wall of some celestial city. Along the top and extending a good way down, was a rich pearly-gray belt of snow; below it a belt of blue and dark purple, marking the extension of the forests; and stretching along the base of the range a broad belt of rose-purple; all these colors, from the blue sky to the yellow valley smoothly blending as they do in a rainbow."

Rich, flowing brush strokes of words came easily to Muir when he was describing natural wonders. Such was not the case, however, when he tried to write about himself. Struggling with an autobiography he never finished, Muir confided to friends that, "my life on the whole has been level and uneventful," and he found he had little to say to the "moiling, squirming, fog-breathing public."

Muir produced his best work when he was investigating geological or botanical riddles, such as the origins of Yosemite Valley. He challenged the eminent California geologist Josiah Whitney, who had theorized that Yosemite was the product of an earthquake cataclysm. Muir, however, correctly concluded that the deep valley had been sculpted by glaciers. His articulate treatise convinced the scientific community.

Muir was also an engaging raconteur, whether it was by a park campfire or in the corridors of power. When legislators were wrestling over whether to make Yosemite a national park, Muir

Yosemite Valley in the 1860s

contacted the powerful president of the Southern Pacific Railroad, with whom he had traveled in Alaska, and had him line up the votes. He didn't always win—the construction of Hetch Hetchy Dam was his most heartbreaking failure—but he never shied away from a fight.

Still in the end, Muir was more mountaineer than politician, philosopher, writer, and scientist combined. Ralph Waldo Emerson, who had visited him at Yosemite, wrote often urging Muir to end his lonely mountain "probation" and come warm up with his circle of intellectuals in Boston.

But Muir was too imbued with the wilderness ever to retire from it. "I never saw a discontented tree," he wrote. "They grip the ground as though they liked it, and though fast rooted they travel about as far as we do. They go wandering forth in all directions with every wind, going and coming like ourselves, traveling with us around the sun two million miles a day, and through space heaven knows how fast and far!" ■

Monarch, which appears full of life despite lying on its side.

A number of backcountry trails originate from the Wawona Information Station, including the 5-mile (one way) switchback **Chilnualna Fall Trail** up to this spectacular cascade just north of Wawona Dome, where you'll also find beautiful pot-hole pools.

For a much longer backcountry excursion, you can go beyond the fall and create a 21-mile multi-day hike on a series of unnamed trails. As you circle **Buena Vista Peak,** you'll climb through stands of pine and juniper, and wildflower meadows ablaze in the spring with white shooting stars. You'll also pass several high altitude lakes including Crescent and Royal Arch before returning to Chilnualna. En route, you're likely to see scrub jays, mountain quails, and acorn woodpeckers overhead. You might also spot rock squirrels, bobcats, black bears, or mountain lions.

Tioga Road

The southernmost route through the Sierra reaches an elevation so high near Tioga Pass—9,945 feet—that snows keep it closed from November to May. Beginning near the Big Oak Flat Entrance, the 62-mile road (Calif. 120) climbs through evergreen forest, past dazzling mile-long Tenaya Lake, and through **Tuolumne Meadows.**

This subalpine meadow, with the blue ribbon of the Tuolumne River flowing through, is surrounded by more of Yosemite's monumental dome rocks and horned peaks. There is a visitor center here, and trailheads that lead to the wilderness of the park's little-visited north section.

To see the **Grand Canyon of the Tuolumne River**—a spectacular, steep-sided gorge of sculpted rock and waterfalls that offers dramatic, sweeping vistas—you start north from Tuolumne Meadows on a segment of the **Pacific Crest National Scenic Trail,** then head down the canyon. Day-hikers can turn back at Glen Aulin, after a cool-off swim below the tumbling falls.

North of Tioga Pass is also a good starting point for a multi-day visit to the park's numerous jewel-like alpine lakes nestled in the rugged high country above 10,000 feet. With a backcountry camping permit, you can settle down for a night under the stars next to one of these intimate crystal pools, most of which can be circumnavigated in 15 minutes. ∎

Rock climber on El Capitan

Calaveras Big Trees State Park

■ 6,500 acres ■ East central California, 75 miles east of Stockton on Calif. 4
■ Best seasons spring and summer ■ Camping, hiking, guided walks, white-
water rafting and kayaking, fishing, cross-country skiing ■ Adm. fee ■ Contact
the park, P.O. Box 120, Arnold, CA 95223; phone 209-795-2334.
www.sierra.parks.state.ca.us/cbt/cbt.htm

ESTABLISHED IN 1931, this state park harbors more than a thousand old-
growth giant sequoias in two large groves. More than 60 million years
ago these trees covered large areas of North America, but climate change
reduced the sequoia forests to a few isolated pockets on wet mountain
slopes. In the last two centuries logging has claimed most of those that
remained. California's forests today are predominantly pine, making
preserves like Calaveras all the more rare and delightful.

From the visitor center head south on the main park road, a scenic
drive that will take you over the Stanislaus River Bridge. In 9 miles you'll
come to a parking area for the **South Grove.** You'll find the largest
sequoia in the park, called the **Agassiz Tree** and standing more than 250
feet tall, located midway along the 5-mile **South Grove Loop Trail.** This
lovely walk passes several other giants as well, including the burned-out
but still-living **Chimney Tree.** The
North Grove gets more visitors
because it's next to the visitor center parking lot and the **loop trail** is
only 1 mile long. With a brochure
in hand, you can identify the rich
plant life of the redwood understory, including monkeyflowers,
dogwood, lilies, and the Pacific yew,
here in its southernmost habitat.

This region was the setting for
Mark Twain's "Celebrated Jumping
Frog of Calaveras County" (Angels
Camp is just down the road), and
its history is studded with over-the-
top tales. In the park is the stump
of the **Discovery Tree,** a 30-foot-
wide sequoia cut down in 1853.
The stump was used as a dance
floor and the trunk became California's first bowling alley.

The **North Fork Stanislaus
River** runs through the park and
offers Class III and IV rapids. The
state stocks the river with rainbow
trout for anglers. ■

Fallen Giants

When a giant sequoia keels
over, the earth shakes and
people tremble. It happened
in April 2000 in the North
Grove at Calaveras when visitors reported hearing a "huge
crash." Rangers found that
tree No. 115, a sequoia with
a 17-foot diameter, had fallen.

The tree was nicknamed
"Anna Mehlig" after a European pianist whose U.S. tour
was a big hit almost a century
ago. The tree made a big hit,
too, toppling several smaller
sequoias and taking a big
gouge out of a hillside.

Once down, though, the
fallen tree becomes a nurse
log, providing a home for
ferns and insects and a bed
for new sequoia seedlings.

Lake Tahoe Basin

■ 72 miles of shoreline ■ East central California, near Truckee via Calif. 89 or Calif. 267 ■ Best seasons spring-fall ■ Camping, hiking, boating, swimming, waterskiing, fishing, biking ■ Contact U.S.F.S. Lake Tahoe Basin Management Unit, 870 Emerald Bay Rd., Suite 1, South Lake Tahoe, CA 96150; phone 530-573-2600. www.r5.fs.fed.us/ltbmu

YOU MIGHT SAY THAT LAKE TAHOE has a split personality: a clear, blue mountain lake of enormous size and depth in a forested, peak-rimmed basin...pervaded by logging, condominiums, casinos, and speedboats. If you come upon the lake from a high ridge in the Desolation Wilderness early on a fall morning, you see almost none of the surrounding develop-

Sailboat race on Lake Tahoe

ment. The resilient lake lives, and there are steps underway that may make it healthier still in the future.

Tahoe is the second largest alpine lake in North America, after Oregon's Crater Lake, 22 miles long with a depth as great as 1,643 feet and 122,000 acres of surface. Before pollution became a problem, the water was so clear you could see objects on the lake's floor in 130 feet of water.

Wedged between the Sierra Nevada and the Carson Range right on the California-Nevada border, the Lake Tahoe Basin is the product of volcanism and plate tectonics. It lies in a depression between two active faults—the steep-sided Sierra Nevada Crustal block on the west side of Lake Tahoe is still moving in a north-westerly direction. Lava from Mount Pluto blocked the basin's northern outlet two million years ago, and the lake began to fill. More recently, glaciers carved deep gouges in the surrounding land and the growing lake flowed into them as well. Emerald Bay is among the more scenic of these flooded valleys.

Since the days when pioneers' wagons rolled through Donner Pass just to the north, Tahoe has attracted visitors. With the construction of several ski resorts nearby—and casinos on the Nevada side in and around Reno—in the 1950s, the lakeshore began attracting permanent residents. Now after 40 years of rapid growth in the area, efforts to curb more damaging activities are underway.

In 1999, the Tahoe Regional Planning Agency banned two-stroke jet skis from Lake Tahoe in a controversial move to cut pollution; the agency also mandated a 5-mph speed limit within 600 feet of the shore. But further steps to curtail some of the basins's other pollution problems—construction, for instance, or automobile traffic—will face opposition from local businesses.

Folks around here are serious about their recreation, which means popular areas like Emerald Bay fill up quickly with boats on summer weekends, and even trails in nearby wilderness areas are relatively busy thoroughfares. Whether you're in a kayak or on a water ski, when you look down through the bracing snowmelt water, you will not see as far as paddlers a century ago, though it will still be a beautiful sight.

What to See and Do

You can take a 72-mile scenic drive around the lake—a three-hour trip usually lengthened by road construction—but this means navigating the clots of overbuilt commerce at the south and north shores. You can rent various types and sizes of boats in the towns along the shoreline and explore by water, remaining watchful for sudden weather changes. Or you can stop at one of the state parks on the lakeshore for a swim, a hike, or a picnic.

On the California side, Calif. 89 passes above **Emerald Bay,** a deep sheltered cove flanked by forested peninsulas. Several breathtaking pullouts along here include one where you can take a short walk to **Eagle Falls** as it drops down to the bay; another accesses a moderate switchback drop to **Vikingsholm,** a 1920s mansion on the shore in

Emerald Bay State Park. A little farther north on Calif. 89 is **D. L. Bliss State Park.** Here you can pick up the scenic 3-mile **Rubicon Trail,** which follows the shoreline south to Emerald Point.

If the lake seems too crowded or commercial, head up into Lake Tahoe's surrounding backcountry. One of the most accessible areas is Eldorado National Forest's **Desolation Wilderness,** small in size at 63,475 acres, but packed with alpine meadows, granite cliffs, and a few peaks nearing 10,000 feet above sea level.

A popular day hike is the **Ralston Trail** to the top of Ralston Peak. The trailhead lies just a half mile east of Twin Bridges on US 50; the parking lot is across the street from Camp Sacramento. Be advised that the trail is described as moderate to strenuous with considerable elevation gain. There is a self-registration box located at the trailhead.

A 12-mile segment of the **Tahoe Rim Trail** crosses Desolation Wilderness. The 150-mile loop follows ridges and mountaintops around Lake Tahoe, passing alpine lakes, through dense red fir woods, and past Basque shepherds' carvings in tree trunks. This section of the trail surpasses most other stretches for the stark beauty of its subalpine terrain with a mixture of high alpine meadows. Exit US 50 at Echo Summit and follow the signs to the parking lot.

Roughly 3 miles of the trail at the north end of the lake have not been completed. The trail, begun in 1984, is largely the work of volunteers, and you're welcome to put in some time on a trail crew—call the Tahoe Rim Trail office *(775-588-0686)*.

On the Nevada side, **Lake Tahoe Nevada State Park** is a 14,242-acre preserve that includes shoreline, dense forest, and **Marlette Lake** reached by trail.

Yuba-Donner Scenic Byway

More in keeping with the unhurried, uncrowded, and unstreamlined travel style of the gold rush era, this beautiful circuit loops north of Tahoe over **Yuba Pass,** through **Tahoe National Forest** and a promenade of sparkling lakes, jagged granite peaks, and picturesque old mining towns. It makes for a wonderful day-long sightseeing excursion.

From Tahoe City on the northwest shore of the lake, follow Calif. 89 north; the scenic byway begins at Truckee. Continue north on Calif. 89 past Sierraville, then take Calif. 49 west to Nevada City, and return to Truckee via Calif. 20 and I-80. The entire loop is less than 160 miles, but they are twisty miles with welcome distractions, such as hiking, fishing, and swimming.

Calif. 49 is considered by many to be the most scenic stretch of the byway. From Calif. 89 it meanders through the grassy Sierra Valley before climbing steeply to Yuba Pass. Just beyond, the **Sierra Buttes** serrate the skyline, looming more than 4,000 feet over the **Lakes Basin.** If heights don't bother you, make the 7-mile round-trip climb via the Pacific Crest Trail to the Sierra Buttes fire lookout, affording fabulous views over the Sierra. Its trailhead, as well as others that access the area's many alpine lakes, can be found off Gold Lake Highway west of Bassetts. Some of the more popular hikes visit Long Lake, the Sardine Lakes, and Gold Lake. Throughout the Lakes Basin, campgrounds and primitive lodges provide options for accommodations.

Continuing on Calif. 49 brings you to the old mining towns of Sierra City and Downieville. These towns cling to mountainsides and riverbanks, and also to the 19th-century artifacts of their boomtown days. If you want to see how mine ore was crushed and processed, visit the **Kentucky Mine Museum** *(530-862-1310)* east of Sierra City.

The towns grow larger and more spruced up as you continue along the byway. Still, you'll find in the steep canyons and lake basins a world surprisingly untainted by the haste and waste that has engulfed so much of California. ∎

Lassen Volcanic National Park

■ 106,000 acres ■ North-central California, 50 miles east of Red Bluff and Redding ■ Year-round ■ Hiking, backpacking, boating, swimming, fishing, cross-country skiing, snowshoeing ■ Adm. fee ■ Contact the park, P.O. Box 100, Mineral, CA 96063-0100; phone 530-595-4444. www.nps.gov/lavo

MOUNT LASSEN BECAME A NATIONAL PARK in 1916, the year after it vented a huge mushroom cloud of steam and ash, part of a seven-year cycle of volcanic activity that included eruptions, mudflows, and avalanches. Some of that turbulent action was recorded by locals in vivid photographs, which you can view today at the park's Loomis Museum. Lassen has been inactive since 1921, but generations of visitors have come to appreciate its other charms: glaciated canyons, pristine lakes, abundant wildflowers, and forests teeming with wildlife.

Scientific interest in the volcano is undiminished, because it provides a useful 60-year model for what might be expected from other volcanoes in the Cascade Range. The park is especially interesting because it includes four different types of volcano: the big peak's plug volcano; an older, layered stratovolcano; shield volcanoes, where basalt forms low, smooth domes; and cinder cones. All can be found on and around the Cascades' other dominant peaks. Volcanologists know eruptions will continue in this very young and active system, and they hope that studying Lassen might help them better determine where and when.

Mount Lassen began as a growth on the north shoulder of an older volcano, Mount Tehama, about 11,000 years ago. Brokeoff Mountain, in the southwest corner of the park, is a remnant of Tehama, which earlier left traces of its own eruptions and lava flows, as well as several periods of glaciation. Lassen grew by expelling a thick, light-colored lava called dacite, which formed a plug and dome. Glaciers later moved some of the loose rock and left it in surrounding moraines; no glaciers remain today, and the peak has a rather dull, dark visage without them. Lassen's location near the intersection of the Sierra Nevada and Cascade Range provides it with a great variety of vegetation, which feeds herds of mule deer and a black bear population.

What to See and Do

One-day visits to national parks tend to shortchange visitors, but you can actually see and do a lot at Lassen if you're on a tight schedule. Pick up a road guide at the **Loomis Museum** and drive **Lassen Park Road** *(closed in winter),* the primary thoroughfare through the park. Beginning at the northwest entrance near Manzanita Lake, the road loops around Lassen Peak, with opportunities to see and explore on foot mud pots, hot springs, and some roadside lakes.

East of the lake, a short, self-guided, handicapped-accessible

Snowshoeing in Lassen Volcanic National Park

trail takes you to the **Devastated Area**—a site wrecked by the massive 1915 eruption.

Climbing the peak involves a round-trip hike of about five hours with a rise of 2,000 feet in elevation over 2.5 miles to the 10,457-foot summit. From the top you get an aerial view of the park's famous features, as well as Mount Shasta, Lassen's 14,162-foot neighbor 75 miles to the northwest. Just south of the peak, and easily accessible from the road, are the boiling lakes, steam vents, and mud pots of **Bumpass Hell,** which you can visit on a 3-mile (round-trip) trail.

Lassen Park Road is very steep, yet popular with physically fit cyclists. Snow closes the road early and keeps it closed late, which means a long season for cross-country skiers. The Forest Service grooms many trails just outside the park boundaries.

Areas on the park's east side get fewer visitors; this is where you go for backcountry backpacking. From I-5, take Calif. 36 to Chester, a small community on Lake Almanor. Then drive up Warner Valley from the south to trailheads and easily accessible hot springs and steam vents like **Devils Kitchen.** Trails connect the many lakes that are nestled in the older, glaciated lava flows on this side of the park, but there are no catchable fish, since many of the lakes have no stream connections. ■

Ahjumawi Lava Springs State Park

■ 6,000 acres ■ Northern California, 62 miles east of Redding off Calif. 299
■ Best season summer ■ Primitive camping, boating, fishing, bird-watching
■ Access by boat only ■ Contact California State Parks, 24898 Hwy. 89, Burney, CA 96013; phone 530-335-2777. www.parks.ca.gov/north/nobutes/alssp190.htm

FRESHWATER SPRINGS GUSH everywhere from the volcanic rock that surrounds **Big Lake, Horr Pond,** and the **Tule River.** Today this primeval landscape survives, thanks largely to the absence of roads into beautiful Ahjumawi Lava Springs State Park. That means few visitors and little disturbance for the many species of birds that visit or live here, including western grebe, marsh hawk, quail, osprey, bald eagle, and great blue heron near **Crystal Springs.**

Plan to bring your own canoe, kayak, or small powerboat, as there are no rentals in the area. From the launching area, called the Rat Farm, paddle in a northwest direction across Horr Pond, where the fly-fishing is excellent, to the park on the north bank.

The park sits on lava flows that make up only a small portion of the extensive volcanic activity that pushed up the peaks of the Cascade Range over the last 20 million years. From here you can see Mounts Shasta and Lassen to the west and south. Lava tubes and fields of jagged black basalt—not easy to walk on—cover much of the park.

But there are also fields of grass and sagebrush, forests of oak and pine, and wetlands, all providing habitat for mule deer, black bears, mountain lions, and yellow-bellied marmots. The Indian word *ahjumawi* means "coming together of waters," and the springs emerging from the lava beds constitute one of the largest freshwater spring systems in the entire country. Meander among the bubbling springs and you will marvel at the amazingly clear water. In the deeper pools it takes on a rich cobalt or aquamarine color.

In the little lava rock coves where the springs emerge, you can see the remnants of fish traps used by Native Americans to catch suckers and native rainbow trout. Big lava rocks were put in the water around the springs to form wing dams with narrow openings downstream; once a good number of fish were within the enclosure, the outlet was closed off and the fish were speared or netted.

There are nine primitive, or "environmental," campsites in the park, centered around Crystal Springs and Ja She Creek. Though these are the most popular spots in the park, even on big vacation days, campsites are often empty. Several trails traverse the park; from Crystal Springs, it's a short 1-mile walk to Horr Pond. From there you can head north on the 3-mile **Spatter Cone Loop Trail,** where you'll view lava tubes, lava flows, and the trail's namesake, a volcanic formation similar to a plug dome.

South and west of Ahjumawi on Calif. 299 is **McArthur-Burney Falls Memorial State Park** *(530-335-2777),* an 800-acre park surrounding the falls, which drops 129 feet over a basalt shelf. The flow of the spring-fed falls never drops below 100 million gallons per day, and various birds, including black swifts, nest in the greenery behind the cascade. ■

McArthur-Burney Falls

Mount Shasta Wilderness

■ 38,200 acres ■ Northern California, east of Weed via Everitt Memorial Highway to trailheads at Bunny Flats or Panther Meadow ■ Year-round ■ Camping, hiking, mountain climbing, mountain biking, cross-country skiing ■ Fee for summit climb ■ Contact Mt. Shasta Ranger District, Shasta-Trinity National Forest, 204 W. Alma St., Mount Shasta, CA 96067; phone 530-926-4511. www.r5.fs.fed.us/shastatrinity

THE TREELESS SUMMIT OF Mount Shasta, with its lustrous cloak of eight separate glaciers, rises dramatically above the surrounding forests. The unobstructed size of the 14,162-foot peak strikes awe in visitors; and then they want to climb it. The first climbers to reach the top, in 1854, found steamy sulphur springs just below the summit, "hot enough to cook an egg in five minutes." Shasta has somewhat cooled since then, but it's still

Mount Shasta at sunset

among the most active mountains in the young, volatile Cascade Range. That's one reason it has a sharper, more distinct outline than its brethren to the north, Mount Rainier and Mount Hood; that, and a drier climate, producing less eroding moisture.

Geologists call Mount Shasta a stratovolcano. Over the centuries, from various vents and cones, it has belched lava, ash, cinder, and gas, building and rebuilding itself with a series of rock layers. Lava has emerged at different times in many different places on the mountain. Shastina, a secondary peak on the south side of the mountain, grew from a vent that opened about 10,000 years ago. And just west of Shasta, right next to I-5, is Black Butte, a plug dome that is related to the same period of volcanic activity.

John Muir described Shasta's glaciers as: "a down-crawling mantle of ice upon a fountain of smoldering fire." The rubble mounds pushed by the ice, called moraines, indicate that the glaciers at one time reached

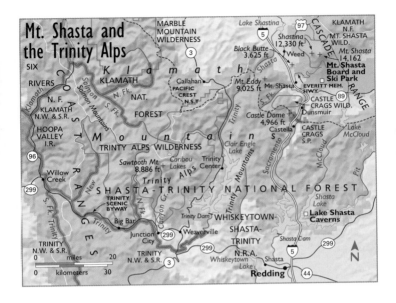

Mt. Shasta and the Trinity Alps

Bigfoot Watch

Despite a lack of bones or other hard evidence, a cadre of true believers is convinced there are hairy apelike creatures wandering the woods in the vicinity of Mount Shasta. A controversial 1967 videotape claims to show Sasquatch—also called Bigfoot—wandering in the Bluff Creek area of the Klamath Mountains. Reports of 18-inch footprints crop up regularly, which would jibe with descriptions of a creature 8 feet tall.

If you plan a bigfoot expedition, take note that the month of August has produced the most sightings. And if you're lucky enough to snap a clear photo of one, contact the International Society of Cryptozoology (P.O. Box 43070, Tucson, AZ 85733).

all the way down the sides of the mountain to the present-day town of Dunsmuir along the banks of the Sacramento River.

Today the eight glaciers on Shasta, which probably date back roughly 3,000 years, reach down to an altitude of about 9,000 feet. At all times of the year, except during the late summer, climbers must spend some of their time crossing snow.

Though the peak dominates people's imaginations, there are springs, waterfalls, and interesting lava flows lower down. Past logging on the mountain's slopes has left open areas of chaparral, but above 5,500 feet are fir and pine forests, including the Shasta red fir and white bark pine near timberline, about 8,000 feet above sea level.

In the spring, the meadows explode with colorful columbine, monkeyflower, and blue gentian. Also look for chubby gold-mantled ground squirrels and pine marten.

What to See and Do

Not everybody aspires to climb a 14,000-foot mountain, but most visitors want to get up close to it. Stop at the Forest Service's **Mount Shasta Ranger District office** in the town of Mount Shasta for maps, advice, and permits. Then drive east on the **Everitt Memorial Highway,** with stops at viewing areas where you can see Eddy Peak and the Sacramento River Canyon. The twisty, 11-mile-long road will take you above timberline on the mountain, and provides access to the 2-mile (one way) **Sand Flat Trail** and the 1.7-mile (one way) **Bunny Flat Trail.**

From these trailheads you can begin climbs up **Avalanche Gulch,** the easiest and most popular way

Improvised hot tub, Mount Shasta Wilderness

to reach the summit, a 5,000-foot change in elevation from the start of the trail. Even on this route, you will definitely need crampons and ice axes. More challenging routes, including **Casaval Ridge** or **Hidden Valley,** are plentiful, but should only be attempted by experienced climbers or with a guide. Several other routes on the north and east sides of the mountain require glacier experience.

Most climbers go up the mountain between May and July, but many prefer the earlier months of the climbing season, when the snow is firm but not icy and you don't have to scramble in loose rock. You must register and pay a fee, leave the dog at home, and pack out any human waste.

Day Hikes and Other Activities

Not every hike must lead to the summit. There are easier day hikes to lesser knobs like **Grey Butte;** as well as the popular hike from Bunny Flat (on Everitt Memorial Hwy.) to the Sierra Club's timberline cabin at **Horse Camp.** A particularly beautiful route is the **Clear Creek Trail** on the mountain's southeast side. Take Pilgrim Creek Road to Clear Creek Road and continue for 8 miles to the parking lot. The trail starts there, at 6,500 feet. You'll follow red fir-trimmed Mud Creek Canyon, gaining 1,100 feet in elevation to emerge in an area of spring-fed, fragile alpine meadows.

John Muir recommended going around Shasta rather than up it. It's a 5-day trip across glaciers and canyons with a lot of bushwhacking (a trail is planned but not completed), but you'll

Signing the log atop Mount Shasta

really know the mountain when you're done. For a terrific view of Mount Shasta and the surrounding terrain, climb atop **Black Butte.** The 2.5-mile, rocky, very steep trail begins off Everitt Memorial Highway east of the city of Mount Shasta.

Winter and spring, you can ski in the backcountry and snowboard on the mountain; again, you might want to use a guide service to learn your way around. The Mt. Shasta Board and Ski Park *(800-754-7427)* sits on the southern flank of the mountain, just outside the wilderness area boundary off Calif. 89.

Logging on Shasta's north side and fire on the south slope have left some scars. But these events, both man-made and natural, also left dirt roads cut into the mountain that are ideal for mountain biking. Bikes can be rented in Mount Shasta City at the House of Ski *(530-926-2359)* and the 5th Season *(530-926-3606)*. ■

Castle Crags State Park

■ 4,000 acres ■ Northern California, 45 miles north of Redding, 6 miles south of Dunsmuir ■ Best seasons spring and summer ■ Camping hiking, backpacking, climbing, fishing ■ Adm. fee ■ Contact the park, P.O. Box 80, Castella, CA 96017; phone 530-235-2684. http://parks.ca.gov

THE GRANITE SPIRES OF Castle Crags emerge like a bundle of spear points from a quiver of forest along the Sacramento River. They form a dramatic skyline, an array of knobs, spires, and sheer faces. In geological terms the crags are a pluton, granite that hardened underground and then was pushed up through old seabed sediments. This happened about 200 million years ago; then the crags were sculpted by glaciers and weather into the jagged shapes of today. They make a memorable sight for drivers along I-5, some 2,500 feet below.

The higher crags are part of Castle Crags Wilderness, which is in **Shasta-Trinity National Forest** *(530-964-2184)*. They are easily reached by trail through the state park, and provide some of the best hiking and climbing in the region. On the east side of I-5, the park includes a few miles of the upper Sacramento River, where you can catch-and-release good-size rainbow trout from late April through November. You can obtain maps and detailed information on trail conditions from a small visitor center at the ranger station near the park entrance.

From the visitor center, drive up to the Vista Point parking area to the trailhead for the 2.7-mile (one way) **Crags Trail.** It's not a long hike, but the route is very steep—2,200 feet elevation change. The reward at the end is 4,966-foot **Castle Dome,** and it is well worth the exertion. Many who make this hike will scramble about on the rocks around Castle Dome and then head back down the trail. Serious climbers will stick around for the face climbs on fairly solid rock. Castle Dome has numerous exciting routes, and there are tough climbs on **Mount Hubris** (the Ogre) and **Six Toe Rock.** Since this is wilderness, top-roping or sport acrobatics are not allowed, just solid traditional climbing.

If you're not going all the way to Castle Dome, at least get past Bob's Hat Trail, which is where you'll stop hearing traffic sounds from I-5. Views along the way are of the Trinity Mountains, the crags above, and the valleys and ridges stretching west and south. The trees thin out on top—though some tenacious pines grow right out of the rock—and the 360-degree views include Mount Shasta to the north. Backpackers can pick up the **Pacific Crest Trail** from the Crags Trail and hike into the high country west of the crags and the alpine lakes of the Trinity Mountains.

The **Flume Trail** is a relatively level 2.5-mile (one way) hike that starts at the ranger station and passes through several different types of habitat, such as dry chaparral, pine forest, and oak woodland. From spring through the summer your path will be brightened by blossoming wildflowers, including many species of rare California orchids. Watch for American kestrels and acorn woodpeckers among the trees. ■

Backcountry camping, Trinity Alps Wilderness

Trinity Alps Wilderness

■ 502,764 acres ■ Northern California, west of Redding on Calif. 299 to Big
Bar or Weaverville ■ Best season summer ■ Camping, hiking, backpacking,
white-water rafting and kayaking, swimming, fishing ■ Contact Big Bar Ranger
Station, Shasta-Trinity National Forest, Star Route 1, Box 10, Big Bar, CA 96010;
phone 530-623-6106. www.rs.fs.fed.us/shastatrinity

POCKET WILDERNESS AREAS protect key habitat and natural wonders, but
it's the big wilderness preserves that strike a primordial chord. Deep in
the Trinity Alps, with no roadhead near and no shelter but the arbor of
evergreens and the big slabs of granite, you can experience the sort of
untethered wild experience that once was typical of California's northern
forests. The Trinity Alps Wilderness is an exquisite collection of rivers,
lakes, alpine meadows, and peaks over 8,000 feet.

Neither as tall as the Sierra Nevada, nor as volcanic as the Cascades,
the Trinity Alps get less attention, which is often beneficial to wilderness.
In part because these mountains are nearer the wet ocean air, and in part
because they never rose as high as the Sierra Nevada, they retain remnants of ancient North American forests and nurture an amazing variety

of plants and trees. The Trinity Alps have been called a "living fossil forest," with 20 species of conifer, including, at the higher elevations, the foxtail pine, found elsewhere only in the southern Sierra Nevada.

Two federally designated Wild and Scenic Rivers, the **New River** and the **North Fork Trinity River,** cut deep canyons in the wilderness area as they flow south into a third Wild and Scenic River, the Trinity's main stem. Salmon, steelhead, and brook trout still make spawning runs up these rivers, and the fishing is good. The Trinity itself lies outside the wilderness area, easily accessible to rafters and kayakers as it runs along Calif. 299 on the south edge of the wilderness, its Class III rapids kept up even during the dry summers by an upstream dam. Farther downstream, around **Burnt Ranch Gorge,** the paddling gets much tougher.

To get a better understanding of the history and natural beauty of this region, take the 175-mile scenic drive that begins north of Yreka on Calif. 96. Following the Klamath River most of the way, the route goes through historic mining towns, over a series of passes, and down along the river bottom, including sections of dry chaparral, dense forests of Douglas-fir, and occasional sprays of redbud in the early spring. At Willow Creek, head east on Calif. 299, which ambles along the Trinity River to Redding.

The most popular route into the wilderness is along the **Canyon Creek Trail,** from a trailhead in Junction City on Canyon Creek Road. The journey up Canyon Creek through pine and fir trees with manzanita bushes is easy to moderate (about a 16-mile round-trip), and gets you to lakes set like diamonds beneath Sawtooth Mountain.

A century ago, the only thing that brought people into this remote country was the hope of gold strikes or a logging expedition. Scars remain from the hydraulic mining that blasted mountainsides with pressurized water, even in the wilderness areas. Much of the timber is second growth, and areas in the north of the Trinity Alps Wilderness are still open to livestock grazing. ■

Fording a tributary of the Trinity River

Great Basin and Modoc Plateau

Wheeler Peak, Great Basin National Park

THE GREAT BASIN IS NOT the round-bottomed receptacle we think of as a basin, but rather a huge spread of alternating valleys and mountain ranges, walled off to the west by the Sierra Nevada and to the east by Utah's Wasatch Mountains. Its mountains, lining up north-south in parallel ranks, rise steeply from the desert plain and possess a subtle charm most appreciated by landscape painters and desert hermits—a charm that can be erased now and then by a howling blizzard or merciless summer sun. There is

Canada geese and goslings, Lower Klamath National Wildlife Refuge

no pretending it is always a comfortable place, but the opportunities for wilderness solitude are extraordinary.

Before there were mountains here, there was a struggle between land and sea, the rise and fall and rise again of a long, westward-sloping continental shelf that emerged from the ocean layered with sediments formed by erosion and the settling of the skeletons of marine organisms. The push and shove of tectonic plates began in earnest some 200 million years ago, as the Farallon plate thrust under the North American plate, a continental friction that tore open faults and volcanic vents. The subduction of the Northern Pacific plate raised and stretched the plains until they cracked into broken pieces of crust, tilted on their sides to form dozens of small mountain ranges, whose eroding sediments collected in between. Periods of intense volcanism accompanied this plate tectonic activity.

Finally, the modern Sierra Nevada uplifted ten million years ago, creating a meteorological tollgate in the west that extracts much of the water from Pacific storms. The Great Basin was left high and dry. Fresh water that flowed from the mountains during the ice ages had no outlet to the sea. It would accumulate in giant freshwater bodies such as Lake Lohantan and Lake Bonneville, and slowly evaporate, leaving remnants such as Pyramid and Walker Lakes today.

Elsewhere in the country, every little rivulet eventually joins bigger streams on a long journey that takes it to the sea, where it will evaporate and return as rain or snow, part of the world's great hydrological cycle. In the Great Basin no stream connects to the continent's enormous drainage

Old Homestead, Kinney Camp, Sheldon National Wildlife Refuge

system, no water drains to the oceans. The most distinctive feature of the Great Basin is that, as distinguished Western author Wallace Stegner put it, "wherever you live in it you flow toward every other part."

It's a world unto itself, threadbare in a way, but inhabited by creatures well adjusted to its scarcity, like the Shoshone who once roamed the basin in small bands. Their hardscrabble hunter-gatherer lifestyle was viewed by some white settlers as pathetic and destitute, but they were a peaceful and autonomous people, and they made their way in the Great Basin's arid world with a self-reliance few of the newcomers would attain.

Thin-air peaks and white-water rivers may be the sort of wilderness that makes your heart pound fast, but the remote corners of the Great Basin can make it pound faster. On a hot afternoon hiking the high country of Jarbidge Wilderness, or caught in a howling blizzard on the high plains north of Pyramid Lake, you know what it is to be alone with nature's full and pitiless force.

This chapter actually begins in northeast California, where the Modoc Plateau forms the western boundary of the Great Basin. Hidden amid the long, desert vistas of this country are extraordinary remainders of ancient volcanic eruptions, such as Lava Beds National Monument and Medicine Lake, and rich pockets of water and wildlife, such as Lower Klamath and Tule Lakes National Wildlife Refuges. We then move east into Nevada and the Great Basin, making our way south to discover some extraordinary mountain wilderness where few would think to look for it, and finishing at Great Basin National Park, one of the newer additions to the nation's park system. ∎

Lower Klamath and Tule Lake National Wildlife Refuges

■ 86,016 acres ■ Northern California, 31 miles south of Klamath Falls, Oreg., off Calif. 139 ■ Best seasons spring and fall ■ Walking, canoeing, bird-watching, wildlife viewing, auto tours, petroglyphs ■ Contact Klamath Basin NWR Complex, Rte. 1, Box 74, Tulelake, CA 96134; phone 530-667-2231. www.klamathnwr.org

HUGE SHALLOW LAKES AND MARSHES once covered northeast California and southern Oregon, creating an "Everglades of the West" where millions of birds traveling the Pacific flyway could set down and feed. But the Klamath Basin wetlands, like so much other California bird habitat, were seen as a nuisance by farmers who arrived during the late 19th century. As the farmers drained, dyked, and planted the land, what had been 350,000 acres of bird habitat shrank by more than half. The birds kept coming, though, and in 1908, outdoors enthusiast President Theodore Roosevelt moved to protect them by creating the nation's first waterfowl refuge.

The U.S. Fish and Wildlife Service has since added some key pieces of the mosaic straddling the California-Oregon border, stretching from Tule Lake near Lava Beds National Monument (see pp. 226-28) to Klamath Marsh near Crater Lake National Park. Today the Klamath Basin refuges are six in number: Upper Klamath, Bear Valley, and Klamath Marsh are in Oregon; Lower Klamath, Tule Lake, and Clear Lake are in California. (The Clear Lake refuge is closed to the public except for limited waterfowl and pronghorn hunting in season, to reduce disturbance of nesting birds such

Sunset, Tule Lake National Wildlife Refuge

as the American white pelican, which produce an average of 1,400 fledgling pelicans each year.) To maintain these fragile habitats, the refuges' staff work with the growers in surrounding agricultural land, leasing refuge lands for crops, some of which are left unharvested for the birds.

What to See and Do

Like many of the lakes on the east side of California's taller mountains, these lakes have shrunk considerably from their historic levels. You can see the former waterline of Tule Lake at **Petroglyph Rock**, where ancient artists worked from boats, high on the rock. Still, the birds seem intent on stopping in. In spring come the waterbirds, including herons and double-crested cormorants. In November, the refuges teem with Canada geese, ducks of many varieties, and tundra swans. Hundreds of bald eagles spend winter days at the Lower Klamath refuge, and white-faced ibises, escaping from the rising waters of the Great Salt Lake, have returned to nest there as well.

Both **Lower Klamath** and **Tule Lake refuges** have 10-mile auto tours with informational signs. At the **Tule Lake Visitor Center** *(on Hill Rd., 5 miles W of Tulelake)*, you can view slide shows and exhibits, then start a driving tour just outside the door, or take the steep but short 0.3-mile hike up **Sheepy Ridge** to view the entire basin. You can also reserve time in photographic blinds at both refuges *(530-667-2231)*. A 2-mile canoe trail at Tule Lake allows you to paddle through cattails and bulrushes of the marsh wren nesting area in **Tule Marsh**, where you might also see American bitterns and great blue herons—and, with luck, beavers, muskrat, and river otters, too. ■

Spelunking, Lava Beds National Monument

Lava Beds National Monument

■ 46,567 acres ■ Northeast California, 50 miles south of Klamath Falls, Oregon, off Calif. 139 ■ Year-round ■ Camping, hiking, backpacking, walking, guided walks, biking, bird-watching, wildlife viewing, spelunking, petroglyphs ■ Adm. fee ■ Contact the monument, Box 867, Tulelake, CA 96134; phone 530-667-2282, ext. 232. www.nps.gov/labe

IN THIS REMOTE NORTHEAST corner of California lava poured forth from the earth 30,000 years ago, but instead of blasting from a peak like Mount Lassen, it flowed from low-lying vents and spread across the Modoc Plateau in sheets and channels. As the lava surface cooled and hardened, molten rock continued to flow beneath, forming tubes inside the hardening mass. These lava tubes—now broken up into caves—are the most striking feature of Lava Beds National Monument, abutting the south side of Tule Lake National Wildlife Refuge (see pp. 224-25). The phenomenon is called a shield volcano, featuring layers of lava flows that form a gently curving surface first described in Iceland as resembling a warrior's shield laid on the ground. There have been many eruptions here over the last million years, the most recent only a thousand years ago. The 1800°F lava took many shapes as it covered the landscape, popping up in cinder cones and chimneys, spreading in both smooth basalts (called pahoehoe) and rough-edged clinker (aa), and forming tubes atop older tubes.

The roofs of the lava tubes have collapsed in places, allowing easy access from the surface, and lava tube caves tend to run horizontally, requiring less technical skill of spelunkers than do caves formed by percolating water. There are so many known caves at Lava Beds—the tally is 440 now, and counting—that explorers pick from a wide variety of environments, from ice caves to fern grottoes. Various life-forms have taken up residence, including colorful lichens and Townsend's big-eared bats, for which certain caves are closed to humans during the spring nursery season.

Above ground, the jagged surface of the lava flows requires thick-soled shoes, but there are grasslands and pine forests as well. Deer, mountain lions, and hawks abound in the monument, which includes the bluffs and cliffs where raptors thrive. Migrating birds fly through from adjacent wildlife refuges. Bighorn sheep once lived here, but disease from neighboring domestic sheep killed them off in the early 20th century.

In 1872, the Modoc took advantage of the lava beds topography to resist U.S. Army efforts to move them west to the Klamath Reservation. Led by the resourceful Captain Jack, 52 Modocs made their stand during these Modoc Wars at the "Stronghold," a natural fortress protected by lava formations and Tule Lake, and held off a much larger force armed with mortars and howitzers for six months. Ultimately defeated, the Modocs were eventually moved even farther from their traditional lands to Oklahoma, where the tribe continues today.

What to See and Do

Whether you enter the monument from the main, northeast entrance (4 miles S of Tulelake, off Calif. 139) or from the southeast entrance (27 miles N of Canby, off Calif. 139), it's best to follow the main road first to the **visitor center** in the southern part of the park to get oriented to the monument's historic and geologic sites. **Mushpot Cave,** a 770-foot cave adjacent to the visitor center, has artificial lighting and explanatory signs to orient a first-time spelunker.

From the visitor center you can drive the 1.5-mile **Cave Loop Road,** which takes you by more than a dozen well-marked, easy-access caves (no guide needed; access by ladder in some cases; flashlights available at visitor center). Among the features to look for: the bluish ceiling of the **Blue Grotto Cave,** the "hanging gardens" from the roof holes in the **Sunshine Cave,** and the sparkling yellow walls (caused by slimy bacteria) of the **Golden Dome Cave.**

One of the most beautiful and interesting caves is **Fern Cave** (Check with visitor center for directions), which can be seen only on a guided tour two days a week by appointment. In addition to the ferns beneath the cave's collapsed roof, there are ancient pictographs on the walls.

Visitors interested in ancient Native American art will want also to visit **Petroglyph Point** (Check with visitor center for directions), an outcrop of volcanic tuff where earlier peoples carved over 5,000 images, most of them geometric shapes. No one knows for certain what they mean, or who made them as long as 4,000 years ago, but their location high on the rock face indicates they were carved from boats at a time when a lake lapped against the rock.

For panoramic views of the park and surrounding lands, you can climb the steep **Schonchin Butte Trail** (2 miles N of visitor center on main road to Schonchin Butte Lookout Rd., then 1.5 miles E to trailhead). It's a 1.8-mile round-trip hike to a fire lookout, with about a 500-foot climb.

Pictographs, Symbol Bridge cave, Lava Beds National Monument

History buffs will want to continue north on the main road to a trailhead for the 2.2-mile round-trip hike to the **Thomas-Wright Battlefield,** where the Modoc withstood the assaults of the U.S. Army in 1872. Back on the main road and heading north, you'll pass through and alongside the **Devils Homestead Lava Flow,** and then arrive at **Gillems Camp,** site of a U.S. Army encampment during the Modoc Wars. A short climb up the **Gillem Bluff Trail** gives you an overview of the camp's remnants. From Gillems Camp, the road bends east. In 4 miles you'll reach **Captain Jack's Stronghold,** where two short, self-guided interpretive trails *(inner loop 0.5 mile, outer loop 1.5 miles)* will take you into the heart of the Modoc Wars.

Much of the park is protected wilderness, and several trails lead through the park's backcountry and into the surrounding **Modoc National Forest** *(530-233-5811).* However, near the Indian Well Campground *(1 mile E of visitor center on main road),* a level, 1-mile hike along the **Bunchgrass Trail** will give you a look at the area's typical vegetation and wildlife.

South from the visitor center on a gravel road heading toward Medicine Lake (see opposite) is **Mammoth Crater,** where ponderosa pines shade the 2-mile-long **Hidden Valley Trail** that circles the valley floor, and wildflowers such as lupine and Indian paintbrush proliferate in the summer. You can hike to the rim *(200 yards round-trip from parking lot),* where raptors take in the view, too, and dive for a meal now and then. ∎

Caving Precautions

Wear thick-soled boots, bundle up for the consistently cool temperatures, and don't go alone. Each person should carry several sources of light. If you plan to explore wilderness caves, be sure to register at the visitor center. Also, watch your head: Most injuries in caves occur when people watching their feet fail to see the dips in the ceiling. Hard hats or bike helmets are strongly recommended.

Medicine Lake

■ 200 square miles ■ Northeast California, 14 miles south of Lava Beds National Monument on FR 49, or 35 miles southwest of Tulelake on Cty. Rd. 97 ■ Best seasons summer and winter. Roads often closed by snow in winter ■ Hiking, swimming, bird-watching ■ Contact Modoc National Forest, 800 W. 12th St., Alturas, CA 96101, phone 530-233-5811; or McCloud Ranger District, Shasta-Trinity National Forest, 2019 Forest Rd., McCloud, CA 96057, phone 530-964-2184

MEDICINE LAKE SITS IN a caldera, or basin, that is the collapsed summit of a massive shield volcano—a broad, gently sloped dome with many vents—named for the lake itself. Its western edge is a high and barren landscape so similar to the moon that it was used for training by lunar-bound astronauts in the 1960s. Volcanic activity as recently as a thousand years ago led to the formation of what is now Lava Beds National Monument (see pp. 226-28). Around the rim of the caldera are cinder cones that have erupted at various times over the eons, including **Glass Mountain**, a smooth white dome that stands out amid the black obsidian typical of the area. Various tribes of Native Americans once made annual visits here to collect the sharp-edged volcanic glass for use in tools and weapons.

The best way to tour the volcanic sights is to pick up a self-guided geology tour from the McCloud Ranger District office. From McCloud take Calif. 89 for 17 miles east to the junction with Forest Road 15 and turn north. In 4.3 miles the road will fork. Taking the right fork, Forest Road 49, will give you views of the **Giant Crater Lava Flow,** an unbroken field of jumbled, broken rock that was once lava flowing from **Giant Crater,** 10 miles north. At 20.3 miles from the junction with Calif. 89 is a pull-off on the left side of the road where a short walk will bring you to views of lava caves and bridges, including the 18-mile-long **Giant Crater Lava Tube,** the longest known tube system in the world. At 30.5 miles from the junction with Calif. 89, you'll reach Medicine Lake itself.

Despite its stark setting, the lake is a popular picnic and camping spot, shaded around the edge by pine forests and stocked with trout. Heavy snows from November to May feed its clear blue waters, which remains fresh despite having no known outlet and only a small inlet along the western shore. Vegetation throughout the wider area, known as the Medicine Lake Highlands, consists of red and white fir, sugar pine, and, at higher elevations, lodgepole pine with an understory of manzanita, bitterbrush, and snowbrush.

Taking the left fork, Forest Road 15, will take you past red-white-and-black **Paint Pot Crater,** with **Pumice Stone Mountain** in the background, and eventually to a short spur road west to **Little Glass Mountain,** a striking cone of rhyolite, pumice, and obsidian that geologists believe erupted less than 850 years ago. ■

Following pages: Warren Mountains, Modoc National Forest

Pronghorn, Sheldon National Wildlife Refuge

Sheldon National Wildlife Refuge

■ 575,813 acres ■ Northwest Nevada, 15 miles from Denio on Nev. 140
■ Best seasons summer and fall ■ Primitive camping, hiking, backpacking,
walking, swimming, fishing, mountain biking, bird-watching, wildlife viewing,
wildflower viewing ■ Contact the refuge, P.O. Box 111, Lakeview, OR 97630;
phone 541-947-3315

SHELDON NATIONAL WILDLIFE REFUGE is one of those little-known gems
of the wildlife world, tucked in the northwest corner of Nevada. Even
people from the Oregon coast will come inland to cast a serene fishing
line here. The gentle hills of the refuge were filled in by volcanic eruptions that spread rhyolite and basalt across a landscape that once was wet
enough to fill lakes and water pine forests. Springs and streams have cut
some steep-sided gorges that appear like tears in the tablelands. Explore
a little further in what appears to be a fairly dry landscape and you'll find
lakes and reservoirs, some with sizable fish.

One reason for the fine habitat at Sheldon is that about a decade ago
the U.S. Fish and Wildlife Service took the cattle off the range. Along
with **Hart Mountain National Antelope Refuge** *(541-947-3315)* in
Oregon, Sheldon provides the largest uninterrupted cattle-free habitat in
the Great Basin. Though Sheldon isn't yet fully restored from the effects
of long-term cattle grazing, you'll see an abundance of native grasses
and sedges, bushy and green in wet years. From May to October, you
will find a great diversity of birdlife in both the riparian zones and the
sagebrush-dominated uplands. Nearly 200 species have been spotted,

including Clark's grebe, snowy egret, golden eagle, and the sage grouse, whose elaborate courtship rituals in late winter and spring are always a big attraction. Depending on how wet the year and how high the lakes, ducks and geese abound during the spring and fall, along with avocets and other shorebirds.

The Sheldon refuge was established primarily to protect pronghorn, prairie denizens with a reddish coat, white rump patch, black mask, and black horns with a forward-curling prong. Like the bison, these animals once roamed the grasslands in vast herds, but were decimated by hunting and land-use conflicts in the 19th century. By the time preserves were first set aside for them a century ago, fewer than 15,000 pronghorn were left. Now there are as many as a million nationwide. Though sometimes called an antelope, the pronghorn is not one. In fact, it has no close mammal relatives anywhere in the world. This truly North American species is also known for its speed: Capable of racing in bursts of up to 75 miles per hour, the pronghorn is faster than any other mammal except a cheetah; but a cheetah can't sustain its speed for four minutes as a pronghorn can.

The refuge is a haven during the winter for up to 3,500 pronghorn that come to **Big Spring Table** in the northeastern part of the refuge from as far away as the Hart Mountain refuge, some 40 miles north. Similarly, deer that summer on **Badger Mountain,** on the far southwestern edge of Sheldon, migrate to the **Virgin Valley** on the eastern side for the winter. Other mammals found in the refuge include bighorn sheep, weasel, skunk, coyote, kit fox, mountain lion, bobcat, and more than a dozen species of bat.

Sheldon is home to ten species of fish, most of them introduced, including rainbow trout and largemouth bass. A favorite fishing area, with primitive camping, is **Big Spring Reservoir** (*2.5 miles N of Nev. 140*). More expansive views are a feature of Virgin Valley Camp at the **Dufur-rena Ponds** (*Turn S off Nev. 140 at refuge headquarters sign onto a gravel road along Virgin Creek*), a small campground with a warm spring that flows into a large stone-rimmed pool with a gravel bottom. ■

Opals

Out of the dull, brown sedimentary rock of the Virgin Valley comes a milky gem that can break light into colors like a rainbow. Opals are formed from conglomerations of silica that get left behind when geothermal hot springs bubble through the earth. Though it's related to quartz, it's not a crystal. In some cases, as at Sheldon, it can lodge in fossilized wood, creating a beautiful mix of petrified wood grain and opalescence. There are opals in the ground in the Virgin Valley, often associated with petrified wood. You can collect up to seven pounds of rocks per person per day, except in the Virgin Mining District, whose signs for opal-mining operations you can see from Nev. 140 as it crosses the Virgin Valley. Here you can buy a gem, or pay a fee to dig through their tailings.

Casting for trout, Pyramid Lake

Pyramid Lake

■ 180 square miles ■ Northwest Nevada, 35 miles northeast of Reno on Nev. 445 ■ Best season summer ■ Camping, hiking, backpacking, walking, boating, canoeing, fishing, bird-watching, wildlife viewing ■ Contact Pyramid Lake Marina, P.O. Box 309, Wadsworth, NV 89442; phone 775-476-1156.

EXPLORER JOHN FRÉMONT came over a pass west of the Sierras in 1844 and beheld, between the pastel pinks and grays of the Virginia Mountains and the Lake Range, "a sheet of green water" that "broke upon our eyes like the ocean." From the water rose an oddly shaped island—a mound of tufa, a kind of freshwater limestone left by springs when water levels drop (see p. 187). The mound looked to Frémont like an Egyptian pyramid, so he named the green water Pyramid Lake. More than 10 miles wide at its widest, 27 miles long, and with areas deeper than 350 feet, the lake is fed by the Truckee River flowing from Lake Tahoe. Pyramid has no outlets but loses water through evaporation, dropping the lake level about 4 feet per year and leaving the lake a little alkaline—about one-sixth as salty as seawater.

The Kooyooe Tukaddu Paiute who lived in the area had their own name for the lake, of course: *Ku-ui pah nu nah,* or "cuui-ui pond," named for the cui-ui, a large lakesucker unique to those waters and a major food source for the Kooyooe Tukaddu ("cui-ui eaters"). Large, plankton-eating fish that average five to six pounds, cui-ui are lake dwellers but stream spawners. For most of the 20th century, water diversion from the Truckee River (for agriculture, urban development, and other commercial water uses) lowered the lake's water level enough to create an impassable delta at the river's mouth, preventing the cui-ui from entering the river to spawn. Only the cui-ui's longevity (they live more than 40 years) has allowed the species to survive—sometimes as long as 19 years without reproducing. Today, the cui-ui are still endangered, but increased flows of the Truckee in recent years have allowed the fish to reproduce naturally. Each spring, cui-ui adults, most of which mature at 8 to 12 years of age, migrate to the mouth of the Truckee, where they wait for sufficient stream flow to enter the river. Several hatcheries, operated under the direction of the Kooyooe Tukaddu Paiute, also raise cui-ui and the threatened Lahontan cutthroat trout, stocking the lake for fishing.

What to See and Do

For a panoramic view from the west side of the lake, take the 35-mile **Pyramid Lake Scenic Byway** (Nev. 445) from Sparks, Nevada, which will deliver you to Sutcliffe, where you can purchase a day-use permit (required by the Pyramid Lake Paiute Reservation) at the **Pyramid Lake Marina and visitor center.** A small museum here explains the history of the lake and its hydrology and wildlife. You can launch your own boat from the marina ramp, or rent boats or personal watercraft. Bird-watchers should keep an eye out for common loon; Western, Clark's, horned, red-necked, and eared grebes; and, in summer, double-crested cormorants. At the **Dunn Hatchery** *(775-476-0510)* up the hill southwest of Sutcliffe you can tour the trout and cui-ui tanks.

Heading north past the marina on Nev. 445 for 20 miles, you'll come to the sharp, tufa-coated formation called **Needles** and an old geothermal well. The well vents steam and was once a good spot for a hot pool dip, but it is now closed to the public due to vandalism and disrespect to the environment by some visitors.

Toward the south end of the lake, near the mouth of the Truckee River, are a series of beaches and tufa formations, including **Popcorn Rock** and one that the Kooyooe Tukaddu call the **Great Stone Mother,** whose tears filled the lake. The river delta is a good place to look for grebes, cormorants, gulls, and terns.

To reach the east side of the lake, continue past Popcorn Rock to the intersection with Nev. 447, and head north for 5 miles to Milepost 21, where a rough road will take you along the shore close to **Anaho Island National Wildlife Refuge.** A large colony of endangered American white pelicans nest here from late spring to late summer. The birds are easily spooked—they'll leave their eggs exposed to sun and predators if disturbed—so the island is closed to the public. However, you can camp on the beach just across the water from the island and see plenty of bird activity, including sage sparrow, prairie falcon, and rock wren. If you head south instead of north on Nev. 447, the short **Numana Hatchery Wetlands Trail** *(Follow sign for hatchery)* will give you excellent access to riparian habitat on the lower Truckee River. Look for wood duck, Virginia rail, yellow warbler, and, in winter, Lincoln's sparrow. ∎

Arc Dome Wilderness

■ 115,000 acres ■ Central Nevada, 60 miles from Tonopah, accessible from Rte. 89 on the west side and Nev. 376 on the east ■ Best months July-Sept. ■ Primitive camping, hiking, backpacking, mountain climbing, fishing, horseback riding ■ Contact Tonopah Ranger District, 1400 S. Erie Main St., P.O. Box 3940, Tonopah, NV 89049. 775-482-6286

THE LARGEST OF EIGHT WILDERNESS AREAS in the Humboldt-Toiyabe National Forest, Arc Dome Wilderness includes the highest summits of the rugged Toiyabe Range, a spine of mountains that runs at a sustained elevation above 10,000-feet for more than 50 of its 125 miles. Arc Dome itself, rising to 11,788 feet, dominates the area. An outstanding example

View from Toiyabe Crest National Trail, Arc Dome Wilderness

of the Basin and Range topography typical of the state, the barren Toiyabes rise steeply from broad, flat-bottomed valleys with virtually no foothills. Like the Toquima and Monitor Ranges to their east, the Toiyabes are fairly bald, with pinyon-juniper forests down low and limber pine and mountain mahogany up high, and an occasional streak of aspen. Rainfall is light, and the rivers are small but good for trout fishing.

What to See and Do

Exploring this wilderness, which occupies the southern one-third of the Humboldt-Toiyabe National Forest, requires a willingness to rough it—but the views, and the peace, are worth the exertion. Probably the most popular access point is the **Cow Canyon trail-**

head, in the Reese River Valley on the west side of the range. (Anglers may want to stop to check out the trout fishing in the **Reese River.**) To reach the trailhead, go north from Tonopah on Nev. 95 to the Gabbs Poleline Road and take this road to the Cloverdale turnoff, heading east. One mile past the old Cloverdale Ranch, take a turnoff east for 30 miles to 1 mile beyond the Cloverdale Summit. Take a turnoff to the south for less than a mile and take the first turn to the left to Cow Canyon trailhead. The trail heads 1 mile downhill to the Reese River. From here, you can follow the river along a 12-mile portion of the 72-mile **Toiyabe Crest National Trail,** a designated National Recreation Trail constructed by the Civilian Conservation Corps in the 1930s, which runs from Kingston Canyon to South Twin, on the east side of the Toiyabe Range.

Another option might be the 7-mile **Stewart Creek Trail** to **Arc Dome Summit,** which takes off from Columbine Campground (*from Cloverdale Summit, drive on 16 miles, passing through Yomba Indian Reservation, then head E on FR 119 to signs for campground*). The trail passes through stands of aspens in a broad-floored valley before climbing upward. Although the mountains here are a jumble of sedimentary, volcanic, and granite rock, Arc Dome itself is largely volcanic stone, with a reddish tinge. Near the top are two bowl-shaped cirques, gouged out by glaciers more than 10,000 years ago. On a clear day, you can look west across the state of Nevada to California's White Mountains and can usually spot the outline of the Sierra Nevada beyond—a distance of more than 100 miles.

Hardier souls can get to the summit via another portion of the Toiyabe National Crest Trail. Access to this end of the trail is from a parking lot at South Twin off Nev. 376 in the Big Smoky Valley. ■

"The Loneliest Road in America"

When two-lane US 50 across central Nevada was declared the "loneliest road in America" by *LIFE* magazine in 1986, communities along the route immediately went to work publicizing it, pointing out such attractions as museums and wildlife areas, as well as such tongue-in-cheek "must-sees" as large mounds of sand and abandoned open-pit copper mines. But experienced Nevada travelers have long considered US 50 a fine alternative to the interstate— uncrowded, fast, and closer to the landscape. The view from the road can be downright beautiful, in fact, as when the highway edges around the peaks of Great Basin National Park (see pp. 244-47), or climbs into the mountains outside Eureka. The irony is that all the publicity has lured more travelers, making the road a lot less lonely. Still, if you're planning a long trip on US 50, bear in mind that towns can be 70 miles or more apart. Make sure your car has been well serviced before you depart.

A family ranch, east side of Ruby Mountains

Ruby Mountains Wilderness

■ 90,000 acres ■ Northern Nevada, southeast of Elko ■ Year-round. Peak season July-Aug. ■ Camping, hiking, backpacking, walking, rock climbing, swimming, fishing, biking, mountain biking, horseback riding, snowmobiling, cross-country skiing, snowshoeing, wildlife viewing, wildflower viewing ■ Roads not maintained in winter, may be closed by snow even as late as July ■ Contact Ruby Mountains Ranger District, Humboldt-Toiyabe National Forest, 140 Pacific Ave., Wells, NV 89835; phone 775-738-5171 or 800-715-9379

THE LURE OF THIS REMOTE WILDERNESS AREA is profound. Formed 20 million years ago by tectonic folding and scoured by glaciers during the last ice age, the Ruby Mountains offer visitors 10 peaks 10,000 feet or more, sculpted alpine valleys, and more than two dozen lakes surrounded by craggy cirques. Rising in a long, narrow north-south ridge about 60 miles long and rarely more than 10 miles across, the mountains are a magnet for precipitation. Storms moving up from the south travel northwest across Nevada, stack up against the high ridge, and render the Rubies the wettest, greenest range in the state. The abundant rainfall, moist soils, and diverse geology nourish habitat for nearly 190 plant species in the alpine ecosystem, including aspen, white bark pine, limber pine, and isolated patches of bristlecone pine. Lower down you'll find cottonwood, pinyon pine, mountain mahogany, bitterbrush, sagebrush, and some juniper. Among the area's abundant wildflowers you'll see snow spring parsley, yellow monkey flower, Indian paintbrush, bluebells, and three plants endemic to these mountains—King's buckwheat, the small-flowered penstemon, and the Ruby Mountain primrose.

The state's largest mule deer population roams the Rubies, and hikers are also likely to spot bighorn sheep, mountain goats, deer, sage grouse, and one species not found anywhere else in the United States—the Himalayan snowcock.

What to See and Do

The most popular introduction to the Rubies is along the 12-mile **Lamoille Canyon Scenic Byway** (*FR 660; 20 miles S of Elko on Nev. 227, follow signs for Lamoille Canyon Recreation Area. Road closed in winter*), a two-lane road that wends its way up into U-shaped **Lamoille Canyon,** where a late spring carpet of yellow

Vandalized aspen, Humboldt-Toiyabe NF

monkey flower and purple lupine belies the year-round snowfields on the surrounding peaks. The byway ends at 8,800 feet elevation in a glacial cirque known as **Road's End,** a fine spot for taking in the views of alpine meadows and dramatic peaks. Rest rooms and a parking lot are nearby. Trails leading from Road's End offer a variety of day hikes and longer treks.

An easy hike for families with younger children, for instance, is the 3.5-mile round-trip to **Island Lake.** Switchbacks make it a gradual climb. Also popular are day hikes along the first 7 miles of the 40-mile long Ruby Crest National Recreation Trail (*access via either of two trails from Road's End*).

For those who like to fish, a 4-mile round-trip to well-stocked **Lamoille Lake** is often the day's goal. Of course, the best fishing is in the early morning and evening, so camping may be in order.

More ambitious hikers might attempt the 6-mile round-trip to 10,400-foot **Liberty Pass,** offering views of the spires of **Ruby Dome,**

Jarbidge Wilderness

Created in 1964 and the first wilderness area designated in Nevada, the Jarbidge is northeast of Elko, near the Idaho border (Ruby Mountains Ranger District, 775-752-3357). With eight peaks higher than 10,000 feet, the wilderness gets some heavy weather: thunderstorms and sudden, unseasonal snow. The Jarbidge also has 125 miles of trails and air so clean it gets a rare Class I "airshed" rating from the Environmental Protection Agency. One popular entry is via the Snowslide Gulch Trailhead on the northwest side of the wilderness. To get there, take US 93 from Twin Falls, Idaho, or Wells, Nev., to Rogerson, Idaho. Take the Rogerson-Three Creek Highway (County Road 752) and go 65 miles to Jarbidge, Nev. Park near road's end at Pine Creek Campground.

the highest point in the range at 11,387 feet to the northwest.

Ruby Crest National Recreation Trail

The entire length of the Ruby Crest National Recreation Trail is best hiked south-north, from remote 7,324-foot Harrison Pass, to the parking lot at Lamoille Canyon. The more "civilized" lot is a safer place to leave a return vehicle, and hiking in this direction also makes more water available in the later parts of the trip (water is scarce between Harrison Pass and Overland Lake, the first of several lakes en route). To reach the dropoff point at Harrison Pass, drive southeast from Elko on Nev. 227 for 6 miles. Turn left onto Nev. 228 toward Jiggs. After 28 miles, veer left onto Harrison Pass Road (County Road 718). Go 8 miles and turn left onto Forest Road 107. Drive 3 miles north to the Green Mountain trailhead. Call the Forest Service (775-738-5171) to have maps and trail information sent to you.

Ruby Lake NWR

At the south end of the Ruby Mountains is the Ruby Lake National Wildlife Refuge (775-779-2237; Nev. 228 S from Elko to Cty. Rd. 767, go S for 8 miles to refuge headquarters). More than 200 species of birds have been identified around the refuge's bulrush marsh and lake, including sandhill cranes, trumpeter swans, white-faced ibises, and American kestrels.

The 37,632-acre **Ruby Lake** was once part of a huge body of water known as Franklin Lake; millions of years ago during the Pleistocene, the lake was more than 200 feet deep and covered 300,000 acres. Water levels dropped over the eons as Earth's climate grew warmer and drier, but thanks to the establishment of the refuge, this vital habitat is preserved not only for birds but also for wildlife such as coyotes, kangaroo rats, and the occasional pronghorn. A self-guided auto tour runs along the dikes of the central portion of the marsh, and there is good fishing in the lake for brown and rainbow trout and largemouth bass. ■

Following pages: Sunflowers, Angel Falls, Ruby Mountains Wilderness

Ruby-throated hummingbird sampling Indian paintbrush

Great Basin National Park

■ 77,180 acres ■ Eastern Nevada, 5 miles west of Baker on Nev. 488 ■ Best months late June-Sept. ■ Camping, hiking, backpacking, guided walks, mountain climbing, fishing, horseback riding, cross-country skiing, snowshoeing, bird-watching, wildlife viewing, wildflower viewing, spelunking ■ Fee for cave tours ■ Contact the park, 100 Great Basin National Park, Baker, NV 89311; phone 775-234-7331. www.nps.gov/grba

IF YOU IMAGINE THE SURROUNDING sagebrush desert as an ocean, the nature of the Snake Range, home of Great Basin National Park, becomes apparent. The high peaks rise like an archipelago—islands of greater moisture and cooler air that support a rich diversity of plant and animal life that could not survive the hotter, drier climate down below. Indeed, the park is a compact collection of the region's most intriguing features, including alpine lakes and streams, forests of gnarled and ancient bristlecone pines, and the twisting limestone caverns of Lehman Caves.

The park's topography was shaped by the tilting upward of the Snake Range as tectonic plates stretched and lifted the continent's surface. That tilted block was then sculpted during much wetter and cooler eras of the Pleistocene, when glaciers wrapped the mountains' shoulders and pine forests covered the valleys. Utah's Great Salt Lake is a small remnant of an enormous sea of that era—Lake Bonneville—which came within a few miles of what is now the park, depositing lake bottom sediments. About 10,000 years ago the climate warmed, the mountain glaciers here above 8,000 feet began to melt, and the basin began drying out. The only glacier in the Great Basin today is the one patch of ice and snow that remains on the northeast side of 13,063-foot Wheeler Peak. Over most of the region, streams and rivers have no outlet to the ocean, collecting instead in shallow salt lakes, marshes, and mudflats. In fact, there are many basins here not just one, all separated by roughly parallel mountain ranges running north-south.

Great Basin is one of the country's newer national parks, having been set aside in 1986 by President Ronald Reagan. (Lehman Caves National Monument, now incorporated into the park, was created in 1922.)

What to See and Do

The park lies off the beaten track of the interstate highways, so except on peak weekends in the late summer and early fall, you'll rarely find crowds.

Lehman Caves

If you have only a day or two to spend in the park, be sure to stop at the visitor center *(0.5 mile inside the park on Nev. 488)* and buy a ticket for one of the guided tours of **Lehman Caves** *(775-234-7331, ext. 242 for advance purchase).* Tours of 30, 60, and 90 minutes take place throughout the day, with the longer tours going farther along the same route.

The calcium carbonate marine sediments that became the limestone of Lehman Caves are 550 million years old, and thousands of feet thick. After the seas retreated and tectonic uplift raised the limestone bed, rain and snowmelt containing dissolved carbon dioxide percolated through it and started to hollow out a cave. Over millennia, changes in the chemistry and levels of the water in the cave led to the slow deposition of calcite in the form of stalactites and other formations.

A local rancher named Absalom Lehman was the first settler to discover an opening into the cave system in 1885. Lehman explored the caves, and soon was charging a dollar for a candle to let others do the same. Eventually ladders and electric lights were installed. The slowly evolving limestone formations have suffered a few casualties, but their variety remains incredible, including self-descriptive features such as bacon, shields, popcorn, flowstone, columns, and soda straws. The particular formations of this cave once had fanciful names such as the Parachute, the Pearly Gates, the Sailor Kissing his Girlfriend, and Old George and His Pet Dog, which are no longer used today.

For adventure outside the cave, try the quarter-mile round-trip **Mountain View Nature Trail,** which starts at Rhodes' Cabin near the visitor center and offers a pleasant walk in the pinyon-juniper forest and a sense of the area's geology.

Wheeler Peak

Spectacular vistas and a bit more exercise are available if you take the winding 12-mile **Wheeler Peak Scenic Drive** *(Paved road heading NW off Nev. 488 just inside park boundary)* to a parking area and trailhead at the Wheeler Peak Campground. As you climb 3,400 feet in 12 miles, you'll pass from pinyon-juniper woodlands to sub-alpine forest of limber pine, aspen, and spruce, with many places en

Ivory Towers, Lehman Caves, Great Basin NP

route to pause and take in the view. From the campground, the 3-mile round-trip **Alpine Lakes Loop** will take you to **Teresa** and **Stella Lakes,** two small, glacial pools, or tarns, or to the foot of the small glacier that sits in the cirque of Wheeler Peak. Just below the glacier is a remarkable forest of ancient bristlecone pines, home to some of the oldest trees in the world. In the 1960s, prior to the creation of the park, the oldest known bristlecone pine was cut down here—at the age of 4,900 years—as part of a climate study.

A longer, more strenuous trek from the campground is the **Wheeler Peak Summit Trail**—8.6 miles round-trip and 3,000 feet of elevation change to the bald top of the peak. From the 13,063-foot summit you might look around 360 degrees and realize there are areas much less visited where you can get a rich dose of Great Basin solitude. You can take a 13.1-mile round-trip hike on the **Baker Lake/Johnson Lake Loop** *(From park boundary, turn S off Nev. 488 onto Baker Creek Rd; travel 3.6 miles to trailhead. Road is gravel and closed in winter)* to **Baker Lake,** nestled in a cirque on the south side of Wheeler Peak. From here a 6-mile hike heads south around Pyramid Peak and leads to **Johnson Lake.** Both Johnson and Baker Lakes are home to four of the five species of trout that inhabit the park's waters and will be irresistible to any avid angler. Here, as well as in the park's many creeks, you'll find Lahontan cutthroat, brown, rainbow, and brook trout.

If you're up for adventure with a high-clearance vehicle, you can

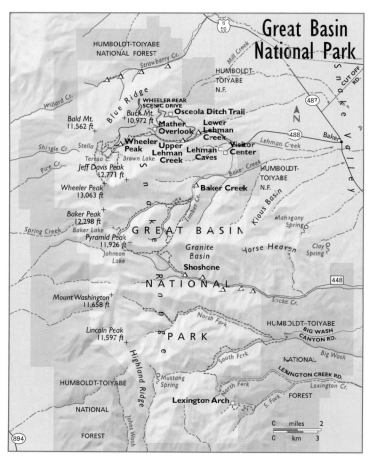

negotiate a rugged dirt road (get directions from the visitor center) into the southern end of the park, where you can take a 3.4-mile round-trip hike to **Lexington Arch**. From beneath this six-story limestone bridge, believed to have once been part of a cave system, you'll have breathtaking views of the Snake Valley to the east. The wilderness deeper in the southern part of the park gets few visitors.

Because many of the park's trails reach elevations above 10,000 feet, you should always be prepared for sudden changes in the weather. If you plan to hike above tree line, be sure to take rain gear and warm clothing. Also, although water is available at the visitor center year-round and at the park's four developed campgrounds during summer, be sure to carry at least one quart of water per person (more for day hikes).

Finally, remember that the alpine world is fragile. At these elevations, plants grow slowly and their margin of survival is narrow. Stay on established roads and trails to avoid inadvertently damaging these areas. ■

Desert and Canyon

Valley of Fire State Park

EVERY HOUR IN LAS VEGAS, millions of gallons of water erupt from the city's fountains while thousands of people bustle by. Yet a mere 20 minutes away, you are in a sagebrush desert that rarely receives more than 6 inches of moisture a year and probably sees fewer than a dozen people in a week. Nowhere in the world will you find a greater contrast between what nature puts on the plate and the meal humanity makes of it than in southern Nevada. Compare the earthen red domes of weathered sandstone at Valley of Fire State Park to the neon architectural sundaes of the city's Strip. Look for a trickle of water in August as you hike among the slabs of Red Rock Canyon, then ride a power-boat across man-made Lake Mead.

For all its neon lights and gushing fountains, however, Las Vegas is a very small spangle in the vast expanse of Mojavean desert. Even Lake Mead, which is arguably a much more powerful manipulation of this ecosystem than the city, seems little more than a thin blue question mark on a vast landscape fractured and worn and baked red and brown.

Some 550 million years ago, what is now Nevada lay at the bottom of a deep ocean basin. Then about 200 million years ago, the Pacific and North American tectonic plates began to collide, the ocean bottom lifted, forming the mountain ranges and draining the sea. Gradually a land that had been covered with water and filled with marine life became desert.

There are three distinct deserts in the Far West: the cactus and mesquite world of the low-elevation Colorado or Sonoran Desert, the sagebrush and pinyon forest of the steeply contoured Great Basin, and the oppressively hot, lower-elevation Mojave, with its petroleum-smelling creosote bushes and the pom-pom arms of Joshua trees. The Mojave is home to some 200 plant species found in neither the Great Basin nor the Sonoran, the most prominent being the Joshua tree.

Most of Nevada lies within the Great Basin, but the southeast corner is part of the Mojave, which

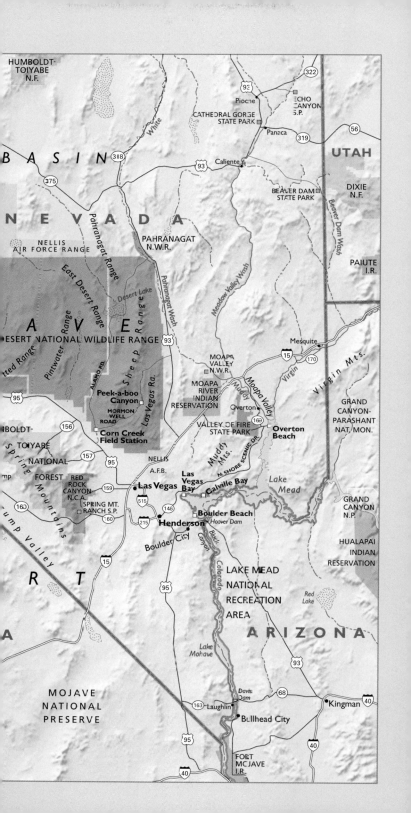

Southwestern thorn apple, Valley of Fire State Park

stretches from Death Valley in California, across southern Nevada, and into Arizona and Utah. Both the Mojave and the Great Basin are part of the Basin and Range Province, a physiographic feature characterized by hundreds of long, narrow, and roughly parallel mountains, separated by deep valleys, which extend southward to include the Sonoran and Chihuahuan Deserts of Arizona and Mexico.

In the Mojave, summers are hot, windy, and dry. What little precipitation there is here falls mostly in winter. It is a desert that for thousands of years admitted only inhabitants with the most conservative appetites for water. Then along came Benjamin "Bugsy" Siegel and his mobster cohorts, who decided to build a city in the desert.

Las Vegas was named for "the meadows," spring-fed splashes of green noted by Spanish explorers. Barely 4 inches of rain falls annually in the Las Vegas Valley, and it evaporates quickly when it lands on pavement or concrete, but the springs tapped an underground aquifer fed by runoff from distant mountains. As the city began to grow, in the 1930s, artesian wells had to be drilled deeper and deeper. Then came a solution perversely typical of the government-phobic West: a big federal water project. The Hoover Dam was completed in 1936, and Las Vegas had a new water supply.

But this is the fastest growing region in the United States, and even a reservoir with nine trillion gallons of water can't supply enough, espe-

Schroeder Lake, Beaver Dam State Park

cially when water rights are divvied up among six states. So in recent years, Vegas officials have gone shopping for water rights in outlying agricultural areas to the north, talked about dams on smaller streams such as the Virgin River and pushed for a bigger share of Colorado River water. (Water from the river is apportioned among seven states—Arizona, California, Colorado, Nevada, New Mexico, Utah, and Wyoming—according to a 1922 compact.)

Touring the wild areas around Las Vegas only reinforces the sense that even a wealthy gambling city can't overpower the environment. The pockets of healthy, well-watered habitat survive by staying small, hidden in high canyon country such as the Spring Mountains or Beaver Dam State Park. Otherwise, wildlife and vegetation make the adjustment, like desert bighorn sheep finding springs in the high, dry country of the Desert National Wildlife Range, or creosote bushes waiting out the droughty periods by dropping leaves.

The sheep have found a niche, too, in the hills above the Hoover Dam, where Lake Mead provides a lot more water than they have any need for. Dipping a toe or a fishing line in that large, man-made pool of Colorado River water, it's worth thinking about a much smaller spot of water far to the west. There, in a forbidding desert landscape, beneath a barren rock outcrop, sits a single pool in which the world's entire world population of the Devils Hole pupfish survives. ■

Cathedral Gorge State Park

■ 1,633 acres ■ Southeast Nevada, 2 miles northwest of Panaca ■ Year-round
■ Camping, hiking, petroglyphs ■ Adm. fee ■ Contact the park, P.O. Box 176,
Panaca, NV 89042; phone 775-728-4460. www.state.nv.us/stparks/cg.htm

WALKING THROUGH THE SILTSTONE and bentonite clay of Cathedral Gorge
is like exploring the icing on a fancy wedding cake, albeit one that's
drooping in the heat. You may wonder if a heavy rain wouldn't simply
knock down the formations, but a lighter mixture of hardened clay
material visible atop the siltstone protects it from rapid erosion.

The material out of which the gorge's cliffs and canyons—called the
Panaca formation—are sculpted was deposited on a lake bottom more
than a million years ago. The lake drained as the climate changed and
made the first cuts into the deep sediments that lined the lake bed.

The intricately carved vertical rock is soft in color and texture, and
shapes suggest everything from tigers to close-packed skyscrapers to
Gothic cathedrals. The formations show a variety of milk-to-coffee colors
that cast a soft light in the middle of the day.

What to See and Do

A regional visitor center at the
southern entrance to Cathedral
Gorge has information on the
many small parks, wildlife, and
petroglyph sites that are found
throughout this area. From the
center, it's about a mile drive along
the main park road to a parking
area. Take the quarter-mile **nature
trail** that begins here. It has informative signs on regional geology
and wildlife. Or venture up **Miller
Point Trail,** a 1-mile steep hike
with a section of metal stairs that
ascend to the **Miller Point Overlook.** You can also reach the point
by car from the south entrance via
US 93 north, a 2-mile drive.

For a longer hike, follow the
signs from the south entrance to
the campground, where the 4-mile
Juniper Draw Trail loops to the
west into the deepest and most

dramatic corner of the gorge.

Near the parking and picnic
areas you'll see gaps in the Panaca
formation wide enough to enter.
Some are described as caves, but
they remain open to the sky. These
peaks, with their resemblance to
cathedral spires, undoubtedly
inspired the gorge's name.

Though the landscape seems
eerily naked at first glance, there is
plenty of wildlife, including deer,
kestrels, and kit foxes. Roadrunners, black-throated sparrows,
ravens, and small hawks are
among the park's resident birds,
which are sometimes joined by
migratory cedar waxwings, hummingbirds, and tanagers. Among
the plants that can be seen here
are purple sage, evening primrose,
yucca, barberry sagebrush, greasewood, and cliffrose. ■

Along Miller Point Trail, Cathedral Gorge State Park

Beaver Dam State Park

■ 2,393 acres ■ Southeast Nevada, 34 miles east of Caliente off US 93
■ Year-round ■ Camping, hiking, fishing, wildlife viewing ■ Adm. fee ■ Vehicles
longer than 25 feet are discouraged ■ Contact the park, HC64, Box 3, Caliente,
NV 89008-9701; phone 775-728-4460.www.state.nv.us/stparks/bd.htm

IN THE REMOTE, DRY HILLS of southeastern Nevada, at 5,000 feet above sea
level, Beaver Dam State Park is something of a secret. Those who venture
here find a beautiful world of ponderosa pine forests, air-conditioned
canyons, and sparkling waterways where rainbow trout dart from the

Schroeder Lake, Beaver Dam State Park

shadow. The creeks are deeply slotted and shaded with cottonwoods, Gambel oaks, and willows (some of which have been cropped off by the park's beavers).

Piute Indians originally settled the area around Headwaters and Pine Creeks (which join to form Beaver Dam Wash above the park's reservoir). Homesteaders arrived in the 1860s. As ranches were carved out of the heavily wooded hills, local residents began coming here for a splash of beauty in the sheltered canyons. The area's popularity grew, and in 1935 it was designated a state park (considered the most beautiful one in Nevada by some people).

You reach the park by driving 6 miles north from Caliente on US 93, then following the park sign east on a graded dirt and gravel road for 28 miles. (People with vehicles and trailers longer than 25 feet are not encouraged to make the drive because of the many treacherous switchbacks.) As you enter the park, the high desert is suddenly morphed into a green, steep world of springs and creeks. A road runs from one end of the park to the other, but you'll want to walk through the cool canyon.

The 0.6-mile **Lake Trail** begins just inside the park entrance at the picnic area and leads to Schroeder Lake. Cast a fishing line or take a refreshing swim in the 15-acre, spring-fed reservoir, which was built in 1962 to control flooding.

From the reservoir, you can hike another 1.5 miles, to the primitive campground at the park's south end, along the prettiest part of **Beaver Dam Wash**. It's a small waterway, easy to wade across when you decide you want to scramble up on a ridge. You will notice the rainbow trout, which are restocked every winter, darting in the clear, cool water. There are also desert suckers and golden shiners in the park's streams.

The canyon walls through which you walk as you follow the wash are steep and colorful—white ashfall tuffs and pink rhyolite that suggest the volcanic past. The water and vegetation sustain mule deer and a variety of birds, including transplanted wild turkeys. At the south end of this hike the canyon opens, and the beaver ponds widen and follow close on one another, their surfaces smooth as silk sheets.

The park road parallels the canyon to the west, rising and falling steeply in and out of tributary washes and finally meeting the trail again at the primitive campground at the bottom of the canyon. Where the road dead-ends—the ranch beyond is private—take the 1-mile **Waterfall Trail** to a small waterfall. The water is warmed by a small hot spring above the falls, which you can reach by hiking a little farther.

Be cautious: The area's steep, unpaved roads can be dangerous when there is snow and rain. Call to check the weather if you're coming between November and April. ∎

Virgin River

The Virgin River, which meets Beaver Dam Wash east of Mesquite in northwest Arizona, is the only river still running free in southern Nevada. It flows for 200 unimpeded miles from southern Utah, through the beautiful Virgin Gorge, across Arizona, and into Nevada and Lake Mead. At its headwaters, the river cuts through steep-walled canyons; as it moves downstream toward Nevada, the terrain changes to broad, open canyons in low desert land.

There are six fish species native to the river. All can be found near the mouth of Beaver Dam Wash. Five are considered endangered or threatened, including the Virgin river chub, the Virgin spinedace, and the woundfin.

For a view of the Virgin River, follow Nev. 170, which loops off I-15 just west of Mesquite and runs along the wide river valley.

Climbing the sandstone walls of Valley of Fire State Park

Valley of Fire State Park

■ 36,800 acres ■ Southern Nevada, 55 miles northeast of Las Vegas via I-15 and Nev. 169 ■ Year-round ■ Hiking, biking, rock formations, petroglyphs ■ Adm fee ■ Contact the park, P.O. Box 515, Overton, NV 89040; phone 702-397-2088. www.state.nv.us/stparks/vf.htm

WHEN THE BRIGHT LIGHTS OF LAS VEGAS threaten to overwhelm you, turn your eyes in the glow of Aztec sandstone at Valley of Fire State Park for a different kind of light show. The spires and slabs and domes change color at the end of day from soft pinks to hot ocher to cool, pale brown. The park is just 55 miles from the Strip, but it's a transformed world of prehistoric gravity and inner radiance.

It's wise to stay overnight, because the rock you thought you knew may turn out to be something else entirely. Not only do the rocks have eerie color-shifting qualities, they also seem to change shapes as the light and shadows move about.

What most of these rocks were, originally, was sand. Like so many stories of the western landscape, this one begins with an enormous ancient sea, which covered this region some 550 million years ago, and layered the remains of marine fossils in deep beds beneath the water. About 200 million years ago, when the Pacific and North American tectonic plates began their seismic jousting, these ocean-bottom sediments were lifted, and the sea drained. Atop this deep bed of sediment, sand accumulated in tall dunes, which then were fossilized and stained by metals such as iron to produce the brilliant colors seen today.

Wind and weather wore unevenly on the tilted rock, forming the twisted humps, arches, tubs, and spires in the park's 6-mile-long valley.

Sandstone sculptures, Valley of Fire State Park

There fanciful shapes have inspried such names as the Beehives, Cobra Rock, and Piano Rock.

Petroglyphs found in the park indicate that early Native Americans, possibly ancient Pueblo people, spent time in the valley and inscribed the sandstone. The areas along the Muddy River north into the Maopa Valley and south into what is now Lake Mead were littered with prehistoric artifacts, some of them inundated today. Exhibits at the **Lost City Museum,** in Overton, do a fine job of telling what we know of the ancient Pueblo people who may have lived here and their mysterious disappearance.

What to See and Do

To reach the park, take I-15 north from Las Vegas for 35 miles then turn east on Nev. 169 for 15 miles to the west entrance of the park.

Inside to the right is a short trail leading to a mass of whittled, swirling sandstone called the **Beehives.** Beyond it, a **loop trail** leads to petrified logs more than 225 million years old (evidence a forest once thrived in this desolate area).

To the left of the entrance is **Scenic Loop Road,** a 2-mile drive offering views of **Arch Rock** and **Piano Rock.** You can stop and take a short climb up the 100-step iron staircase to **Atlatl Rock,** so named because it resembles an atlatl—a notched stick used as a sling to give a boost when hurling a spear. A panel of Indian petroglyphs here serves as a snapshot of early life.

Back out on Nev. 169, go 4 miles farther east to a **visitor center** with exhibits on the geology and archaeology of the area. Displays explain how the creosote bushes and cactuses have adapted to the sparse rainfall. In the spring, marigolds and desert mallow receive enough moisture to brighten the park roads.

From the visitor center, **Mouse's Tank Road** heads north toward the White Domes formation. On the way you can park and hike the short (half-mile round-trip) **Petroglyph Canyon Trail,** an interpreted path passing more stone etchings. The trail leads to **Mouse's Tank,** a sandstone bowl often filled with water from a previous rain. According to legend, Mouse was a Paiute Indian who hid here in the 1890s after local authorities branded him an outlaw. He used the sandstone bowl as a much needed water source.

Farther up Mouse Tank Road, stop at **Rainbow Vista,** a pullover with an extraordinary view of the blazing red canyon and of Silica Dome. Another 4 miles north, the road ends at the **White Domes,** huge concoctions of white silica.

Back at the visitor center, head east on Nev. 169 again for a good look at **Seven Sisters,** red-rock siblings standing sentinel by the road. Ahead are stone cabins built by the Civilian Conservation Corps in the 1930s for travelers. The site is perfect for picnicking.

Just before you reach the park's east entrance, you'll see the valley's best known icon, **Elephant Rock.**

If you wish to extend your visit overnight, there are two campgrounds located outside the west end of the park. ∎

Ash Meadows National Wildlife Refuge

■ 22,000 acres ■ Southwest Nevada, 30 miles northwest of Pahrump on Bell Vista Rd. ■ Year-round ■ Hiking, swimming, wildlife viewing ■ Day use only ■ Contact the refuge, HCR 70, Box 610-Z, Amargosa Valley, NV 89020; phone 702-372-5435. www.r1.fws.gov/desert/ashframe.htm

ONE REASON FOR STOPPING AT ASH MEADOWS is to find out what all the fuss is about. This is the home of the Ash Meadows, the Warm Springs, and the Devils Hole pupfish—three obscure fish that as endangered species have the power to shut down summer-home construction or a big dam-building project. They are minuscule, silver-blue fish with an underslung jaw that have survived in small pockets as the great lakes that once covered the deserts of the Southwest retreated into small corners. These pupfish live here in the desert northwest of Las Vegas, in this small green oasis fed by more than 30 springs.

Although the Ash Meadows and Warm Springs pupfish can be found in many of the springs, the Devils Hole pupfish, the smallest (1 inch), can only be seen in one pool, sunk in a crevasse in the mountainside. This site, which is surrounded by a high fence with barbed wire on top to protect the fish, can be reached by following signs from the refuge headquarters. It holds a few hundred of the endangered little fish.

Springs such as these, isolated in desert uplands, are good candidates for producing endemic species found nowhere else. Biologists count more than 20 unique plants and animals in the area of the refuge in Amargosa Valley, a concentration of indigenous wildlife thought to be greater than anywhere else in the country. Ash Meadows National Wildlife Refuge was established in 1984 to protect this valuable area and help endangered populations such as the pupfish recover. Refuge managers are working to remove exotic plants and fish, such as largemouth bass, which crowd native species.

Visitors can take the self-guided 0.7-mile **Crystal Spring Trail,** a boardwalk that begins near the refuge office and goes through mesquite woods, sand dunes, and wildflower areas. Lean over the springs and get a look at the frisky, silvery pupfish against the green mossy bottom. You'll also see threatened plants such the Ash Meadows gumplant and ivesia.

Although springs can discharge up to 2,600 gallons per minute, most of them run in channels no bigger than an irrigation ditch as they meander around the refuge. Beneath the surface is a huge aquifer of "fossil" water that has been flowing underground for thousands of years, and now bubbles up in a series of springs and seeps. Swimming in the springs is prohibited, but you can take a dip in **Crystal Reservoir,** reached via a short trail from the visitor center. ■

Red Rock Canyon National Conservation Area

Red Rock Canyon National Conservation Area

■ 197,000 acres ■ Southern Nevada, 13 miles west of Las Vegas on Nev. 159
■ Year-round ■ Hiking, rock climbing, mountain biking, horseback riding, wildlife
viewing ■ Adm. fee ■ Contact Bureau of Land Management, HCR 33, Box
5500, Las Vegas, NV 89124; phone 702-363-1921. www.redrockcanyon.blm.gov

GAZING UP AT THE MULTIHUED SANDSTONE BLOCKS of Red Rock Canyon
under a hot summer sun, remind yourself that this was until recently—

merely a few hundred million years ago—the bottom of an ocean. Then it became a very dry desert, with drifting dunes piling sand half a mile deep. The sand solidified, and the forces of erosion began to carve it into interesting shapes.

That is the story of much of the sculpted sandstone in the Mojave Desert, but at Red Rock there is a wrinkle that explains why it remains standing tall while other sandstone is worn down: Approximately 65 million years ago, the Earth's crust snapped and overlapped, throwing the harder gray limestone from the long ago ocean floor over the softer and younger red sandstone. You can clearly see the color change of the rock along the Keystone Thrust Fault, and it is the gray cap of limestone that resists erosion.

The canyon sits in the foreground of the Spring Mountains, a tall wall of rock that closes off the west side of the valley. A great many species find refuge here, not because of the colorful rocks, but because there's a little more water flowing in the creeks and canyons. Mountain lions, kit foxes, red-tailed hawks, and kangaroo rats are here. So is a small band of less than 200 desert bighorn sheep, who keep to the steeper terrain but can sometimes be spotted at springs. Part of the bighorns' problem is competition from burros, imported animals that have made themselves at home. Two well-known refugees, a desert iguana and chuckwalla, can be found at the **Red Rock Visitor Center.** Both are escapees from Las Vegas, where they were poorly kept "pets" before being brought here for a life of ease.

Human escapees from the city can jump in a car and head west on Nev. 159 for 13 miles to reach the visitor center. Here they'll find exhibits covering geology and natural history. This is also the beginning of a 13-mile scenic drive that is the centerpiece of most visits to Red Rock Canyon. From the numerous pullouts and trailheads, you can join the many short hikes into the area, including the 2.5-mile (round-trip) **Ice Box Canyon Trail,** the 2.9-mile (round-trip) **Pine Creek Canyon Trail,** and the short **Calico Hills Trail,** where you'll find deep canyons, natural water-holding tanks, and the remnants of agave roasting pits left by early Native American inhabitants. Ambitious hikers can venture from Sandstone Quarry up the 5-mile (round-trip) **Turtlehead Peak Trail** to the 6,323-foot summit, or along the escarpment atop Wilson Cliffs, which back up to the Spring Mountains along the park's western edge.

Though the rock is mostly soft sandstone, rock climbers come here in droves. They work out of the **Pine Creek Canyon** area, or on routes above the **Sandstone Quarry,** which lies above the scenic loop. There are several outfitters in the area *(contact the BLM for a list).*

The scenic loop area can be extremely busy on weekends, so you may want to shift to less crowded routes at the southern end of the park. You also may want to pay a visit to the cool meadows and old buildings of **Spring Mountain Ranch** *(702-875-4141),* a former cattle ranch that once belonged to Howard Hughes and is now a state park within Red Rock Canyon. ■

Desert National Wildlife Range

■ 1.5 million acres ■ Southern Nevada, 25 miles north of Las Vegas off US 95
■ Year-round ■ Hiking, bird-watching, wildlife viewing ■ Contact the range,
1500 N. Decatur Blvd., Las Vegas, NV 89108; phone 702-646-3401.
www.r1.fws.gov/desert/desframe.htm

BEGINNING ON THE NORTHERN OUTSKIRTS of Las Vegas is the largest
national wildlife refuge this side of Alaska, encompassing valleys dotted
with Joshua trees and six mountain ranges rising to nearly 10,000 feet.
The primary purpose of the preserve is to improve life for the desert
bighorn sheep (see sidebar opposite), though this objective may be
compromised somewhat by the fact that a big portion of the refuge is
still used by Nellis Air Force Base for a bombing range.

More than 50 other mammal species share the refuge with the
bighorn sheep, including several threatened ones such as the Hidden
Forest uinta chipmunk, the long-legged myotis, and Townsend's big-
eared bat. At least 240 species of birds have been seen here, among them
the bald eagle and the peregrine falcon. Some 30 species of reptiles and
amphibians are found at the range, including the endangered Pahrump
poolfish. The minnow-size fish was transplanted to the refuge after it was
discovered to be nearing extinction in the Pahrump Valley north of Las
Vegas. Springs there declined due to wells tapping the aquifer.

The Pahrump poolfish resides in a spring running through a cattail
marsh beside the **Corn Creek Field Station,** a small, unmanned structure
at the southern end of the refuge, the main entryway *(from Las Vegas,
take US 95 N for 20 miles, then at refuge sign turn E for 5 miles).* At the
station, pick up a map to the refuge and view some displays about the
habitat at different altitudes. Then take the short (less than a mile)
Interpretive Trail, which meanders past the springs and marsh.

For trips beyond the field station, be aware there is no potable water
and the unpaved roads are rough in spots. You'll feel more at ease if
you're piloting a vehicle with high clearance and carrying lots of bottled
water. Take binoculars; you'll need them for spotting the sheep. The most
common trip from the station is along **Mormon Well Road,** which runs
about 40 miles up and over the 7,000-foot-high Las Vegas Range through
the east side of the refuge. A printed guide, available at Corn Creek,
points out sheep habitat, an agave roasting pit used by prehistoric inhabitants of the area, and the cave-dotted **Peek-a-boo Canyon.** The refuge
has a full range of desert habitat: from the low, dry realm of the creosote
bush to the pine and fir communities of the high, wetter country. The
lower elevatons of the drive are dotted with mojave yucca and cactus.

An option to enjoy the solitude of the desert can be found by taking
Alamo Road straight north from the Corn Creek Field Station, between
the East Desert Range and Sheep Range. This road runs 65 miles around
a dry lake bed to the northern boundary of the refuge. ■

Desert Bighorn Sheep

With their dignified bearing and crown of curled horn, the desert bighorn sheep are one of the royal families of desert wildlife. They are not easily seen, except with a good spotting scope and a map of watering holes. They stick to the high rocks, avoiding people and livestock, and concentrate on survival and propagation.

The bighorns originated in Asia and made their way to North America during the last ice age, when a land bridge existed between what is now Russia and Alaska. The sheep spread throughout the mountain and desert provinces of the West. But then, in the 19th century, the great tide of human migration began to rush across the West, and the animals' very existence was threatened. First hunters decimated the sheep for food and trophies, then exotic diseases brought by livestock swept through the remaining bighorn populations.

To save the bighorn sheep, a small number of refuges such as the Desert NWR were established in the region stretching from the northern Rockies to the Mexican border. With protection, the great fluctuation in herd size is now caused only by wet and dry cycles.

Desert bighorn sheep found on the Desert NWR are smaller in stature than their cousins to the north (the Rocky Mountain and California bighorns), but their distinctive curled horns tend to be larger. These are true horns, which aren't shed; if you find a set in the wild, it's usually attached to a skull.

Desert bighorn sheep

A ram's horn will form its full distinctive curl by about eight years of age. Like tree rings, the rings, or whorls, on the outside of the horn represent years, the first distinctive ones forming after 4 years of age. The head and horns of a full-grown ram constitute as much as one-fifth of the animal's total weight.

If you're lucky enough to hear the distinctive crack of rams butting heads, it will likely be sometime between midsummer and late fall, when the bighorn sheep breed. Rams that have wandered through the spring in bachelor groups search out as many females as they can, and when two males meet, they'll square off at about 20 feet and try to knock each other silly. Lambs are born in February and March, and grow up in a nursery group of ewes, other lambs, and young males.

Water Overuse in Las Vegas

ON THE FACE OF IT, it's fairly disturbing: a huge growing city in the driest desert country in North America building resort after resort with extravagant water themes. Among them are the Venetian, a miniature canal city; the Bellagio, overlooking an 8.5-acre lake that features dancing fountains; and "O," the sensational Cirque du Soleil entertainment extravaganza set in a 1.5-million-gallon pool.

How can a city receiving only about 4 inches of rain a year—and most of that in a few uncollectable downpours—justify such water usage?

"Actually," says a spokesman for the Southern Nevada Water Authority, "only about 7 percent of our water use goes to casinos and resorts. The biggest use by far is residential—about two-thirds of the water." In fact, the SNWA has made a major effort to educate all water users about the need for conservation and there have been some positive results: a reduction in lawn watering; a move toward more desert landscaping (which doesn't require so much water); and the conversion by golf courses and parks to "gray" water (i.e., recycled from urban use).

But conservation groups such as Citizen Alert in Las Vegas say it's not enough. They point to the 5,000 newcomers moving into the valley every month and a heavily burdened sewage system that may be polluting Lake Mead—not to mention the trampling of delicate desert surfaces, which both hurts the ecosystem and causes dust-related health problems.

Eleven years ago, Las Vegas scared farmers all over the southern part of the state by filing for water rights in rural Nevada allowing the city to import water. Opponents claimed the project would cost billions and might pull down the water table and

Caesars Palace, Las Vegas

damage wetlands. Las Vegas backed off, and experts such as SNWA cirector Pat Mulroy, turned their attention to another water source—the Colorado River.

With the six other states with water rights on the Colorado, Nevada has reached a tentative agreement that will assure southern Nevada of a water supply for probably another 30 years or more. The agreement also allows the state to "bank" a certain amount of its Colorado River water in the underground aquifers of Arizona, to be pumped out in the future as needed.

If the Colorado agreement (which needs approval by the U.S. Department of the Interior) works as planned, the Las Vegas area—even if its phenomenal growth continues—will have enough water to keep the fountains of its resorts spouting.

Interestingly, a public-private group is planning another attraction in the heart of Las Vegas that focuses on water: the 180-acre Las Vegas Springs Preserve *(Valley View Blvd. and Alta Dr., just off US 95)*, complete with visitor center, trails, and boardwalks, opening in 2005. Though the springs, which formed "the meadows" for which the city was named, stopped flowing above ground 50 years ago, they are still there, right at the heart of the city, left largely alone because of a waterworks project in the vicinity. Today you'll find scattered stands of trees and shrubs here. And on the park's north side, you'll see the old springs caretaker's ranch.

The plan is to restore the natural habitat and native flora and fauna, as well as historic facilities such as the ancient redwood pipes of the first settlement, and the row of cottonwoods, still standing, planted by Mormon settlers in the 1850s. "It's our equivalent of Plymouth Rock," said one booster.

Whether the project holds water remains to be seen. ■

Desert National Wildlife Range

Paddle wheeler crossing Lake Mead

Lake Mead National Recreation Area

■ 1.5 million-acre (NRA); 162,700-acre (reservoir) ■ Southern Nevada and northwest Arizona, 27 miles south of Las Vegas on US 93 ■ Year-round
■ Hiking, boating, rafting, swimming, scuba diving, waterskiing, fishing, biking, bird-watching, wildlife viewing ■ Contact the recreation area, 601 Nevada Highway, Boulder City, NV 89005; phone 702-293-8907. www.nps.gov/lame

TAMING THE COLORADO RIVER, which slices through some last wrinkles of the Basin and Range topography that defines most of Nevada, created one of the most popular recreation areas in the state of Nevada: Lake Mead. But it wasn't done easily or without cost to the area's wildlife.

Before 1936, the Colorado River swelled into a raging brown torrent every spring and then subsided in the summer to a meandering trickle, enlivened now and then by a thunderstorm-fueled flash flood. To control this force of nature, the federal government decided in 1931 to construct a 726-foot-high concrete plug at the top of Black Canyon. It took five years and some 5,000 workers to complete the engineering feat known as the Hoover Dam, which backs up water 110 miles, about nine trillion gallons of it, providing flood control as well as electricity, drinking water, and irrigation water.

Although the damming of the Colorado brought benefits, it also brought detrimental side effects. By lowering water temperatures, preventing spawning far downstream, and blocking migration both up- and downstream, the dam contributed to the decline of more than one species of fish. Among them are the Colorado pikeminnow (formerly the Colorado squawfish), the bonytail chub, and the razorback sucker, all endangered now. However, federal managers have made some attempts in recent years to open the gates enough to simulate a mild version of muddy, high-water runoff that aids the various fish species.

Yet, while threatening some creatures, damming the river has helped others. Lake Mead and its sister lake to the south, 67-mile-long Lake Mohave (created in 1953 with the construction of Davis Dam) have attracted numerous species of shore- and waterbirds to the area. Among them are herons, egrets, and pelicans. Bird-watchers can find many different species at the wildlife sanctuary located at the tip of Overton Arm, the lake's northern branch.

Still one look at the bare rocky banks of Lake Mohave and it's clear that backing up a huge basin of water in the canyon of the Colorado River hasn't convinced the surrounding land to give up its desert heart. Fishermen and jet skiers might argue that dams have transformed this corner of southern Nevada, but the rock nettles and chuckwallas suggest it hasn't. The foot-long chuckwalla is the largest of many lizards that were here long before the lake and will likely be here long after. Over thousands of years—millions, in some cases—species such as the lizards, creosote bushes, and the desert verbenas have developed survival strategies in the face of oppressive summer heat and only 6 inches of rain annually.

Lake Mead, Lake Mohave, the surrounding desert, and Arizona's Shivwits Plateau are all a part of the Lake Mead National Recreation Area, which was established in 1964. Terrain ranges from mountain to desert to lake. A wide variety of animals, birds, and plants live here, including desert bighorn, roadrunners, bald eagles, Joshua trees, and cactuses. It is a great place to visit and explore.

What to See and Do

Summer holidays from Memorial Day to Labor Day bring the biggest crowds, and there are areas on the lake where boaters congregate in large numbers. But these are big bodies of water backing up into various canyon arms, so it is not too difficult to get away, on the water, on foot, or in a vehicle.

Most visits begin with a stop at the **Alan Bible Visitor Center,** just north of Boulder City at the intersection of US 93 and Nev. 166. At the center, you can pick up maps and advice, and visit an outdoor botanical garden with information on the vegetation of the area.

To see Lake Mead, you can follow Lakeshore and Northshore Scenic Drives. From these, you'll have access to the various beaches and trails. Off the scenic drives

there are many rough side roads that twist through the desert shrubs to overlooks or canyons dropping down to the water. On these unimproved roads, you'd be wise to have 4WD, take plenty

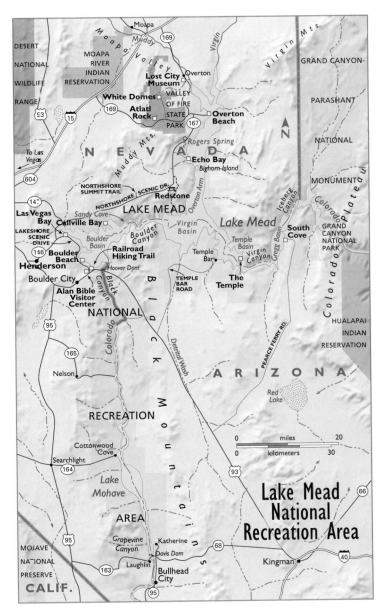

A webbed visitor to Lake Mead

Boating and sunbathing on Lake Mead

of water, and check with park rangers, who have maps showing which roads are open.

This is not particularly popular country for hiking, especially in the lethal summer heat, but there are short hikes and some canyon treks worth taking in the fall, winter, or spring.

Western and Northern Shores

If you are looking for a pebbly beach to sun and swim, or an interesting hike along the lakeshore, head north on Nev. 166 from the visitor center. This is **Lakeshore Scenic Drive,** a 7-mile drive along **Boulder Basin,** on the lake's western shore.

To continue around the lake, turn right onto **Northshore Scenic Drive,** which meanders around the water for another 48 miles to the beautiful Valley of Fire State Park (see pp. 259-261). You can stop along the way for short hikes such as the half-mile (round-trip) **Northshore Summit Trail** *(Access at Milepost 20.5 on Northshore*

Scenic Dr.), with views of the lake and the colorful sandstone rocks called Bowl of Fire.

Go a little farther on the drive to Milepost 27, and you'll find the **Redstone picnic area,** which has a half-mile interpretive loop that explains the geology of the area as it circles red sandstone monoliths.

Another popular option is a dip in shady **Rogers Spring** *(Mile 40).* At the picnic area, you'll find the head of the **Rogers Spring Trail,** a three-quarter-mile round-trip hike across the stream and up to a wonderful overlook.

Southern Shore

If you'd like to explore the southern shoreline first, then venture onto the **Railroad Hiking Trail,** located just south of the Alan Bible Visitor Center, on Lakeshore Scenic Drive. Open to hikers and bicyclists, this pathway toward Hoover Dam winds around the shoreline through old railroad tunnels, a 5.2-mile round-trip. You might spot desert bighorn sheep.

A steep, 4-mile hike on **Liberty Bell Arch Trail** (*Access off US 93*) in Black Canyon leads to a large natural arch of conglomerate rock and a spectacular view of the lake and canyon.

Lake Mohave

For those wishing to see Lake Mohave on foot, inquire at the Alan Bible Visitor Center about scheduled hikes. Several days a week (*Oct.-April*), rangers from the Katherine Landing Ranger Station at Lake Mohave lead hikes (*call NRA headquarters for information*). One of the most popular hikes is along the 1.5-mile **Relay Hill Trail.** The reward for your efforts in making the 600-foot climb is a spectacular view of the lake and surrounding area.

Another interesting site to explore is **Grapevine Canyon,** just west of Lake Mohave and Davis Dam off Nev. 163. Like other canyons in the area, Grapevine shelters hidden springs and lush vegetation. The canyon's water and wildlife attracted ancient rock artists: Petroglyphs dot the rocks at the mouth of the canyon and decorate cliff faces farther in. You'll be able to identify the forms of humans and bighorn sheep.

On the Lakes

The most common way to explore the NRA is by boat. If you don't have your own, commercial outfitters offer tours by paddle wheelers or, on the Black Canyon section where the river actually moves, by raft (*list of concessionaires is available at the visitor center or website*).

You can also rent watercraft at the various marinas that dot the western shore, as well as at Temple Bar in Temple Basin to the east and at Lake Mohave. Boulder Beach is the most popular launch site, because of its proximity to Las Vegas and the dam, which boaters like to gawk at from the upstream side. At various spots along **Boulder Beach,** people water-ski, swim, and scuba dive. Boaters often head upriver toward **Callville Bay** and **Boulder Canyon,** where they can squeeze into scenic **Wishing Well Cove** or stop for some good sunbathing at **Sandy Cove.**

Farther upriver, in **Virgin Basin** and Overton Arm, the crowds thin and the fishing improves. There are deep coves with colorful rock and several petroglyph sites. Lonely **Overton Arm,** where the Virgin River (see sidebar p. 258) comes south into the Colorado, has colorful badlands to the water's edge, with the Black and Muddy Mountains on one side, and the Virgin Mountains on the other. In the middle of the arm is **Bighorn Island,** where, the story goes, a lonely bighorn ram was stranded when the water rose and a butte became an island.

Up the Colorado River arm east, **The Temple** rock rises from the east shore, protected from erosion by a limestone cap. Heading into upper Lake Mead—Temple Bar is the last marina with services—you go through sheer-walled Virgin Canyon, Gregg Basin, and finally Iceberg Canyon. This wild, dry country is good for fishing: Striped bass weighing more than 50 pounds have been caught in Lake Mead, and Lake Mohave is known for its large number of rainbow trout. ■

R ding high on an Air Chair, Lake Mead

Other Sites

The following is a select list of other Far West sites.

North Coast

Fort Point National Historic Site

Constructed to protect San Francisco Bay during the Civil War, Fort Point is located within the Golden Gate NRA in San Francisco's Presidio. It served as the operations base during construction of the Golden Gate Bridge in the 1930s. Tours are offered daily. Contact the site, P.O. Box 29333, Presidio of San Francisco, CA 94129; phone 415-556-1693. www.nps.gov/fopo

Fort Ross State Historic Park

Established in 1812 as a Russian trading outpost, Fort Ross features reconstructed period buildings, including the first Russian Orthodox chapel south of Alaska. A visitor center and museum offer exhibits on the Russian-American Fur Company and the Russian presence in the Pacific Northwest during the 19th century. Contact the site, 19005 Coast Highway 1, Jenner, CA 95450; phone 707-847-3286. http://parks.ca.gov

Mount Diablo State Park

On a clear day, from the summit of 3,849-foot-high Mount Diablo you can see west past the Goden Gate Bridge, south to Mount Loma Prieta in the Santa Cruz Mountains, north to Mount St. Helen's, and east to the Sierra Nevada. Camping, hiking, and horseback riding opportunities are available. Contact the park, 96 Mitchell Canyon Rd., Clayton, CA 94517; phone 925-837-2525. http://parks.ca.gov

Central and South Coast

Castle Rock State Park

Located along the crest of the Santa Cruz Mountains, this park has 32 miles of horseback riding and hiking trails amid 3,600 acres of madrone, Douglas-fir, and coastal redwood forest The 31-mile Skyline to the Sea Trail connects the park to Big Basin Redwoods State Park, with a link to the Pacific at Waddell Beach. Contact the park, 15300 Skyline Blvd., Los Gatos, CA 95033; phone 408-867-2952. http://parks.ca.gov

Oceano Dunes State Vehicular Recreation Area

Adjacent to the Nature Conservancy's Nipomo Dunes preserve, Oceano Dunes is administered by the State of California. Used by enthusiasts for vehicular dune and beach access since the early 1900s, the nearly 4,000-acre site is one of the few legal spots in California for beach driving. Contact the recreation area, 576 Camino Mercado, Arroyo Grande, CA 93420; phone 805-473-7223. www.oceanodunes.com

California Deserts

Imperial Sand Dunes Recreation Area

This 40-mile-long dune system is one of the country's largest; some crests reach heights of more than 300 feet. These formations offer great scenery, opportunities for solitude, rare plants and animals, and, in the dunes south of Calif. 78, dune driving. The Cahuilla Ranger Station on Gecko Road is open weekends October-May. Contact the El Centro Field Office of the BLM, 1661 South Fourth St., El Centro, CA 92243; phone 760-337-4400.

Salton Sea State Recreation Area

Located on the Salton Sea's eastern shore, this recreation area is a haven for swimmers, bird-watchers, fishermen, and boaters. The visitor center is 25 miles southeast of Indio via Calif. 111. Contact the park, 100-225 State Park Rd., North Shore, CA 92254; phone 760-393-3052 or 760-393-3059. http://parks.ca.gov

Trona Pinnacles National Natural Landmark

Trona Pinnacles is a geologic wonderland of more than 500 tufa (calcium carbonate) spires. They rise out of the dry Searles Lake basin in a variety of formations. Some are more than 140 feet high. The landmark is about 20 miles east of Ridgecrest down a 5-mile dirt road off Calif. 178. The best times to visit are fall through early spring. Primitive camping is permitted. Contact the Ridgecrest Field Office of the BLM, 300 S. Richmond Rd., Ridgecrest, CA 93555; phone 760-384-5400.

Central Valley

Cosumnes River Preserve

Off I-5 between Stockton and Sacramento, the Nature Conservancy property protects the only undammed river on the west slope of the Sierra. Hiking, canoeing, kayaking, and bird- and wildlife-watching are all possible in one of the Central Valley's richest biological regions. Call the visitor center for a schedule of naturalist-led tours, or explore the area on one of the interpreted wetland trails. Contact the preserve, 13501 Franklin Blvd., Galt, CA 95632; phone 916-684-2816. www.cosumnes.org

Pacheco State Park

Pacheco State Park, the last remaining section of the 1843 Mexican land grant of Francisco Pacheco, is known for its lovely tapestry of spring wildflowers and the vistas of the San Joaquin and Santa Clara Valleys. More then 28 miles of trails offer opportunities for hiking, mountain biking, and horseback riding. Weekends in spring bring the largest crowds. The park is located 20 miles east of Gilroy on Dinosaur Point Road off Calif. 152. Contact the park, 38787 Dinosaur Pt. Rd., Hollister, CA 95023; phone 209-826-6283. http://parks.ca.gov

San Luis Reservoir State Recreation Area

Seven miles west of I-5 on Calif. 152, near Los Banos, San Luis Reservoir has boating, board sailing, and fishing. Its three lakes are home to bass, trout, and catfish. The California Aqueduct Bikeway begins at the San Luis Creek picnic area and runs 70 miles to Bethany Reservoir. Recommended launch site for less experienced sailors is in the Medeiros area off Calif. 33, just north of Calif. 152. Contact the park, 31426 Gonzaga Rd., Gustine, CA 95322; phone 800-805-4805 or 209-826-1197. http://parks.ca.gov

Sierra Nevada

Marble Mountain Wilderness

Take I-5 to Yreka and continue toward Fort Jones in the Klamath Mountains. The rugged Marble Mountain Wilderness comprises nearly 100 pristine lakes, panoramic ridgecrest vistas, and wildflower meadows. The Pacific Crest Trail runs through the wilderness. Contact Klamath National Forest, 1312 Farlane Road, Yreka, CA 96097; phone 530-842-6131. www.r5.fs. fed.us/klamath/vvc/wilderness/marbles/index.html

Plumas-Eureka State Park

Located in the Lakes Basin, this park offers glacier-gouged lakes and mountains, trout streams, and forests of Jeffrey pines and red firs. In addition to outdoor recreation such as hiking, fishing, and camping, there is a mining museum and assorted mining buildings. Contact the park, 310 Johnsville Rd., Blairsden, CA 96103; phone 530-836-2380. http://parks.ca.gov

Great Basin and Interior

Cave Lake State Park

Nestled in the Schell Creek Range at 7,300 feet, this 32-acre dam-created reservoir is a popular base for summer hiking and winter cross-country skiing into the Humboldt-Toiyabe National Forest, which surrounds the park. Other activities include trout fishing, ice skating, and ice fishing. Contact the park, P.O. Box 761, Ely, NV 89301; phone 702-728-4467. www.state.nv.us/stparks

Ward Charcoal Ovens State Historic Site

During the 1870s, these six 30-foot-high, 20-inch thick beehive-shaped ovens converted timber into charcoal for use in neighboring mines. They fell into disuse in the 1880s and then served as horse shelters and outlaw hideouts. Accessible by dirt road from May-Oct., the park offers primitive camping and great scenery. Contact the park, P.O. Box 193, Ely, NV 89301; phone 775-728-4467. www.state.nv.us/stparks

Desert and Canyon

Echo Canyon State Park

Located in southeast Nevada 12 miles east of Pioche via Nev. 322 and 323, 1,080-acre Echo Canyon and its reservoir attract hikers and fishermen. Early morning, explore the park's backcountry on the 2.5-mile Ash Canyon Trail. The interpretive trail climbs to the valley rim before descending into Ash Canyon. The 68-acre reservoir attracts a variety of waterfowl and shore birds. Contact the park, Star Route, Box 295, Pioche, NV 89043; phone 775-962-5103. www. state.nv.us/stparks

Henderson Bird Viewing Preserve

With 90 acres of ponds and adjacent land, this is one of Nevada's best spots for migrant and nesting birds. Throughout the year, you'll find plenty to see—from resident larks and wrens to migrant waterfowl and terns to nesting hummingbirds and blackbirds. Trails with interpretive signs, observation stations, and benches are excellent for the beginning bird-watcher. It is located at 2400 Moser Dr., off Sunset Road in Henderson (just east of Las Vegas). Contact the Henderson Parks and Recreation Department, 240 Water St., Henderson, NV 89015; phone 702-566-2939. www.cityofhenderson.com/parks/birdpreserve.html

Resources

The following is a select list of resources. Contact state and local associations for additional outfitter and lodging options. For chain hotels and motels operating in the Far West, see p. 283.

CALIFORNIA

Federal and State Agencies

Bureau of Land Management
2800 Cottage Way,
Suite W1834
Sacramento, CA 95825
916-978-4400
www.blm.gov/caso
Provides maps and recreation information on BLM lands in California. For more detailed information on BLM lands in southern California, contact the California Desert District Office (6221 Box Springs Blvd., Riverside, CA 92507; phone 909-697-5200. www.ca.blm.gov/cdd)

California Department of Fish and Game
1416 Ninth St.
Sacramento, CA 95814
916-227-2245
www.dfg.ca.gov
For obtaining licenses, brochures, and other information.

California Department of Parks & Recreation
P.O. Box 942896
Sacramento, CA 94296
916-653-6995
http://parks.ca.gov
Information on California state parks and preserves, including camping.

California Travel and Tourism
800-462-2543
http://gocalif.ca.gov
General resource for travel in California. Eight welcome centers across the state provide maps, brochures, and information about driving tours, special events, lodging, and other travel subjects.

USDA Forest Service Pacific Southwest Region
1323 Club Dr.
Vallejo, CA 94592
707-562-8737
www.r5.fs.fed.us
Source of general information on all national forests in California. For detailed information regarding trails and camping possibilities in a specific forest contact that forest directly.

Outfitters and Activities

All-Outdoors Whitewater Rafting
1250 Pine St., Suite 103
Walnut Creek CA 94596
800-247-2387
www.aorafting.com
A great source for whitewater-rafting trips in California.

Catch a Canoe & Bicycles, Too!
44850 Comptche-Ukiah Rd.
Mendocino, CA 95460
800-320-2453 or
707-937-0273
Rent a kayak, canoe, or bike to access the Big or Noyo Rivers. State-of-the-art-equipment.

Five Brooks Ranch
P.O. Box 99
Olema, CA 94950
415-663-1570
www.fivebrooks.com
Guided rides on 120+ miles of trails in Pt. Reyes area.

Hilltop Stables
2131 Hollister St.
San Diego, CA 92154
619-428-5441
Guided rides on one of the few California county beaches open to horses.

Island Packers
1867 Spinnaker Dr.
Ventura, CA 93001
805-642-1393
www.islandpackers.com
Day or multi-day Channel Island cruises.

Joshua Tree Rock Climbing School
HCR Box 3034
Joshua Tree, CA 92252
800-890-4745 or
760-366-4745
www.joshuatreerockclimbing.com
Offers all levels of instruction year-round in Joshua Tree National Park, ranging from one to four days, for individuals and groups. The school also provides guide services.

Mountain Adventure Seminar
P.O. Box 5102
Bear Valley, CA 95223
209-753-6566
www.mtadventure.com
Multi-day camp-based climbing adventures in Joshua Tree NP and Pinnacles NM. Fully permitted and licensed.

Pacific Crest Trail Association
5325 Elkhorn Blvd.,
PMB#256
Sacramento, CA 95842
916-349-2109 or
888-728-7245
www.pcta.org
Organization protects, preserves, and promotes the trail. An excellent source for planning a hike on the trail, the PCTA provides books, maps, and trail-condition updates.

Truth Aquatics, Inc.
301 W. Cabrillo Blvd.
Santa Barbara, CA 93101
805-962-1127
www.truthaquatics.com
Diving, hiking, kayaking trips in Channel Islands.

Vertical Adventures Rock Climbing School
P.O. Box 7548, Newport Beach, CA 92658
949-854-6250 or
800-514-8785
www.vertical-adventures.com
One- to four-day rock seminars for all skill levels. In summer, climb in the

San Jacinto Mountains; in winter, climb in Joshua Tree National Park.

Yosemite Mountaineering School
Yosemite National Park, CA 95389
209-372-8435 or
209-372-8344
www.yosemitemountaineering.com
Full range of one- and two-day classes for beginners through advanced climbers.

Outdoor Education and Resources

Adventure Outings
417 Cherry St.,
Chico CA 95929
530-898-4011
www.cs4chico.edu/as/adventure
A recreation program of the California State University, Chico, Adventure Outings provides a wide range of excursions and educational programs, including: backpacking, canoeing, fly fishing, mountain biking, snow boarding, rock climbing, and rafting.

Backcountry Seminars
200 Palm Canyon Dr.
Borrego Springs, CA 92004
760-767-4315
www.anzaborrego.statepark.org/seminar.html
California State Parks host educational courses held in Anza-Borrego Desert State Park, Salton Sea State Recreation Area, and Cuyamaca Rancho State Park. Seminars range from a half day to two full days on topics such as geology, paleontology, history, and natural history. All seminars are led by expert instructors.

The Desert Institute
Joshua Tree National Park Association
74485 National Park Dr.
Twentynine Palms, CA 92277
760-367-5525
www.joshuatree.org/field
Weekend adult outdoor classes focusing on sci-

ence, history and the arts in Joshua Tree National Park and the adjacent Mojave Desert.

Oceanic Society
Ft. Mason Center, Bldg. E
San Francisco, CA 94123
415-474-3385
800-326-7491
www.oceanic-society.org
Hands-on expeditions with marine scientists.

Sequoia Natural History Association Field Seminar Program
HCR 89-Box 10
Three Rivers, CA 93271
559-565-3759
www.sequoiahistory.org/sem_info.htm
Year-round seminars in Sequoia and Kings Canyon National Parks that range from one to seven days. The variety of topics is geared toward giving people a greater understanding of nature and the outdoors.

Yosemite Field Seminars
Yosemite Association,
P.O. Box 230
El Portal, CA 95318
209-379-1906
http://yosemite.org/seminars
Seminars on topics such as birding, photography, natural history, and Native American history. Many seminars run over a weekend; they are open to teenagers (16 and older) and adults.

Yosemite Institute
P.O. Box 487
Yosemite, CA 95389
209-379-9511
www.yni.org/yi
Offers hands-on adult and family field seminars, as well as a variety of adventure programs for children age 11 and older. A wide range of natural and cultural history topics are covered.

Lodgings

California Association of Bed and Breakfast Inns
2715 Porter St.
Soquel, CA 95073
831-462-9191

State-wide association of more than 360 establishments, including inns, cottages, and farm stays.

North Coast

Bed & Breakfast San Francisco
P.O. Box 420009
San Francisco, CA 94142
415-899-0060 or
800-452-8249
www.bbsf.com
Wide range of choices among cozy B&Bs.

Mendocino Coast Reservations
1000 Main St.
P.O. Box 1143
Mendocino, CA 95460
707-937-5033 or
800-262-7801
www.mendocinovacations.com
Weekend and vacation rentals in all price ranges.

Central and South Coasts

The Big Sur Lodge
47225 Highway One
Big Sur, CA 93920
831-667-3100 or
800-424-4787
www.bigsurlodge.com
Located in Pfeiffer Big Sur State Park; 61 guest rooms, a restaurant, and a conference center.

Tassajara Zen Mountain Center
39171 Tassajara Rd.
Carmel Valley, CA 93924
831-659-2229
www.sfzc.com/Pages/Tassajara/Tassajara_Controls/zmcdes.html
Open May-Aug. for day and overnight guests. Reservations necessary.

California Deserts

Gateway towns offer a wide range of accommodations; contact the chambers of commerce for area listings. In the Anza-Borrego Desert State Park area contact Borrego Springs (P.O. Box 420, Borrego Springs, CA 92004; phone 800-559-5524 or 760-767-5555); for the Joshua Tree National Park area, Twentynine Palms (6455-A Mesquite Avenue, Twentynine Palms, CA 92277; phone 760-367-3445); and for the Mojave National Preserve area,

Needles
(P.O. Box 7050, Needles, CA 92363; phone 619-326-2050).

Furnace Creek Inn & Ranch Resort
Highway 190, P.O. Box 1
Death Valley, CA 92328
760-786-2345
www.furnacecreekresort.com
The inn offers a timeless elegance, the ranch a charming family-type atmosphere. Both are located in Furnace Creek in the heart of Death Valley National Park.

Central Valley

Contact the Redding Convention & Visitors Bureau (800-874-7562 or 530-225-4100) for complete lodging and activity information in the Shasta Dam area.
http://ci.redding.ca.us/cnvb/cnvbhome.htm

Sierra Nevada

Plantation Bed and Breakfast (Sequoia NP)
33038 Sierra Highway 198
Lemon Cove, CA 93244
800-240-1466
www.plantationbnb.com
Named after characters from Gone with the Wind, the rooms of this scenic B&B range from simple to luxurious.

Yosemite Concessions Services
5410 E. Home Ave.
Fresno, CA 93727
559-252-4848
www.yosemitepark.com
The park concessioner manages the luxurious Ahwahnee Hotel, the modern yet rustic Yosemit Lodge, and the simple tent cabins of Corry Village.

Camping

Many of California's state parks, including Big Basin Redwoods, Pfeiffer Big Sur, Julia Pfeiffer Burns, Del Norte Coast Redwoods, Jedediah Smith Redwoods, and Prairie Creek Redwoods, allow you to reserve a campsite in advance for a fee. Call Reserve America Reservations (800-444-7275) for information and details, or go to www.reserveamerica.com.

The USDA Forest Service operates campgrounds throughout the state's national forestlands. Call specific national forests for details. The National Recreation Reservation Service is a camping service offering more than 49,500 camping facilities at 1,700 different federally managed locations. Call 877-444-6777 or go to www.reserveusa.com. Information on some campgrounds can be found at the Great Outdoors Recreation Page (www.gorp.com).

High Sierra Camps (Yosemite NP)

All lodging in canvas tent cabins. High Sierra camps are reserved on a lottery basis. Applications are available Oct. 15 to Nov. 30 annually. For information, call the High Sierra Desk at 559-253-5674.

NEVADA

Federal and State Agencies

Bureau of Land Management
Nevada State Office
1340 Financial Blvd.,
Reno, NV 89502
775-861-6400
www.nv.blm.gov
Rules and regulations for use and camping on BLM-managed lands. Visitor center open Monday-Friday. Visitors may apply for both BLM and Forest Service permits. Maps, books, and advice are available.

Nevada Commission on Tourism
401 North Carson St.
Carson City, NV 89701
800-638-2328 or
775 687-4322
www.travelnevada.com
General resource for travel in Nevada, including camping and lodging information.

Nevada Department of Transportation
877-682-6237
www.nevadadot.com

Nevada Division of Wildlife
1100 Valley Rd.
Reno, NV 89512
775-688-1500
www.state.nv.us/cnr/nvwildlife
Hunting and fishing licenses as well as site information and recommendations.

Nevada State Parks
1300 South Curry St.
Carson City, NV 89703
775-687-4384
www.state.nv.us/stparks/
Information on parks, including camping.

Public Lands Interpretive Association
6501 Fourth St., NW
Suite 1
Albuquerque, NM 87107
877-851-8946 (toll free) or
505-345-9498
www.publiclands.org
Part of a national network that provides information and educational resources on state and federally managed public lands. Recreation permits, maps, and books may be obtained online.

USDA Forest Service
2035 Last Chance Road
Elko, NV 89801
775-738-5171
www.fs.fed.us/r4/nevada.htm
Maps, as well as camping and trail information, for Humboldt-Toiyabe National Forest.

Outfitters and Activities

Escape the City Streets
8221 W. Charleston,
#101
Las Vegas, NV 89117
800-596-2953 or
702-596-2953
www.escapeadventures.com
Mountain-bike adventures throughout southern Nevada and south and central California, including Lake Tahoe, Mojave Desert, and Red Rock Canyon.

Forever Resorts
HCR 30, Box 1000

Cottonwood Cove,
NV 89046
702-297-1464 or
800-255-5561
www.foreverresorts.com
Year-round rentals from personal watercraft and powerboats to luxurious houseboats for Lake Mead and Lake Mohave.

Hike This!
1982 N. Rainbow Dr.
Suite 264
Las Vegas, NV 89108
702-393-4453
www.hikethislasvegas.com
Offers half-day guided hikes in Red Rock Canyon.

Ruby Mountains Helicopter Skiing
P.O. Box 281192
Lamoille, NV 89828
775-753-6867
www.helicopterskiing.com
Terrain and run-length options. Not for the faint-hearted.

Sagebrush Ranch
12000 West Ann Rd.
Las Vegas, NV 89149
702-645-9422
Fully supported horseback rides through the Red Rock Canyon area. One-hour to multiple-day trips offered.

Seven Crown Resorts
P.O. Box 16247
Irvine, CA 92623
800-752-9669
www.sevencrown.com
Offers multi-day houseboat rentals on Lake Shasta, Lake Mead, Lake Mohave, and the California Delta.

Sky's the Limit, Inc.
HCR 33 Box 1
Calico Basin
Red Rock, NV, 89124
702-363-4533
www.skysthelimit.com
Technical climbing courses and trips in Red Rock Canyon are designed to develop technical skills and confidence on the rock.

Lodging

See Nevada Commission on Tourism.

Nevada Hotel & Motel Association
2901 El Camino Ave.
Suite 202
Las Vegas, NV 89102
702-878-9272
www.nvhotels.com

Desert and Canyon

Las Vegas Convention &
Visitors Authority
3150 Paradise Road
Las Vegas, NV 89109
800-332-5333
www.vegasfreedom.com

Reno/Sparks Convention &
Visitors Authority
1 East First St., 2nd Fl.
Reno, NV 89501
888-448-7366
www.renolaketahoe.com
Accommodations for Lake
Tahoe and surrounding area.

Great Basin

Bre tenstein House Bed &
Breakfast
P.O. Box 281381
Lamoille, NV 89828
702-753-6356
Three rooms in main lodge;
detached cabin with Jacuzzi.

Red Lion Inn
2065 Idaho St.
Elko, NV 89301
800-545-0044
223 rooms, pool, casino.

Lake Mead NRA and Vicinity

Boulder City and Laughlin
are common departure
points for exploration of
Lake Mead and Lake
Mohave. Contact the Boul-
der City Chamber of Com-
merce (702-293-2034,
www.bouldercity.com) or
the Laughlin Visitors Bureau
(702-298-3321, www.visit-
laughlin.com) for lodging
and other activities.

Camping

For a list of private campgrounds around the state,
contact the Nevada Com-
mission on Tourism, Nevada
State Parks, the USDA Forest Service, and the Bureau
of Land Management (see p.
282) also operate camp-
grounds throughout
Nevada. Additional information is available at
www.gorp.com.

National Recreation Reservation Service
877-444-6777
www.reserveusa.com
Camping reservation ser-
vice, offering over 49,500
camping facilities at 1,700
different locations man-
aged by the USDA Forest
Service and the US Army
Corps of Engineers.

**Hotel & Motel Chains
in California and
Nevada**

Accommodations are avail-
able in both states.

Best Western International
800-528-1234

Choice Hotels
800-424-6423

Clarion Hotels
800-252-7466

Comfort Inns
800-228-5150

Courtyard by Marriott
800-321-2211

Days Inn
800-325-2525

Econo Lodge
800-446-6900

Embassy Suites
800-362-2779

Fairfield Inn by Marriott
800-228-2800

Hilton Hotels and Resorts
800-445-8667

Holiday Inns
800-465-4329

Howard Johnson
800-654-2000

Hyatt Hotels and Resorts
800-223-1234

Marriott Hotels and
Resorts
800-228-9290

Motel Six
800-466-8356

Quality Inns-Hotels-Suites
800-228-5151

Ramada Inns
800-272-6232

Red Lion Hotels
800-547-8010

Sheraton Hotels and Inns
800-325-3535

Super 8 Motels
800-843-1991

About the Author/Photographer

Geoffrey O'Gara writes mostly about social and natural resource issues in the American West. His latest book, published by Alfred A. Knopf, is *What You See in Clear Water, Life on the Wind River Reservation.* O'Gara lives with his wife, Berthenia Crocker, and son Nicholas in Lander, Wyoming.

Freelance photographer **Phil Schermeister** has traveled to Mexico's Copper Canyon, Canada's Banff National Park, and numerous locations throughout the United States on assignments for the National Geographic. Schermeister and his wife, Laureen, live in Sonora, California, in the Sierra Nevada foothills.

Illustrations Credits

Photographs in this book are by Phil Schermeister except for the following:

p. 49 - Amy Wiles/Wales/Index Stock Imagery
p. 55 - Robert Houser/Index Stock Imagery
p. 87 - Norbert Wu/Norbert Wu Photography
p. 200 - Royal Geographic Society
p. 266 - Mark Gibson/Index Stock Imagery
p. 269 - John Luke/Index Stock Imagery

Index

Abbreviations

National Forest=NF
National Monument=NM
National Park=NP
National Recreation
    Area=NRA
National Wildlife
    Refuge=NWR
State Park=SP
State Reserve=SR

National Geographic Guide to America's Outdoors: Far West
by Geoffrey O'Gara
Photographed by Phil Schermeister

Published by the National Geographic Society
John M. Fahey, Jr., *President and Chief Executive Officer*
Gilbert M. Grosvenor, *Chairman of the Board*
Nina D. Hoffman, *Senior Vice President*

Prepared by the Book Division
William R. Gray, *Vice President and Director*
Charles Kogod, *Assistant Director*
Barbara A. Payne, *Editorial Director*

Guides to America's Outdoors
Elizabeth L. Newhouse, *Director of Travel Books*
Cinda Rose, *Art Director*
Barbara A. Noe, *Associate Editor*
Caroline Hickey, *Senior Researcher*
Carl Mehler, *Director of Maps*
Roberta Conlan, *Project Director*

Staff for this Book
Roberta Conlan, Jim Lynch, Jarelle S. Stein, *Editors*
Dorrit Green, *Designer*
Marilyn Gibbons, *Illustrations Editor*
Nora Gallagher, Victoria Garrett Jones,
    Keith R. Moore, Jane Sunderland, *Researchers*
Lise Sajewski, *Editorial Consultant*
Matt Chwastyk, Jerome N. Cookson, Sven M. Dolling, Thomas L. Gray,
    Joseph F. Ochlak, Nicholas P. Rosenbach, Gregory Ugiansky, Martin S. Walz,
    National Geographic Maps, Mapping Specialists, *Map Edit, Research, and Production*
Tibor Tóth, *Map Relief*
R. Gary Colbert, *Production Director*
Janet Dustin, *Illustrations Assistant*
Deborah Patton, *Indexer*
Robert Della Vecchia, *Project Assistant*
Deb Antonini, *Contributor*

Ed Hastey, *Consultant*

Manufacturing and Quality Control
George V. White, *Director;* John T. Dunn, *Associate Director;* Vincent P. Ryan, *Manager;*
Phillip L. Schlosser, *Financial Analyst*

Library of Congress Cataloging-in-Publication Data
O'Gara, Geoffrey.
    Guide to America's outdoors: Far West / Geoffrey O'Gara; photography by Phil Schermeister.
        p. cm
    ISBN 0-7922-7751-1
        1. West (U.S.)—Guidebooks. 2. National parks and reserves—West (U.S.)—Guidebooks. 3.
Outdoor recreation—West (U.S.)—Guidebooks. I. Title: Far West. II. Schermeister, Phil. III. Title
    F590.3 .O37 2000
        917.9404'54—dc21   00-063824
                                                                            CIP